VISUAL QUICKSTART GUIDE

ADOBE ACROBAT 9

FOR WINDOWS AND MACINTOSH

John Deubert

 Peachpit Press

Visual QuickStart Guide
Adobe Acrobat 9 for Windows and Macintosh
John Deubert

Peachpit Press
1249 Eighth Street
Berkeley, CA 94710
510/524-2178
510/524-2221 (fax)

Find us on the Web at: www.peachpit.com
To report errors, please send a note to: errata@peachpit.com

Peachpit Press is a division of Pearson Education.

Copyright © 2009 by John Deubert

Editor: Becky Morgan
Production Coordinator: Myrna Vladic
Compositor: Christi Payne
Copyeditor: Jacqueline Kan Aaron
Indexer: Jack Lewis
Cover Design: Peachpit Press

ISBN-13: 978-0-321-55295-2
ISBN-10: 0-321-55295-4
9 8 7 6 5 4 3 2 1

Printed and bound in the United States of America

Dedication

For (in order of height) Barbara, Elizabeth, Gigi, and Julia.

Acknowledgements

I have come to the conclusion that in updating an existing book, pretty much everyone else works harder than the author, who gets to put his or her name on the cover. Accordingly, I celebrate everyone who slaved over this project who don't get to put their names in a highly visible place.

While this book could arguably have been updated without me, it absolutely wouldn't be in your hands without the following people: Becky Morgan, my editor, who is thoughtful in her commentary, tolerant of my peculiar schedule, and not the least bit sarcastic when my text appears to have been written by gremlins; Production Editor Myrna Vladic made sure I actually supplied all the bits and pieces that go into the book; Copyeditor Jacqueline Kan Aaron cleaned up my prose, undangled my participles, and continued working on this project even after she noticed the Castilleja connection; Compositor Christi Payne assembled an intertangled mass of text and image files into a remarkably nice looking book (Christi, how are you at jigsaw puzzles?); Indexer Jack Lewis does a wonderful job at a task that requires both creativity and a tolerance for tedium; and marketer Sara Jane Todd ensures that people know about the book, like what they see, and ultimately give someone money for it. My heartfelt thanks to everyone!

At home, as always, I thank my wife for her patience when I stop responding to external stimuli for hours on end.

TABLE OF CONTENTS

Chapter 1   **Starting with Acrobat**   **1**

Opening and Quitting Acrobat 9 3
Examining the Initial Screen 4
Examining the Menus 6
Examining the Toolbars 8
Customizing Toolbars 11
Working with Navigation Panes 12
Setting Preferences 15

Chapter 2   **Viewing a Document**   **17**

Opening a PDF File 18
Moving from Page to Page 19
Moving from View to View 20
Zooming In and Out 21
Choosing a Page Layout 28
Searching for Text 30
Arranging Documents on the Screen 33
Using Reading Mode 34
Using Links and Bookmarks 36
Measuring Sizes and Areas 38

Chapter 3   **Saving and Printing Files**   **43**

Saving a PDF File 44
Exporting to Other Formats 45
Minimizing File Size 50
Printing a Document 52
Print Options 54
Printing Multiple Pages per Sheet 57
Printing a Booklet 58

Chapter 4   **Making PDF Files**   **59**

Printing to a PDF File 60
Using PDFMaker in Microsoft Office
    (Windows) 62
Converting Images and Other Files to PDF 64
Scanning Directly to PDF 65
Converting Web Pages to PDF 66
Converting Screen Shots to PDF 67
Merging PDF Files 69

Chapter 5   PDF Portfolios   71

Creating a Portfolio 73
Choosing a Layout 77
Adding a Welcome Page. 79
Adding a Header 81
Choosing a Color Scheme. 83
Setting File Information 84
Publishing Your Portfolio. 85
Sharing with Acrobat.com. 87

Chapter 6   Adding Comments to a Document   89

Examining Acrobat's Commenting Tools. 90
Adding a Sticky Note Comment 92
Adding a Text Box Comment. 94
Adding a Callout Comment. 97
Adding Lines and Arrows. 98
Drawing Ovals and Rectangles 99
Adding Polygons and Clouds 100
Text Edits 102
Adding a Stamp Comment 104
Creating Your Own Stamp. 106
Checking Spelling in Comments 108
Exporting and Importing Comments. 109
Enabling Commenting in Adobe Reader. 110

Chapter 7   Reading Commented Documents   111

Examining the Comments List. 112
Replying to a Comment 114
Marking Comments. 115
Managing the Comments List 116
Searching for Text in Comments. 117
Printing Comments 119
Migrating Comments 122

Chapter 8   Reviewing PDF Documents   123

Starting an E-mail–Based Review 124
Reviewing an E-mailed Document 126
Receiving E-mail–Reviewed Documents. 127
Starting a Shared Review 128
Reviewing a Shared Document. 132
Receiving Server-Based Reviews 133
Real-Time Collaborative Reviews 134

TABLE OF CONTENTS

Chapter 9   Manipulating Pages   139
Rearranging Pages 140
Extracting Pages 141
Inserting One File into Another.............. 142
Replacing Pages............................. 143
Rotating Pages.............................. 144
Cropping Pages 146

**Chapter 10   Adding and Changing Text
and Graphics   149**
Touching Up Text........................... 150
Modifying Line Art.......................... 152
Adding Headers and Footers................. 156
Adding a Background 159
Adding a Watermark........................ 161
Redacting a Document 163

Chapter 11   Adding Simple Navigation Features   169
Adding Bookmarks.......................... 170
Creating Links 173
Modifying Existing Links 176
Making Automatic Web Links............... 177
Creating Articles 178

Chapter 12   Creating an Acrobat Presentation   181
Setting Open Options 182
Creating a Full-Screen Slide Show............ 184
Creating a Next Page Button................. 186
Creating a Self-Running Presentation 188
Placing a Movie on a Page 190
Playing a Movie 196
Placing a Flash Animation on the Page 199
Adding Sound to a PDF Page.................... 200

Chapter 13   Organizing Documents   203
Examining the Organizer.................... 204
Using the History Pane...................... 206
Using the Places Pane 207
Using the Collections Category 208

Chapter 14 Creating Forms with Acrobat Pro   211

About LiveCycle Designer 212
Creating a Form from a Template 213
Editing Forms with LiveCycle Designer........ 216
Converting Electronic Documents to Forms... 219
Distributing Forms............................ 223
Responding to a Distributed Form 228
Receiving and Viewing Results................ 229

Chapter 15 Password Protection   233

Restricting File Access 234
Restricting Reader Activities.................. 236

Chapter 16 Digital Signatures   239

About Adobe Self-Sign Security.............. 240
Creating a Digital ID 241
Creating a Certificate from an ID............. 243
Importing a Certificate as a Trusted Identity... 245
Signing a PDF Document..................... 247
Creating a Signature Appearance 249
Creating a Signature Field 251
Validating a Signed Document................ 253

Chapter 17 Converting Paper to PDF   255

Typing on a Paper Form...................... 256
Creating a Searchable Image.................. 258
Converting a Scan with ClearScan............ 260

Index   262

Starting with Acrobat

Acrobat 9 is the latest and—really—greatest version of Adobe Systems' software for viewing, managing, and manipulating PDF files. At this point in its evolution, Acrobat incorporates more than a decade of Adobe's experience and experimentation with what people want to do with PDF files and how best to do that.

What will you find new in Acrobat 9? Well, new features, of course: portfolios, Flash integration, real-time collaborative document reviews. But, at least as important, Acrobat 9 streamlines and simplifies the use of its features; it's easier than it has ever been to create forms, send files out for review, and combine PDF files into a single document.

"More capability, less effort" was clearly one of Adobe's design goals in this newest version of Acrobat, and there is much to make us happy.

This book describes the purpose and use of Acrobat 9's most important features, new and old. Like all Visual QuickStart Guides, this book emphasizes the practical application of the program's features and provides step-by-step instructions on how to use those features.

Continues on next page

It'll be fun.

We'll start with the basics: how to open Acrobat, what you'll be looking at when you do so, and how to quit the application. You'll also learn how to customize some of the Acrobat user interface to your taste.

We'll explore the details and use of Acrobat 9's toolbars, menus, and other interface items throughout this book. Here, we orient you so you become comfortable with the layout of the software's windows.

STARTING WITH ACROBAT

Opening and Quitting Acrobat 9

You open and quit Adobe Acrobat 9 the way you open or close any application on the Macintosh or Windows.

To open Acrobat 9:

◆ Do one of the following:
  ▲ Double-click the Acrobat 9 application icon (**Figure 1.1**).
  ▲ Double-click a PDF file icon.
  ▲ On the Macintosh, click the Spotlight icon, type *Acro,* then click on Acrobat 9 when it appears in the list of hits.
  ▲ In Windows, choose Acrobat 9 in the Start menu's Programs submenu.

In all cases, Acrobat 9 launches.

If you started Acrobat by double-clicking a PDF file icon, Acrobat presents you with that document's first page.

If you double-clicked the Acrobat 9 application icon, then what you see depends on your computer platform:

◆ On the Macintosh, the toolbar at the top of the screen changes to the Acrobat 9 toolbar.

◆ In Windows, you are presented with an empty document window.

✔ Tip

■ You may notice that Acrobat 9 is much faster to start up than earlier versions. Adobe put a lot of effort into reducing the application's launch time.

To quit Acrobat 9:

◆ Do one of the following:
  ▲ On the Macintosh, choose Acrobat > Quit Acrobat.
  ▲ In Windows, choose File > Exit.
  ▲ On either platform, press Command/Ctrl-Q.

You can also quit the application by unplugging the computer or bashing it with a hammer, but this probably isn't the best way to quit. But it can be strangely satisfying in certain moods.

Figure 1.1 Launch Acrobat 9 by clicking either the application icon or a PDF document icon.

OPENING AND QUITTING ACROBAT 9

Examining the Initial Screen

When you open a document in Acrobat (you'll see how to do this in Chapter 2) or just launch Acrobat 9 in Windows, you see a window similar to that in **Figure 1.2**. The parts of this window are as follows:

Drag bar. This is a standard Macintosh or Windows drag bar. It contains the name of the PDF document and all the controls you'll find in any application's document window, including the Close, Minimize, and Zoom buttons.

Document pane. This is where Acrobat displays the pages of your PDF document.

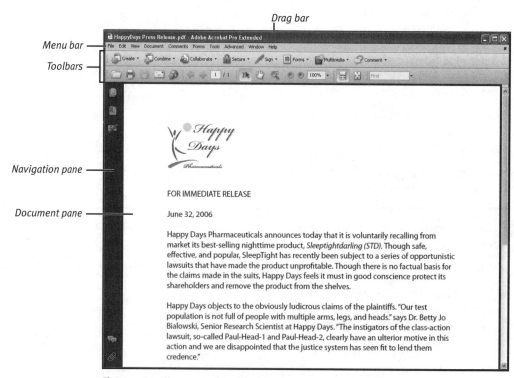

Figure 1.2 You'll see something like this when you open a document in Acrobat 9.

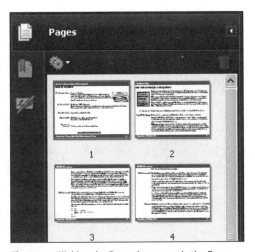

Figure 1.3 Clicking the Pages icon reveals the Pages navigation pane, which displays thumbnails of the document's pages.

Menu bar. The location of the menu bar conforms to your platform's standards. In Windows, the menu bar is at the top of the document window (as shown in Figure 1.2); on the Macintosh, the menu bar runs along the top of the screen, as usual.

Toolbars. In Acrobat 9, each document window has its own collection of toolbars. You may customize the exact set of toolbars that is visible and the contents and location of each toolbar; we'll see how to do this shortly.

Navigation pane. This contains a bunch of icons that, when clicked, reveal a variety of tools and information, such as thumbnails of all the pages (**Figure 1.3**), all the document's comments, and bookmarks to locations within the document.

✔ Tip

- The drag bar's Close button behaves differently on the Macintosh and Windows. On the Macintosh, the Close button closes the document window but doesn't exit the Acrobat application. In Windows, if no other documents are open, the Close button closes the document and also exits Acrobat. These are standard behaviors on the Macintosh and in Windows.

Examining the Menus

Acrobat has ten menus stretching the width of each document window in Windows; on the Macintosh, it has 11 menus spanning the screen (**Figure 1.4**). You'll eventually be using items from every one of these menus. For the moment, let's see what these menus are and what kinds of tasks they make possible:

Acrobat menu. This Macintosh-only menu contains items that affect the operation of the application as a whole. In particular, this is where you set the application preferences and exit Acrobat on the Macintosh.

File menu. This menu lists the commands to open, close, save, and otherwise manipulate the PDF files on your computer's hard disk. This menu is similar to the File menu in other applications. In Windows, this is where you exit the application.

Edit menu. This is a reasonably standard Macintosh or Windows Edit menu, containing Cut, Copy, Paste, and other common commands. In Windows, this is where you set the application preferences.

View menu. The commands in this menu let you change how Acrobat presents your documents. You may choose such things as page display and zoom level. This is also where you specify which toolbars and navigation panes are visible.

Document menu. Here you may choose commands that manipulate the document's structure, delete or rearrange pages, add headers and footers, and more.

Acrobat	File	Edit	View	Document	Comments	Forms	Tools	Advanced	Window	Help

Figure 1.4 The Acrobat menu bar provides access to all the capabilities of the application.

Figure 1.5 Use the Help menu to access Acrobat's excellent help system.

Comments menu. This has all the commands you'll use for commenting on a PDF document and reading the comments of others.

Forms menu. The items in this menu let you create and distribute interactive forms.

Tools menu. This menu contains a set of submenus that provide access to features that are otherwise available only through toolbars, such as creating articles or measuring areas and lengths of items on a page. Other submenus enable features important to specific professions, such as prepress.

Advanced menu. Offering features mostly for advanced users, this menu lets you do such things as create a searchable index spanning a collection of PDF files and preflight a document.

Window menu. This menu lets you specify the details of document windows. For example, you can tile or stack the windows, bring a particular document to the front, and choose a zoom level.

Help menu. This menu provides access to Acrobat's extensive help system, which includes a full Acrobat reference (**Figure 1.5**). It also lets you check for updates and register your Acrobat software.

✔ Tip

■ The Help menu is your friend. Adobe has done a remarkably good job of describing the purpose and use of every part of Acrobat, and you should take advantage of this information at every opportunity. Not sure what a trusted identity is? Here's where you'll find out. Need to add page numbers to a PDF file? The Help system will guide you through the process. (Though not, I hasten to add, with nearly as much style or panache as this book.)

Examining the Toolbars

Acrobat 9 has a very large number of toolbars that supply access to the application's many features (**Figure 1.6**). These toolbars are initially attached to the top of each document window, though they may be moved to any of the windows' four sides.

Most of Acrobat's toolbars aren't initially visible. Showing a toolbar and then hiding it again entails the simple selection of a menu item.

All the toolbars may be "torn off" the document window to become stand-alone palettes.

To make a toolbar visible:

1. Choose a toolbar in the View > Toolbars submenu (**Figure 1.7**).

   Acrobat makes the toolbar visible as a stand-alone palette (**Figure 1.8**).

2. If you want the toolbar docked, drag the palette to the collection of toolbars at the top of a document window. (We talk more about toolbars and palettes next.)

   Acrobat adds the palette to the window as a toolbar.

✔ Tips

- You may want to leave the toolbar in its palette form; this is useful if you're going to use the toolbar only once or twice and then hide it again.

- You can actually drag a toolbar palette to any of the four sides of a document window and it will adhere there.

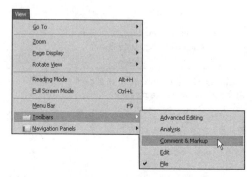

Figure 1.6 Acrobat 9's toolbars are fixed to document windows.

Figure 1.7 You specify the toolbars you want visible by selecting them in the Toolbars submenu.

Figure 1.8 A toolbar may be displayed as a stand-alone palette. Here is the File toolbar.

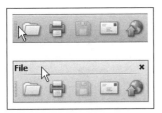

Figure 1.9 The vertical dotted lines at the left of a toolbar indicate the drag area.

Figure 1.10 The Analysis toolbar contains tools to let you examine and measure items on a page.

Figure 1.11 The Multimedia toolbar lets you embed movies, Flash animation, or other multimedia on a page.

To convert a toolbar into a palette:

1. Click and hold toolbar's drag area.

   This is the pair of vertical dotted lines at the left edge of each toolbar, indicated in the top image of **Figure 1.9**.

2. Drag the toolbar off the collection of toolbars at the top of the document window.

   Acrobat converts the toolbar into a palette, as in the bottom image of Figure 1.9.

Acrobat 9 toolbars

Here are the toolbars that we'll be using as we discuss this book's topics.

Advanced Editing. This contains tools for advanced Acrobat features, such as placing movies and adding links on a page.

Analysis. These tools let you examine page contents for a variety of purposes, such as to measure the size or area of drawings (**Figure 1.10**).

Comment & Markup. Here are the tools for adding comments to a page.

Edit. These tools let you perform a variety of tasks that change the contents of the page, such as adding articles and links, placing movies, and cropping.

File. Here you'll find the tools to open, close, and otherwise work with files.

Find. This contains a text field you may use to search in the current document.

Multimedia toolbar. This allows you to embed movies, sounds, or other multimedia in your document (**Figure 1.11**).

Continues on next page

Page Display. This toolbar lets you specify whether Acrobat displays your pages one at a time, as a scrolling column of pages, or as a spread.

Page Navigation. Here are the controls that let you move from page to page within your document.

Print Production. This contains a number of tools with features important to professional printing.

Redaction. These tools let you mark sensitive text within your document for hiding or removal.

Select & Zoom. This toolbar contains the most routinely used tools: the Hand, Selection, and Zoom tools.

Tasks. Here's a set of drop-down menus that allow convenient access to frequent tasks, such as creating a PDF or accessing commenting tools.

Typewriter. This toolbar has tools that let you fill in a scanned paper form without explicitly adding PDF form fields to the document.

Properties bar. Not properly a toolbar, the Properties bar presents information that is useful when you are creating links, form fields, and other objects within Acrobat.

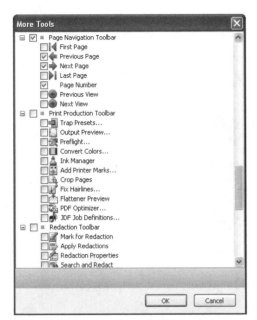

Figure 1.12 Select or deselect each of the tools to make them visible or hidden in Acrobat's toolbars.

Customizing Toolbars

You can control which tools appear in a toolbar. Each toolbar has a set of tool buttons associated with it, and you can choose which of these buttons are visible. The new collection of tools you specify will appear in every new document window you open.

To add or remove toolbar tools:

1. Select View > Toolbars > More Tools.

   Acrobat displays the More Tools dialog box (**Figure 1.12**). This dialog box displays all the tools that can appear in each of the toolbars.

2. Select the check box next to each of the tools that you want visible in your toolbars.

3. Deselect the check box next to each of the tools that you don't want visible.

4. Click OK.

✔ Tip

- A couple of common tools are inexplicably missing in the default setup of their corresponding toolbars. I strongly recommend that you enable the following tools: in the Select & Zoom toolbar, Actual Size, Fit Width, and Fit Page; in the Page Navigation toolbar, Next View and Previous View.

Toolbar Philosophy

People differ in their philosophies regarding toolbars. Some people like to have a toolbar button for every command the application is capable of. On the other hand, I prefer to have toolbar buttons for only the commands I use a lot and that are inconvenient to invoke with the keyboard.

The nice thing about Acrobat 9 is that it lets you set things up just the way you like.

Working with Navigation Panes

The navigation panes occupy an area along the left side of every document window. Normally, the panes are retracted, showing only a column of icons—one for each available pane (**Figure 1.13**). When a pane is opened, it allows you to move around within your document in a specific way, such as moving from page to page using thumbnails (as shown earlier in Figure 1.3), moving among the document's bookmarks, and so on.

To open and close a navigation pane:

1. Click the tab of a closed navigation pane to open it.

   Acrobat opens the navigation pane (**Figure 1.14**).

2. Click the tab of an open pane to close it again.

   The navigation pane collapses down into a tab.

✔ Tip

- The pane panel has a gear icon that, when clicked, displays a pop-up menu of commands appropriate to the current pane (**Figure 1.15**). The collection of commands in this menu varies from one navigation pane to another.

Figure 1.13 The navigation panes are initially visible as a column of icons along the left edge of each window.

Figure 1.14 Clicking one of the navigation tabs exposes the pane associated with that tab.

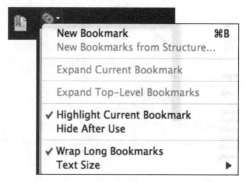

Figure 1.15 Clicking the gear icon at the top of a navigation pane yields a drop-down menu with commands appropriate to that pane.

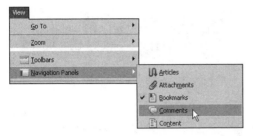

Figure 1.16 The Navigation Panels submenu lets you toggle the visibility of navigation panes.

Acrobat defines a large number of navigation panes that may be available to the user. Most of them aren't initially visible; Acrobat starts out showing only the most commonly used panes.

It's easy to choose which panes Acrobat makes visible in document windows so that you have convenient access to them.

To customize the list of navigation panes:

◆ Choose the pane you want to make visible in the View > Navigation Panels submenu (**Figure 1.16**).

Acrobat toggles the visibility of the navigation tab you choose; if it's visible, it will become hidden, and vice versa.

Acrobat 9 navigation panes

Many of the navigation panes have a specialized purpose and won't be covered in this book. Here we list the navigation panes that are the most useful.

Articles. This navigation pane lists all the articles that exist in the document. Articles are useful for making documents readable; we'll discuss them in Chapter 11.

Bookmarks. This pane lists all the bookmarks placed in the document. These form a clickable table of contents for the PDF file. In Chapter 11, you'll see how to make and use bookmarks.

Continues on next page

WORKING WITH NAVIGATION PANES

Comments. The Comments pane lists all the annotations that have been placed on pages in the document.

Pages. The Pages pane presents thumbnail views of each page in the document. Double-clicking a thumbnail takes you to that page.

Signatures. This pane lists all of the document's electronic signatures.

Any of the navigation panes may be converted to a stand-alone palette, as in **Figure 1.17**.

To convert a navigation pane into a palette:

◆ Click and drag the pane's tab away from the left edge of the window.

Acrobat converts the pane into a palette.

To convert a palette into a navigation pane:

◆ Click and drag the palette into the navigation pane area of a document window.

Acrobat converts the palette into a navigation pane.

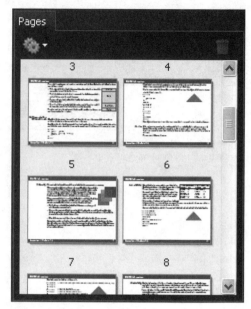

Figure 1.17 All the navigation tabs may be converted to stand-alone palettes.

Setting Preferences

Like all applications, Acrobat maintains a set of preferences that determine how the application should behave when you start a session. This can include such things as the default zoom, the color to be used for comments, and whether Acrobat should report distances in pixels, inches, or centimeters. Some of the tasks in this book require you to set preferences relevant to that task. In the meantime, you may find it useful to look at the preference controls available in Acrobat. (There are a lot of them.)

To set Acrobat's preferences:

1. On the Macintosh, choose Acrobat > Preferences. In Windows, choose Edit > Preferences.

   Acrobat displays the Preferences dialog box (**Figure 1.18**).

   Continues on next page

SETTING PREFERENCES

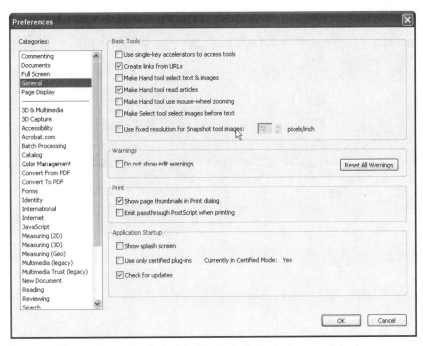

Figure 1.18 You can change Acrobat's default behavior in the Preferences dialog box.

2. Click a category name in the list running down the left side of the dialog box.

   Acrobat presents the controls that apply to that category.

3. Make whatever changes you wish to the preferences controls in that category.

   Repeat steps 2 and 3 for as many categories as you want.

4. Click OK.

✔ Tip

- In your idle moments, you should browse the preference controls available in the Preferences dialog box. It may not sound entertaining, but you'll be surprised how much you can learn about an application's capabilities from its preference controls.

SETTING PREFERENCES

VIEWING A
DOCUMENT

Once you've launched Acrobat and have become familiar with its interface, you're ready to navigate the pages of an open document. This chapter describes the tools in Acrobat 9 that you use to view a PDF document. We'll look at some routine things, such as all the ways to move from page to page and how to zoom in and out, as well as some of Acrobat's more exotic capabilities, such as measuring the length and area of items on the page.

Opening a PDF File

The most basic activity you can carry out in Acrobat is opening a PDF file. You can do this several ways, most of them identical to the way you open files in other applications.

To open a file from the Finder or Windows Explorer:

♦ Do either of the following:

   ▲ Double-click the icon of a PDF file.

   ▲ Drag the icon of a PDF file to the Acrobat application icon.

   Acrobat opens the file.

To open a file from the File menu:

1. Choose File > Open (Command/Ctrl-O) (**Figure 2.1**).

   Acrobat presents you with the standard select-a-file dialog box.

2. Navigate to the file you want to open, and click OK.

   Acrobat opens the file.

To open a file from the File toolbar:

1. Display the File toolbar, if necessary, by choosing View > Toolbars > File.

   Acrobat displays the File toolbar (**Figure 2.2**).

2. Click the Open File icon in the File toolbar.

   The standard select-a-file dialog box opens.

3. Choose the file you want to open, and click OK.

   Acrobat opens the file.

Figure 2.1 You can open a PDF file in Acrobat by choosing File > Open.

Figure 2.2 The File toolbar contains handy tools for opening, printing, saving, e-mailing, and uploading files.

Figure 2.3 The Page Navigation toolbar contains the following tools: Previous Page, Next Page, and a Page Number field.

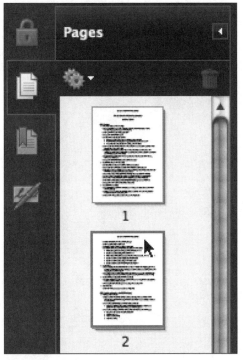

Figure 2.4 Move to an arbitrary page by double-clicking a thumbnail in the Pages navigation pane.

Figure 2.5 The View menu's Go To submenu contains useful commands that let you navigate through pages.

Moving from Page to Page

Once you've opened your document, you'll want to move around among the pages. Here, too, you have several ways to do so, most of them familiar from other applications.

To move to the next or previous page:

◆ Do one of the following:

▲ Press the right or left arrow key on your keyboard to move to the next page or previous page, respectively.

▲ Click the Previous Page or Next Page icon in the Page Navigation toolbar (**Figure 2.3**).

▲ Press the Page Down or Page Up key on your keyboard.

To move to a particular page:

◆ Do either of the following:

▲ Type the page number to which you want to go in the Page Number field in the Page Navigation toolbar (Figure 2.3).

▲ Click the Pages navigation tab to expose the Pages navigation pane, and then double-click the thumbnail of your desired page (**Figure 2.4**).

To move to the first or last page:

1. To go to the document's first page, choose View > Go To > First Page (**Figure 2.5**) or press the Home key.

2. To go to the document's last page, choose View > Go To > Last Page or press the End key.

✔ Tip

■ You can add tools to the Page Navigation toolbar for First Page and Last Page. I recommend you do so; they are very handy. Chapter 1 tells you how to add tools to a toolbar.

Moving from View to View

A *view* in Acrobat parlance includes the document, page number, and zoom. You change to a new view whenever you go to a new page, zoom in or out, or open a new document.

Acrobat has menu items and associated key shortcuts for moving to the previous and next views. If you jump ahead 15 pages by double-clicking a thumbnail, the Previous View command returns you to your original page. These controls are very handy.

To move to the previous or next view:

◆ Do either of the following:

▲ Choose View > Go To > Previous View, or View > Go To > Next View.

▲ Press Command/Ctrl–left arrow key or Command/Ctrl–right arrow key on your keyboard.

✔ Tip

■ I recommend that you add to the Page Navigation toolbar the tools for First and Last Page and for Next and Previous View (**Figure 2.6**). These functions are so frequently used that you'll want to make access to them as convenient as possible. Chapter 1 tells you how to add tools to a toolbar.

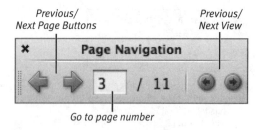

Previous/Next Page Buttons

Previous/Next View

Go to page number

Figure 2.6 You can add to the Page Navigation toolbar tools for First and Last Page and for Next and Previous View.

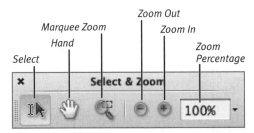

Figure 2.7 The Zoom toolbar contains all the tools you need to zoom in and out of your PDF pages.

Zooming In and Out

Acrobat provides a Select & Zoom toolbar with tools that let you get a closer look at an area of the page or to look at a broader region of the page (**Figure 2.7**). It also has a Select tool, which you use to edit, examine, and otherwise manipulate items on the page; we shall refer to this tool periodically throughout this book.

In Acrobat's default configuration, the Select & Zoom toolbar contains the zoom tools you will use most often. Acrobat's menus also offer less frequently used zoom functions.

Broadly, Acrobat lets you zoom three different ways:

- ◆ Zoom by a specific amount.
- ◆ Zoom so that the page fits in the document window in a particular way (for example, the page width fills the window).
- ◆ Dynamically select the degree of zoom visually.

✔ Tip

- ■ You can add the extra zoom tools to the Zoom toolbar. **Figure 2.8** shows the Zoom toolbar fully loaded with all the zoom tools. See Chapter 1 for a reminder of how to add tools to a toolbar.

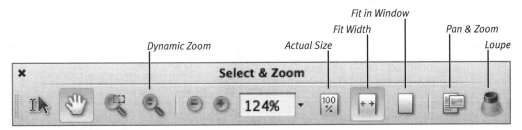

Figure 2.8 The fully loaded Select & Zoom toolbar features five extra tools in addition to the basic ones.

To zoom by a fixed amount:

◆ Do one of the following:

▲ Click the Zoom In (+) or Zoom Out (−) tool on the Select & Zoom toolbar.

Acrobat zooms in to a predetermined zoom level. Starting at 100%, for example, repeated clicks of the + button take you to zooms of 125%, 150%, 200%, and so on, up to a maximum of 6400%.

▲ Type a zoom percentage in the Select & Zoom toolbar's text field.

▲ Click the small, down arrow next to the Select & Zoom toolbar's text field, and choose a predefined zoom percentage from the resulting Zoom Amount menu (**Figure 2.9**).

To zoom the page to fit the document window:

◆ Do one of the following:

▲ Choose Fit Page from the Zoom Amount menu on the Select & Zoom toolbar or press Command/Ctrl-0 to zoom out until the page fits entirely inside the document window (**Figure 2.10**).

▲ Choose Fit Width from the Zoom Amount menu or press Command/Ctrl-2 to zoom in until the document's pages exactly fit the width of the window (Figure 2.10).

▲ Choose Fit Height from the Zoom Amount menu to zoom until the document's pages exactly fit the height of the window.

▲ Press Command/Ctrl-3 to zoom until the text and images on your pages exactly fit the document window.

▲ To return to 100% zoom, choose Actual Size in the Zoom Amount menu or press Command/Ctrl-1 to zoom to 100%.

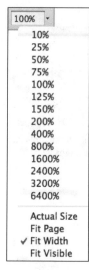

Figure 2.9 The drop-down menu in the Select & Zoom toolbar lets you conveniently choose a zoom amount.

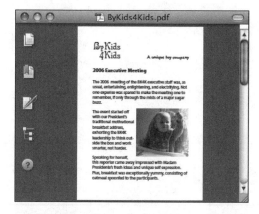

Figure 2.10 Two useful zoom amounts are Fit Page (top) and Fit Width.

Figure 2.11 When you use the Marquee Zoom tool, the mouse pointer normally is a magnifying glass with a plus sign. You can zoom out (and change the point pointer to a minus sign) by holding the Shift key.

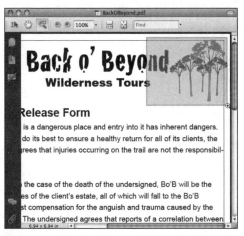

Figure 2.12 Using the Marquee Zoom tool, click and drag a rectangle.

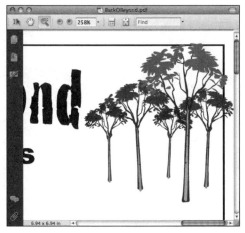

Figure 2.13 Acrobat zooms in until the rectangle fills the window.

The Marquee Zoom tool

The Marquee Zoom tool is the best tool to use when you want to get a better look at a particular part of the page. It lets you intuitively zoom in on a specific area of the page.

To zoom with the Marquee Zoom tool:

1. In the Select & Zoom toolbar, click the Marquee Zoom tool.

   The mouse pointer turns into a magnifying glass with a plus sign in it (**Figure 2.11**).

2. Click in the document window, and drag a rectangle around the area you want to zoom in on (**Figure 2.12**).

   Acrobat zooms in until the area you enclosed in the marquee fills the document window (**Figure 2.13**).

ZOOMING IN AND OUT

✔ Tips

- If you click in the document window without dragging a rectangle, Acrobat zooms in by a predefined amount. The point on which you clicked is centered on the resulting zoomed page.

- You can use the Marquee Zoom tool to zoom out of the page, as well. Repeat the steps in the previous task while holding down the Shift key. Acrobat zooms out, showing you more of the page.

- You can get temporary access to the Marquee Zoom tool anytime by holding down Command/Ctrl-spacebar on your keyboard. Acrobat activates the marquee zoom feature, allowing you to zoom in on the page. If you also hold down the Alt/Option key (Command-Option-spacebar/Ctrl-Alt-spacebar) you can temporarily zoom out.

- If the Select & Zoom toolbar isn't visible, you can get to the Marquee Zoom tool by choosing Tools > Select & Zoom > Marquee Zoom (**Figure 2.14**).

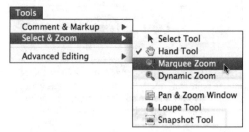

Figure 2.14 The Tools > Select & Zoom submenu gives you access to the Marquee Zoom and Dynamic Zoom tools.

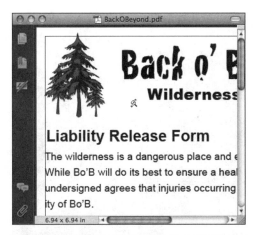

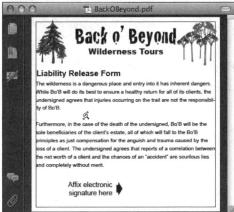

The Dynamic Zoom tool

The Dynamic Zoom tool lets you zoom in and out of your document page by clicking and moving your mouse. Dragging the mouse to the upper left zooms in on the document; dragging to the lower right zooms out (**Figure 2.15**).

To zoom with the Dynamic Zoom tool:

1. Choose Tools > Select & Zoom > Dynamic Zoom (Figure 2.14).

   The mouse pointer changes to the cursor shown in **Figure 2.16**.

2. Click and hold the mouse button anywhere in the document window.

3. Drag up and to the left to zoom in on the document.

4. Drag down and to the right to zoom out.

✔ Tip

- When the Dynamic Zoom tool is selected, you can temporarily gain access to the Marquee Zoom tool by holding down the Shift key. The reverse is also true.

Figure 2.15 The Dynamic Zoom tool lets you zoom in and out of your document by clicking and dragging your mouse. In the figure, we zoom out by dragging the mouse toward the lower left.

Figure 2.16 The mouse pointer looks like this when the Dynamic Zoom tool is active.

ZOOMING IN AND OUT

The Loupe tool

The Loupe tool gives you a close-up of the area on the screen surrounding the mouse pointer. As you move the pointer around the document window, a floating loupe window shows a continually updating close-up.

Unfortunately, this useful tool does not appear on the Select & Zoom toolbar by default. You must select Loupe Tool in the Tools > Select & Zoom submenu (Figure 2.14). You can, of course, add it to the Select & Zoom toolbar using the procedure described in Chapter 1.

To zoom with the Loupe tool:

1. Choose Tools > Select & Zoom > Loupe Tool.

   The mouse pointer changes to a small crosshair.

2. Click in the document window.

   Acrobat displays a *target rectangle* in the document window, and a floating Loupe Tool window that shows a close-up of whatever is in the rectangle (**Figure 2.17**).

   You can drag this rectangle around the document window to see different parts of the page.

✔ Tip

■ Note that the Loupe Tool floating window has controls that let you specify such things as the degree of magnification and the color of the target rectangle (Figure 2.17).

Figure 2.17 The Loupe tool lets you drag a target rectangle around the page and view a close-up of the rectangle's contents in a dialog box.

Figure 2.18 When you click the Pan & Zoom tool, Acrobat presents you with a floating thumbnail view of your page enclosed in a target rectangle (hard to see in this figure).

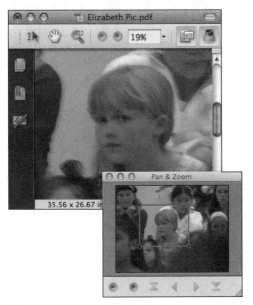

Figure 2.19 As you move and resize the target rectangle, Acrobat zooms the main document window so the rectangle's contents fill the window.

The Pan & Zoom tool

Acrobat's final zoom tool is Pan & Zoom. This is the opposite of the Loupe tool. Acrobat presents you with a floating window containing a thumbnail view of your page. You drag and resize a target rectangle in the thumbnail, and Acrobat zooms the main document page so that the target rectangle fills the page.

Like the Loupe tool, the Pan & Zoom tool is initially available only through the Tools > Select & Zoom submenu (Figure 2.14). You can add it to the Select & Zoom toolbar, as described in Chapter 1.

To zoom with the Pan & Zoom tool:

1. Choose Tools > Select & Zoom > Pan & Zoom window.

   Acrobat displays a floating Pan & Zoom window containing a thumbnail image of your document page. The floating window also has a target rectangle initially set to encompass the entire page (**Figure 2.18**).

2. Resize and move the target rectangle so that it encloses the area on the thumbnail that you want to see close up.

   As you do so, Acrobat continuously zooms the document window so that it's filled with the area enclosed by the target rectangle (**Figure 2.19**).

   You resize the rectangle by grabbing its handles at its corners and sides when the mouse pointer rolls over it.

   If you wish, you can use the controls on the Pan & Zoom thumbnail window to specify a percentage scale, change the color of the target rectangle, or move from page to page within the document.

Choosing a Page Layout

Acrobat can organize your document's pages on the screen a number of ways, such as one page at a time or side by side. These layouts are in the View > Page Display submenu (**Figure 2.20**); some of them are available by default in the Page Display toolbar (**Figure 2.21**) as well.

To change the page layout:

◆ Do either of the following:

▲ Select the desired layout from View > Page Display.

▲ Click the layout button in the Page Display toolbar.

By default, only two layouts—Single Page and Single Page Continuous—are available in this toolbar. You can add the other layouts to the toolbar; see Chapter 1 for instructions on how to customize a toolbar.

Acrobat page layouts

The Page Display submenu allows you access to the following layouts:

Single Page displays one page at a time in the document window (**Figure 2.22**).

Single Page Continuous displays the pages in the document as a single, scrollable column (Figure 2.22).

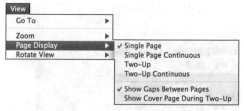

Figure 2.20 You select a page layout from the View > Page Display submenu.

Figure 2.21 Two layouts are available by default in the Page Display toolbar.

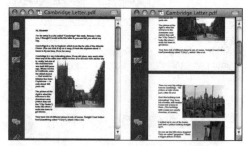

Figure 2.22 Two of the layouts in the Page Display submenu are Single Page (left) and Single Page Continuous (right).

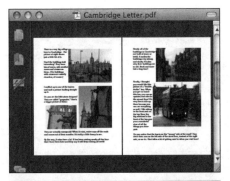

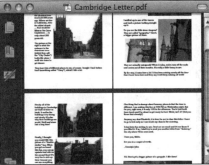

Figure 2.23 The Two-Up (top) and Two-Up Continuous (bottom) layouts are useful for seeing how printed documents will look when the pages are bound.

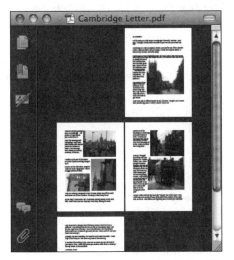

Figure 2.24 The Show Cover Page During Two-Up option forces the first page to be a right-hand page, matching the way the document pages will look when bound.

Two-Up displays two pages at a time, side by side (**Figure 2.23**).

Two-Up Continuous displays two columns of side-by-side pages (Figure 2.23).

✔ Tips

■ The Two-Up and Two-Up Continuous layouts are particularly useful for PDF files that are intended to be bound in a book; they allow you to see how the pages will look when the book is open.

■ If you select Show Cover Page During Two-Up in the View > Page Display submenu, Acrobat displays two-up pages with a blank cover page. The net result of this is to make the first page of the PDF document a right-hand page, as in **Figure 2.24.** This page display can be incredibly useful if your document is going to be bound, since it shows the actual pairing of the document's pages.

Searching for Text

Acrobat has an effective mechanism for searching for a particular piece of text within a document. It's similar to the search features in other applications.

Acrobat has two distinct mechanisms for finding text in a document:

Find looks for text within the current document. Acrobat lets you step through successive instances of the found text one at a time.

Search looks for text in one or more PDF files in locations you specify on your computer's disk. Acrobat presents you with a clickable list of all the instances of that text within the documents.

To find text in a document:

1. If the Find toolbar isn't visible, choose Edit > Find (Command/Ctrl-F).

   Acrobat makes the Find toolbar visible, if it doesn't already reside in the document window (**Figure 2.25**).

2. Type into the text field the word or phrase you want to find.

3. Press the Enter or Return key.

   Acrobat searches the document for the text, stops when it finds an instance, and highlights the text on the page (**Figure 2.26**).

4. To go to the next instance of the text in the document, click the Find Next button on the Find toolbar.

   Note that the Find Next and Find Previous buttons are not initially visible on the toolbar.

5. To go to the previous instance of the text, click the Find Previous button.

Figure 2.25 The Find toolbar has a text field for the text you want to find, a Find Previous button, and a Find Next button.

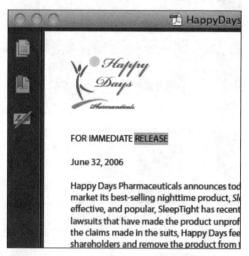

Figure 2.26 When the Find function discovers an instance of the word, it moves the document window so the word is visible and highlights the text on the page.

✔ Tip

■ The Find feature ignores case and diacritical marks in its search; for example, *Jose, José,* and *jose* are considered identical.

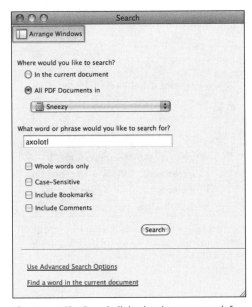

Figure 2.27 The Search dialog box lets you search for a word or phrase in all the PDF files in a particular location.

Figure 2.28 The pop-up menu in the Search dialog box lets you specify where Acrobat should look for PDF files in its search.

To search for text in one or more documents:

1. Choose Edit > Search or press Command/ Ctrl-Shift-F.

   The Search dialog box opens (**Figure 2.27**).

2. Type into the text field the word or phrase you want to search.

3. Click one of the radio buttons to specify where Acrobat should search for the text: in the current PDF document or in all PDF documents in a particular location.

   In the latter case, you may choose a location from the pop-up menu (**Figure 2.28**).

4. Select the check boxes associated with the options you want for the search (Figure 2.27):

   ▲ **Whole Words Only:** Acrobat ignores the text if it's preceded or followed by other alphanumeric characters. Thus, in searching for *wait*, Acrobat ignores *waiting*.

   ▲ **Case-Sensitive:** Acrobat considers case in its search; thus, *Wait* and *wait* are considered different.

   ▲ **Include Bookmarks:** Acrobat searches the titles of the document's bookmarks as well as page contents.

   ▲ **Include Comments:** Acrobat searches comments.

Continues on next page

SEARCHING FOR TEXT

5. Click the Search button.

Acrobat searches all the documents for the specified text. It then creates a list showing all the instances it finds (**Figure 2.29**).

6. To examine any of the found instances, click that instance in the list.

The document window shows you the found text; if that text resides in a different PDF file, Acrobat opens that file.

7. Click the New Search button to start a new search, or click the dialog box's Close button to close the Search dialog box.

✔ Tip

Note that Acrobat can search all the PDF files on all your disks (Figure 2.28). This can take a while. Go get coffee; play with the dog; paint the house.

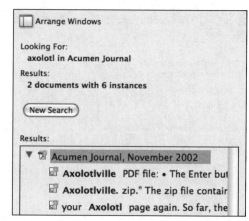

Figure 2.29 The Search feature returns a list of all of the instances it finds. Click one of the instances to see the page on which it resides.

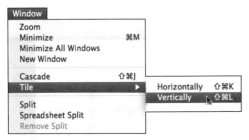

Figure 2.30 You can tile or cascade open document windows via the Window menu.

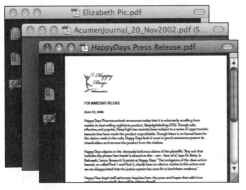

Figure 2.31 Cascading the document windows is useful when you want to see only one of them at a time.

Figure 2.32 Tiling the windows is helpful when you want all the documents to be visible simultaneously for comparison.

Arranging Documents on the Screen

Acrobat lets you tile or cascade the currently open document windows. When you choose one of these options, the document windows are resized so that your entire screen is filled.

These options are available through the Window menu (**Figure 2.30**).

To arrange documents on the screen:

◆ Do one of the following:
  ▲ Choose Window > Cascade.
    Acrobat zooms the document windows to full-screen and offsets them so that the title bars of all the windows are visible (**Figure 2.31**).
  ▲ Choose Window > Tile > Vertically.
    Acrobat tiles the windows top to bottom (**Figure 2.32**).
  ▲ Choose Window > Tile > Horizontally.
    Acrobat tiles the windows across the width of the page.

Using Reading Mode

In Reading mode, Acrobat tries to make a document as easy as possible to read onscreen. To do this, Acrobat hides the toolbars and navigation tabs, and zooms the document so that it fits across the width of the document window (**Figure 2.33**). Additionally, each click of the mouse moves you down the document by one screen.

✔ Tip

■ Reading mode is particularly useful for reading documents that were originally formatted for print. It makes it easy to read the small text used in such documents.

To enter and exit Reading mode:

1. To enter Reading mode, choose View > Reading Mode (**Figure 2.34**).

2. To exit Reading mode, choose View > Reading Mode or press the Escape key.

Figure 2.33 In Reading mode, Acrobat hides the toolbar and navigation tabs, and zooms the document so that its width stretches across the window.

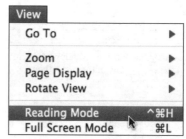

Figure 2.34 Enter Reading mode using the View menu.

To navigate pages in Reading mode:

1. To move forward in the document, do either of the following:
    - ▲ Press the right arrow key on your keyboard.
    - ▲ Scroll down with your mouse's scroll wheel.

2. Seems unnecessary and, furthermore, Acrobat behaves differently, depending upon whether you are in single-page or continuous-pages mode. To move backward through the document, do either of the following:
    - ▲ Press the left arrow key on your keyboard.
    - ▲ Scroll up with your mouse's scroll wheel.

✔ Tip

- ■ Reading mode is much like Full Screen mode. It hides extraneous controls, toolbars, and other distractions; it also automatically moves ahead in the document with a click of the mouse button. Reading mode, however, leaves you with access to the rest of your computer; you can click outside the document window to look briefly at your e-mail or do some other task. In Full Screen mode, nothing is visible except the PDF document; you must leave Full Screen mode to do anything else on your computer. We'll talk about Full Screen mode in detail in Chapter 11.

USING READING MODE

Using Links and Bookmarks

Acrobat gives the author of a PDF file the ability to add navigation features that make it easy for a reader to move around a document. In Chapter 11, you'll see how to create these navigation features. Here, you'll learn to use these features when viewing a PDF document.

Again, the author must build these features into the PDF document for them to be available to the reader.

Using links

Links in Acrobat work just like links in Web pages. You click them, and the document does something: moves you to another location in the document, plays a movie, or performs some other activity determined by the document designer.

It's up to the creator of the PDF file to make a page's links visible to the reader. You will generally see the same range of visual clues that you find on a Web page, such as blue text and button icons (**Figure 2.35**).

✔ Tips

- As in a Web browser, you can always tell when the mouse cursor is hovering over a link because the cursor changes to a pointing finger.

- The destination associated with a link may be in a different file. Some documents are distributed as a set of PDF files, one for each chapter; clicking a link in a Table of Contents file takes you to the file that contains that topic.

- A link's destination can also be a Web site. When you click on such a link, Acrobat opens that Web page in your browser.

Figure 2.35 Links and buttons in PDF pages usually look like those in their Web-page equivalents.

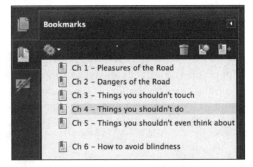

Figure 2.36 Clicking the Bookmarks tab exposes the document's bookmarks.

Using bookmarks

Bookmarks reside in the Bookmarks navigation pane, one of the tabs along the left side of your document windows. The bookmarks form a clickable table of contents provided by the document's author.

Clicking a bookmark takes you to a predetermined location in the document.

To use a document's bookmarks:

1. Click the Bookmarks tab to open the Bookmarks navigation pane, if necessary.

   You see all of the document's bookmarks (**Figure 2.36**).

2. Click a bookmark.

   Acrobat takes you to the location associated with that bookmark.

Measuring Sizes and Areas

Acrobat provides a set of tools that you can use to measure the sizes and areas of items on a page. These measurements can be reported in any units you wish; you specify a scale (so many millimeters equals so many feet, for example), and Acrobat reports its results in real units. This makes these tools extremely useful for working with maps, floor plans, and other scale drawings.

You get to the measuring tools from the Analysis toolbar (**Figure 2.37**). You can reach this toolbar by choosing View > Toolbars > Analysis, then clicking on the Measuring tool icon. Acrobat displays the Measurement palette (**Figure 2.38**).

The Measurement palette

The Measurement palette has three measurement tools and four buttons for "snap types." We shall discuss the tools first and the then talk about what a snap type is.

The palette's three measurement tools, on the right side of Figure 2.38, are as follows (from left to right in the palette):

◆ The **Distance** tool, for measuring the distance between two points.

◆ The **Perimeter** tool, for measuring the length of an area's border on the page.

◆ The **Area** tool, for measuring the area of a region on the page.

The Snap Types buttons on the left side of Figure 2.38 specify that when you click on the page with a measuring tool, the cursor should move, or *snap*, to the nearest significant point. The buttons let you specify any combination of four types of "significant points," all reasonably self-explanatory (from left to right in the palette):

◆ Snap to **Paths**

◆ Snap to **Endpoints**

◆ Snap to **Midpoint**

◆ Snap to **Intersection**

✔ Tips

■ All the Snap Types are turned on by default. I can think of no reason why they shouldn't be left on. Generally you are measuring something that is drawn on the page, and the Snap Tool feature is extremely convenient.

■ A measuring tool will snap to a path, endpoint, and so on, only if the tool is already within a few screen pixels of that point when you click. This is a good thing, since having the tools jump to an endpoint that is halfway across the page would get really annoying after the thirtieth time.

Figure 2.37 The Analysis toolbar contains the Measuring tool.

Figure 2.38 The Measurement palette contains three measurement tools on the right and four snap-type buttons.

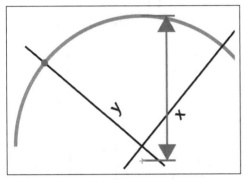

Figure 2.39 The Measuring Info window provides ongoing measurement information when any of the measuring tools are active.

Figure 2.40 As you drag the Distance tool's crosshair, a double arrow shows the distance you are measuring.

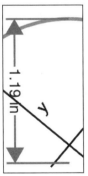

Figure 2.41 The Distance tool leaves a special-purpose annotation—a *measurement markup*—on the page, displaying the double arrow and the distance value.

To measure the distance between two points:

1. Select the Distance tool in the Measurement palette.

   The mouse pointer becomes a crosshair, and the Measuring Info floating window opens (**Figure 2.39**).

2. Click once on the starting point for the distance you want to measure.

   Now, wherever you move your mouse, Acrobat draws a double-arrow line that shows the distance between the mouse's current position and the starting point (**Figure 2.40**). The Measuring Info window also continually reports the distance from the starting point to the mouse's current position.

3. Click the second endpoint for the distance you want to measure.

   The endpoints of the distance you want to measure are now frozen in place. The crosshair is still "live," and now lets you position the double arrow against the page background.

4. Move the crosshair around until the double arrow is positioned where you want it, and click a final time to end the measurement.

   The Measuring Info window reports the distance between your endpoints (Figure 2.39). The double arrows remain on the page as a special annotation called a *measurement markup* (**Figure 2.41**).

MEASURING SIZES AND AREAS

The Perimeter tool

The Perimeter tool measures the distance around the edge of an object or a region on the page.

To measure the perimeter of a region:

1. Select the Perimeter tool in the Measurement palette (Figure 2.38).

   The mouse pointer becomes a crosshair, and Acrobat displays the Measuring Info window (Figure 2.39).

2. Click at the starting point for the distance you want to measure.

3. Click successively on points around the perimeter of the area you want to measure.

   As you do so, Acrobat shows you the set of straight lines connecting your points as well as a running total of your distance so far (**Figure 2.42**). This distance also appears in the Measuring Info window.

4. Click twice on the final point of your perimeter to let Acrobat know you're done.

   Acrobat freezes the values displayed Measuring Info window. It also adds the polygon you created to the page as a measurement markup annotation (the diamond-shaped border shown in **Figure 2.43**).

✔ Tip

■ Having clicked around the perimeter of your region, you can then double-click the resulting polygon annotation with the Hand tool, and Acrobat displays a comment window with the perimeter measurement (**Figure 2.44**).

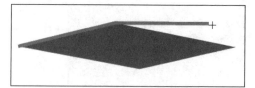

Figure 2.42 The Perimeter Tool window displays the distance around a perimeter you define. Just click points on the edge of the area you are measuring.

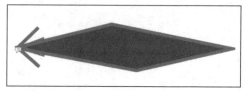

Figure 2.43 The Perimeter tool finishes by adding a measurement markup to your page.

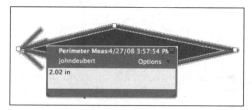

Figure 2.44 Double-clicking the measurement markup displays a pop-up window containing the perimeter value.

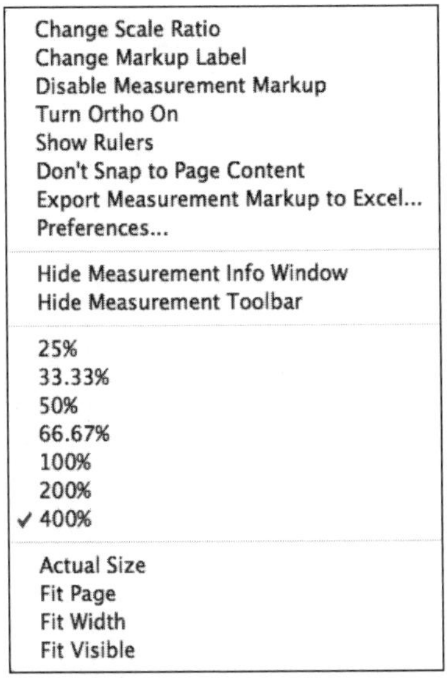

Change Scale Ratio
Change Markup Label
Disable Measurement Markup
Turn Ortho On
Show Rulers
Don't Snap to Page Content
Export Measurement Markup to Excel...
Preferences...

Hide Measurement Info Window
Hide Measurement Toolbar

25%
33.33%
50%
66.67%
100%
200%
✓ 400%

Actual Size
Fit Page
Fit Width
Fit Visible

Figure 2.45 Right-clicking the page with a measuring crosshair displays a pop-up menu with useful settings.

The Area tool

The Area tool works identically to the Perimeter tool, except that it reports the area of the enclosed space you map out with your line segments.

To measure the area of a region:

1. Select the Area tool in the Measurement palette (Figure 2.38).

   The mouse pointer becomes a crosshair, and the Measuring Info window opens (Figure 2.39).

2. Click at the starting point for the region whose area you want to measure.

3. Click successively on points around the perimeter of the region.

   As you do so, Acrobat shows the set of straight lines connecting your points, as in Figure 2.42. Unlike with the Perimeter tool, there's no running total.

4. Click the starting point to close the region.

   The Measuring Info window displays the area of the region enclosed by your line segments. As before, Acrobat adds the polygon to the page as a measurement markup annotation (Figure 2.43).

Measurement settings

Anytime the measuring crosshair is visible, you may right-click on the page and get a contextual menu that lets you change the settings used by the measuring tools (**Figure 2.45**).

MEASURING SIZES AND AREAS

There are several items you can select in this menu, but the ones I find to be the most generally useful are:

Change Scale Ratio. This presents you with a dialog box (**Figure 2.46**) that lets you specify how distances on the PDF page translate into real-life distances. Thus, if your PDF file shows a map of your living room, you can tell the measuring tools that each inch on the page represents 2 feet in real life and have the tools report the actual distance.

Disable Measurement Markup.
Sometimes I'm measuring distances or areas in a diagram, but don't want the double arrows added to the PDF page. This menu item tells the measuring tools not to add the measurement markup comment to the page. The area or distance is reported in the Measuring Info window as usual, but no permanent mark is put on the page.

25%, 33.33%, Fit Page, and so on. These let you zoom in and out of the page while in the middle of a measurement. This can be extremely handy at times. I frequently find myself two-thirds of the way through measuring a spectacularly fussy border and discovering that the rest of the area falls beyond the border of the document window; with Acrobat 9 I can zoom out and continue measuring.

✔ Tips

- I nearly always turn off the measurement markup. Generally, when I'm measuring the size of something on a PDF map or chart, I'm going to put that number into a spreadsheet; I don't usually want the big double arrows and distance value drawing on top of the page contents.

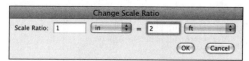

Figure 2.46 The Change Scale Ratio dialog box lets you set the scale for your distance, perimeter, and area measurements.

- If you get an unwanted measurement markup on the page (I often forget to turn off this feature), you can easily remove it by clicking it with the Hand tool or Selection tool (both in the Basic toolbar) and pressing Delete.

SAVING AND PRINTING FILES

3

A document in your computer's memory is impermanent. For your document to trot even a short distance down the sands of time, you need to be able to save it to disk and print it.

Remarkably, Acrobat lets you save your PDF documents to a wide variety of formats. If you need to convert a PDF file to a TIFF file or an EPS file, just select one of those formats when you save the file.

At print time, Acrobat gives you a lot of control over the details of how your document is placed on paper. You can even make a booklet out of your PDF file directly from Acrobat.

In this chapter, you'll see how to use all of Acrobat's file saving, conversion, and printing capabilities.

Saving a PDF File

Many of the tasks in this book describe how to modify the documents you're working with; commenting, touching up text, and adding links all change the file. To make these changes permanent, you must save the file back to your hard disk.

Acrobat does this the same way as most other applications.

To save a document to disk:

◆ Choose File > Save.

Acrobat saves the PDF file onto your hard disk with its existing name.

To save a document with a new name:

1. Choose File > Save As, or click the Save button on the File toolbar (**Figure 3.1**).

   In either case, a standard Save As dialog box opens (**Figure 3.2**).

2. Navigate to the folder on your disk in which you want to save the file.

3. Type a new name for your document into the File Name field.

4. Click Save.

   Acrobat saves your file in the location you specified.

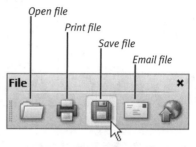

Open file
Print file
Save file
Email file

Figure 3.1 The File toolbar contains tools that let you save or distribute your document.

Figure 3.2 When you choose File > Save As, a standard Save As dialog box opens.

SAVING A PDF FILE

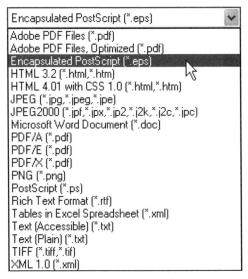

Figure 3.3 The file-type pop-up menu lets you choose from a large number of file formats to which Acrobat can convert a PDF file.

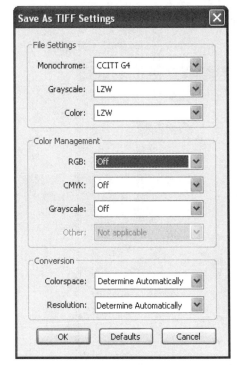

Figure 3.4 Each output file format has a set of controls that dictate the details of the conversion.

Exporting to Other Formats

Acrobat can save a PDF document to a variety of other formats, such as TIFF, PNG, and EPS. This is easily done through the Save As dialog box.

To save a file to a different format:

1. Choose File > Save As, or click the Save button on the File toolbar (Figure 3.1)

   In either case, Acrobat presents you with a standard Save As dialog box (Figure 3.2).

2. Choose a file format from the file-type pop-up menu.

   Acrobat offers a large number of file formats to which it can export (**Figure 3.3**).

3. If you want to change settings, click the Settings button, and choose any of the options you need.

   A Settings dialog box opens for the file format you selected (**Figure 3.4**). You can usually use the defaults with no problems. (See the sidebar "TIFF and EPS Options.")

4. Navigate to the folder on your disk in which you want to save your file.

5. Click Save.

   Acrobat saves your document in the file format you specified.

TIFF and EPS Options

Of all the file types to which Acrobat can convert PDF, only two are routinely useful for most people: TIFF and EPS. These are widely used as illustration formats by high-end page-layout and graphics software such as Adobe InDesign and Adobe Photoshop.

Most of Acrobat's defaults for these formats' file-type settings are perfectly good. For each of them, however, you should change a couple of these settings. These are sticky; once you change them, Acrobat will use the new values until you change them again.

TIFF settings (Figure 3.4):

Change the resolution (at the bottom of the dialog box) to match that of the device on which the illustration will be printed or displayed:

◆ For a printed document, choose 300 dpi for laser printers or 1200 dpi for high-resolution printers.

◆ For onscreen presentations, choose 72 dpi.

EPS general settings (Figure 3.5):

◆ Choose ASCII to ensure compatibility with all networks.

◆ Choose Embedded Fonts to eliminate problems with missing fonts.

◆ Check Convert TrueType to Type 1 to eliminate problems associated with TrueType fonts.

◆ Check Include Preview so that importing applications can more easily work with the file.

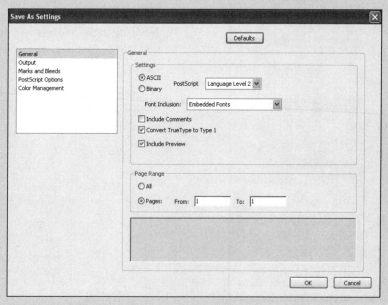

Figure 3.5 The EPS settings shown here always work well.

TIFF AND EPS OPTIONS

Export file types

Acrobat can export PDF files to a variety of other file types, listed in the Save As dialog box's file-type pop-up menu (Figure 3.3). Unfortunately, in most cases the conversion changes the document's appearance: items move around, fonts change, illustrations come out pixilated, and other problems occur. The conversions work best for simple documents.

That said, there are reasons you may want to save a PDF file to some of these formats. Following is a list of the file types to which Acrobat converts most successfully and the purpose of each.

Adobe PDF Files (vector). Acrobat's default file format. Acrobat saves the PDF file as-is.

Adobe PDF Files, Optimized (vector). Still a PDF file, but internally reorganized for viewing in a Web browser. Use this type if you'll be posting your PDF file on the Web for people to read online.

Continues on next page

EXPORTING TO OTHER FORMATS

Vector vs. Bitmap

Each export file type is identified as either vector or bitmap.

Vector files retain their quality regardless of the display or printing device. In particular, edges never become jagged, regardless of the zoom level or the printer's resolution (dpi). On the other hand, vector files are prone to missing fonts and images, and other problems that are often hard to diagnose.

Bitmap files consist of a series of full-page images of all the document's pages. This makes them immune to missing fonts and other problems to which vector formats are prone. However, bitmap files are inherently tied to a device resolution. If the bitmap is intended for a device of one resolution and you print it on a device of another resolution, the results may look bad (**Figure 3.6**).

You should use vector file types unless you have consistent problems with fonts or other hard-to-fix printing problems.

Figure 3.6 Vector file images (left) always look smooth. Bitmap file images (right) become jagged if you zoom in on them.

Encapsulated PostScript (vector). A file format used for illustrations in high-end graphics and page-layout software. EPS is usually your best choice if the PDF file will be used as an illustration (**Figure 3.7**, top).

JPEG (bitmap). A compact bitmap format widely used for images, including digital photography. It's useful only for photographs; it's particularly bad for general PDF files, because line art and text usually become surrounded by a halo of *artifacts,* as in the bottom text in Figure 3.7.

PDF/A (vector). A PDF file that is organized so it is useful for long-term archiving of a document. If you are creating a PDF file that must still be readable in 20 years or more, this is the recommended format.

PDF/E (vector). A PDF file that has a variety of information embedded in it so it is useful for engineering documents. Use this if the document consists of construction plans or other engineering content.

PDF/X (vector). A PDF file that is internally organized for use in prepress. Select this if you will send the PDF file to a print shop for high-quality, professional print.

Rich Text Format (vector). A format that's commonly understood by a wide range of applications, although conversion to it isn't always successful. If you want to convert your PDF file into a word-processing document, this is worth trying.

Figure 3.7 Here is PDF text exported to (from top to bottom) EPS, TIFF, and JPEG. The JPEG artifacts appear somewhat exaggerated because the text was created with the nondefault Low Quality setting.

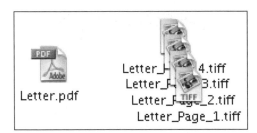

Letter.pdf

Letter_H___4.tiff
Letter_F__3.tiff
Letter_F____2.tiff
Letter_Page_1.tiff

Figure 3.8 When you save a PDF file to a bitmap format, such as JPEG or TIFF, Acrobat creates an image file for each page.

Text (Accessible). A format that extracts the text from the PDF file and attempts to preserve threading and other internal information that makes it easier to use the text with Braille readers. This information must have been put into the PDF file by the creator and is usually absent.

Text (Plain). A format that extracts the text in the PDF file, removing all formatting information and illustrations. The text may come out scrambled if it's formatted in multiple columns.

TIFF (bitmap). The best format if you need to convert your PDF pages to a series of images. The format is reasonably compact, and text and line art look much better than in JPEG (Figure 3.7).

✔ Tips

- If you need to export your pages as illustrations in page-layout or other software, use either EPS or TIFF. EPS is the better choice generally, but if you're having trouble with fonts in the EPS file, go back and resave the PDF file as a TIFF. Keep in mind that because it's a bitmap, the TIFF illustration will become ugly if you scale it. That said, many high-end page-layout programs can use PDF files directly as illustrations, without conversion to other formats.

- If you save a multipage PDF file in one of the bitmap formats, such as JPEG or TIFF, Acrobat creates one bitmap file per page (**Figure 3.8**).

EXPORTING TO OTHER FORMATS

Minimizing File Size

Once you've saved your document, you can use an Acrobat feature that looks through the PDF file and makes changes to minimize the size of the file. This process entails rearranging the internal structure of the document and storing repeated graphics in a more efficient form.

You should always use this feature with PDF files you're going to distribute electronically. It often makes little difference, but sometimes it results in an impressive reduction in file size.

To reduce the size of a PDF file:

1. With your document open, choose Document > Reduce File Size.

   The Reduce File Size dialog box opens (**Figure 3.9**).

2. From the version-compatibility pop-up menu, choose the earliest version of Acrobat with which your file must remain compatible (**Figure 3.10**).

   Choosing higher versions of Acrobat may result in a smaller file, but it will also prevent people from reading the file if they haven't upgraded their version of Acrobat. The default value is Retain Existing; this means the new file should have the same Acrobat compatibility as the original.

3. Click OK.

   The Save As dialog box opens.

4. Provide a name for the new, slimmed-down file, and click OK.

   After a few moments, Acrobat saves the reduced file with the new name.

Figure 3.9 The Reduce File Size dialog box lets you choose the earliest version of Acrobat with which your file must be compatible.

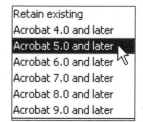

Figure 3.10 Pick the earliest version of Acrobat that your readers might own.

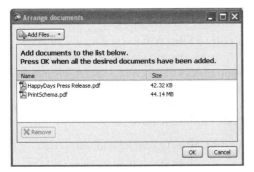

Figure 3.11 Acrobat can reduce the size of several files at once, applying the settings you selected in the Reduce File Size dialog box (Figure 3.9).

✔ Tips

- You can save the reduced file with the same name as the original if you wish. Doing so replaces the original file.

- For optimum trade-off between small file size and broad compatibility, I recommend choosing Acrobat 5 for your compatibility setting. This presumes your file won't be read with an electronic book reader or other device that requires specialized internal information.

- If you click the Apply to Multiple button in the Reduce File Size dialog box (Figure 3.9), Acrobat presents you with another dialog box that lets you select several PDF files to reduce all at once (**Figure 3.11**).

Printing a Document

Visions of the paperless office notwithstanding, PDF is routinely used to distribute printed documents. After you open a PDF file and peruse it on screen, you may want to print it for reading at your leisure.

To print a PDF document:

1. Choose File > Print, or click the Print tool in the File toolbar.

   Acrobat presents you with the Print dialog box (**Figure 3.12**).

2. Choose the options you want.

   In most cases, it's fine to accept the default values for these controls. Most of them are at least occasionally important, however, and we'll discuss them next.

3. Click OK.

   Acrobat prints your document.

Miscellaneous settings

Print to File (Windows). This is a standard Windows check box that tells Acrobat to send the printer code to a file rather than to the printer. This option is occasionally used in professional printing to capture PostScript code for the document.

Print Color As Black (Windows). This option converts colors to black. It may be useful if you're printing diagrams with a lot of thin, light-colored lines.

Printing Tips. If you're connected to the Internet, clicking this button launches your Web browser and takes you to troubleshooting Tips in Adobe's Knowledgebase.

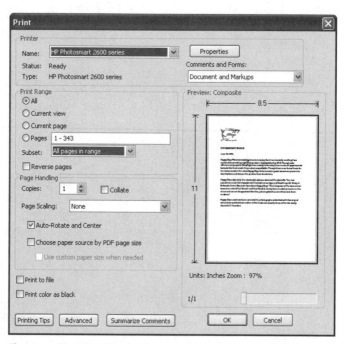

Figure 3.12 The Print dialog box lets you choose from a wide range of options. In most cases, the default values work fine.

PRINTING A DOCUMENT

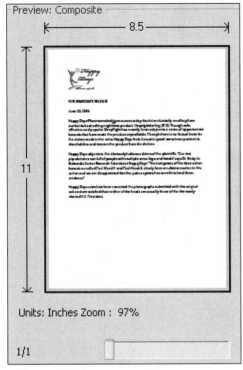

Figure 3.13 The preview picture in the Print dialog box shows you how your printed pages will look. The slider beneath the picture lets you move among the pages.

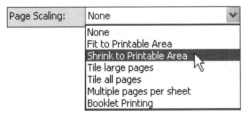

Figure 3.14 The Shrink to Printable Area and the Fit to Printable Area settings may change the size of your page contents.

✔ Tips

- Don't ignore the preview picture in the Print dialog box (Figure 3.12 and **Figure 3.13**). A quick examination of this picture can tell you whether your document will print as you expect.

- The slider control beneath the preview picture in the Print dialog box (Figure 3.12) lets you step through the pages in your document.

- Selecting the Collate check box in the Print dialog box (Figure 3.12) can significantly slow your printing speed, because Acrobat must resend the printing code for each copy of each page in your document. I suggest you routinely leave it unselected and collate by hand.

- If the size and position of items on your printed page seem off by a small amount, check to make sure you didn't print the document with Shrink to Printable Area selected in the Page Scaling menu (**Figure 3.14**). This option may reduce the size of the page contents by a few percent.

Print Options

The Print dialog box (Figure 3.12) presents you with a large collection of choices that determine the details of how your document prints. Although you can usually accept the default values for these options, sometimes you'll need to change some of them.

The Macintosh and Windows versions of this dialog box look different superficially, but the Acrobat-specific controls are entirely identical. The dialog boxes differ only in the controls that are standard to the two environments' Print dialog boxes. For example, the top of the Macintosh version of this dialog box (**Figure 3.15**) has pop-up menus for Presets and Option categories, whereas Windows has printer status text and a Properties button.

Let's look at the controls and see how they affect your print job. Note that the dialog box's preview always reflects the controls' current settings:

Printer controls

Printer Name. This is the standard menu of printers available to your computer. Choose the printer you want to use.

Comments and Forms. This pop-up menu lets you specify whether annotations and form field contents (generically called *markups* in Acrobat) should be printed along with the document pages (**Figure 3.16**).

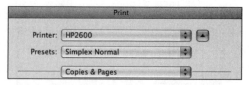

Figure 3.15 The Macintosh Print dialog box has Mac-standard controls at the top, but otherwise has the same Acrobat-specific controls as in Windows.

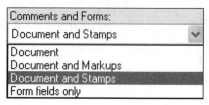

Figure 3.16 The Comments and Forms pop-up menu lets you decide whether to print the contents of annotations and form fields.

Figure 3.17 The Pages text field accepts hyphens to indicate a contiguous range of pages, and commas to separate individual pages.

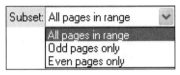

Figure 3.18 The Subset pop-up menu lets you print even, odd, or all pages.

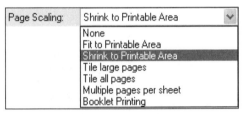

Figure 3.19 The Page Scaling menu tells Acrobat to scale the document pages at print time in a variety of useful ways.

Print-range controls

All, Current View, Current Page, Pages. These four radio buttons choose the pages within your document that you want to print. They're self-explanatory, with one possible exception: The Pages text field (**Figure 3.17**) accepts a hyphen to indicate a contiguous range of pages, and commas to separate discontinuous pages. Thus, 1-4 prints pages 1 through 4, and 1,4,7 prints pages 1, 4, and 7.

Subset. This pop-up menu lets you choose to print even pages, odd pages, or both (**Figure 3.18**). It's useful for manually printing duplex documents.

Reverse Pages. Acrobat prints the pages in reverse order. This is convenient if your printer delivers its pages face-up; the stack of output ends up in correct order.

Page-handling controls

Copies. Specify the number of copies you want of each page.

Collate. If you print multiple copies of a document, the pages are collated.

Page Scaling. This menu lets you resize the document pages in a variety of ways (**Figure 3.19**). The most routinely useful selections are as follows:

◆ The None option prints the document in its native size; this is usually what you want.

Continues on next page

PRINT OPTIONS

- Fit to Printable Area shrinks or expands the page so it fits within the printer's native printable area. This makes the document page as large as it can be without losing information off the edges of the paper (**Figure 3.20**).

- Shrink to Printable Area shrinks the page so it fits within the printer's native printable area. This ensures items near the edges of your pages (such as headers and footers) print successfully.

We'll look at other selections in this menu later in this chapter.

Autorotate and Center. This option repositions the page so it's centered on the paper (**Figure 3.21**). It may also rotate the page if Acrobat thinks it's necessary (usually not). This may be useful if you want to center a small document page on a large piece of paper.

Choose Paper Source by PDF Page Size (Windows). This option overrides the printer's default paper size and uses each page's paper size as specified in the PDF file. It's useful if you have a document whose pages vary in size and a printer with multiple paper trays; Acrobat selects the paper from whichever tray most closely matches the page's size.

Figure 3.20 Fit to Printable Area scales the page up or down until it exactly fits within the current paper area.

Figure 3.21 Autorotate and Center moves the contents of the document page so they're centered on the paper.

Printing Terminology

Here are some terms you may encounter when reading about printing:

Duplex. Printing on both sides of a sheet of paper.

Simplex. Printing on only one side of each sheet of paper.

2-up, 3-up, and so on. Printing more than one page on each sheet. The number is the number of pages per sheet.

Imposition. Rearranging pages for printing a book. The verb is *impose*.

Using these terms, you can say that to make a booklet, your document is printed 2-up, duplex, imposed.

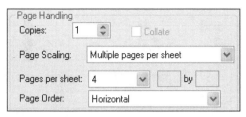

Figure 3.22 When you choose Multiple Pages per Sheet from the Page Scaling menu, Acrobat displays additional controls.

Figure 3.23 The Preview picture in the Print dialog box reflects the number of pages you're printing on each sheet of paper.

| Pages per sheet: | Custom... | 3 | by 2 |

Figure 3.24 If you choose Custom from the Pages per Sheet menu, you can specify how many pages you want across and down each sheet.

Printing Multiple Pages per Sheet

You'll sometimes want to print two or more pages of your document on each piece of paper. Acrobat's Print dialog box lets you do this easily.

To print multiple pages on each printed page:

1. Choose File > Print.

    The Print dialog box opens.

2. In the Page Scaling pop-up menu, choose Multiple Pages per Sheet (**Figure 3.22**).

    Acrobat displays additional controls beneath the Page Scaling pop-up menu (Figure 3.22). In addition, the Print dialog box's Preview reflects the multiple pages (**Figure 3.23**).

3. From the Pages per Sheet menu, choose the number of pages you want on each sheet of paper.

    As always, the Preview picture shows the change.

4. Click OK.

    Acrobat prints your document with the specified number of pages on each sheet of paper.

✔ Tips

- If you choose Custom from the Pages per Sheet pop-up menu, you can specify how many pages you want across and down each sheet (**Figure 3.24**).

- I often make a reference page with thumbnails of all of my document's pages by printing with 16 pages per sheet. The text is unreadable, but it provides me with a usable overview of my document's layout.

Printing a Booklet

Sometimes, when proofing a document, it's useful to turn a PDF file into a booklet. When you choose this feature, Acrobat prints your document two pages per sheet of paper, double-sided, reordering the pages as needed to make a booklet (**Figures 3.25** and **3.26**).

To print a document as a booklet:

1. Choose File > Print.

   Acrobat displays the Print dialog box .

2. In the Page Scaling pop-up menu, choose Booklet Printing.

   Acrobat displays additional controls beneath the Page Scaling pop-up menu (**Figure 3.27**). As always, the Preview reflects the new arrangement of the pages.

3. From the Booklet Subset pop-up menu, choose Front Side Only or Back Side Only if you want to print only one side of each sheet of paper (**Figure 3.28**).

   These options let you print a booklet on a printer that can't print double-sided. You can print the front sides of all the pages, put the paper back into the printer, and then print the back sides.

4. In the "Sheets from ... to" fields, type the beginning and end of the range of paper sheets you want to print.

   Confusingly, entering a zero in both of these fields means "print all the sheets." This is what you'll usually want.

5. In the Binding pop-up menu, specify whether the booklet will be bound on the left or the right.

6. Click OK.

   Acrobat prints your document as a booklet.

Figure 3.25 To turn a 4-page document into a booklet, Acrobat prints pages 4 and 1 on one side of the paper and pages 2 and 3 on the other.

Figure 3.26 Fold the paper to make your booklet. For longer documents, stack the paper, and staple the stack in the middle before folding.

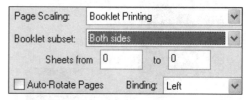

Figure 3.27 When you choose Booklet Printing, Acrobat displays additional controls that let you specify the details.

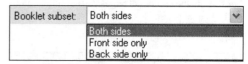

Figure 3.28 Printing the front and back sides separately allows you to print a booklet on a printer that doesn't print double-sided.

MAKING PDF FILES

PDF is arguably the best file format for storing and distributing documents. It's compact, it supports a wide variety of content (including text, images, line art, and multimedia), and you can use it for free without incurring licensing fees. However, all this capability is useless unless you can conveniently create PDF files. This is the topic we address in this chapter.

When you install Acrobat, you also install features into your computer system that make it easy and quick to generate PDF files from within virtually any Macintosh or Windows application. Furthermore, Acrobat has many powerful features that let you create PDF files: you can convert many common file types to PDF, scan paper documents directly into PDF, convert Web pages to PDF files, and combine several PDF files into a single document.

In this chapter, you learn how to do all of these.

Printing to a PDF File

Acrobat makes it easy to create PDF files from any application. When you install Acrobat 9, you also install onto your computer system a virtual printer called Adobe PDF 9.0 (**Figure 4.1**). When you print to this printer, it converts the document being printed into a PDF file rather than producing sheets of paper.

The nice thing about this feature is that it works with any Macintosh or Windows application that allows you to print.

Figure 4.1 Acrobat installs onto your system a virtual printer named Adobe PDF 9.0. When printed to, this printer creates a PDF file.

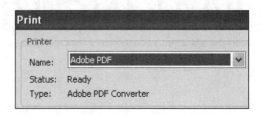

To print to a PDF file:

1. Choose File > Print in your application.
   Your system's standard Print dialog box opens.

2. In the Printer pop-up menu, choose Adobe PDF 9.0 on the Mac or Adobe PDF on Windows (**Figure 4.2**).

3. Click Print.
   A standard Save dialog box opens.

4. Type a name for your PDF file.

5. Click OK.
   After a short while, you will see a newly created PDF file on your disk.

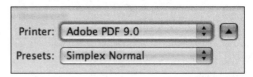

Figure 4.2 You use the Adobe PDF printer by choosing it as the current printer in the standard Print dialog box.

Adobe PDF Options

Adobe PDF defines a set of options, available through the Print dialog box, that affect the PDF it produces. Although Acrobat's default values for these options are the most sensible choices in most cases, you may want to look them over.

You access the PDF options from the standard Print dialog box by clicking the Properties button in Windows or, on the Mac, by choosing PDF Options in the pop-up menu just below the Presets menu (**Figure 4.3**).

See the Acrobat Help files for the meanings of each of these controls.

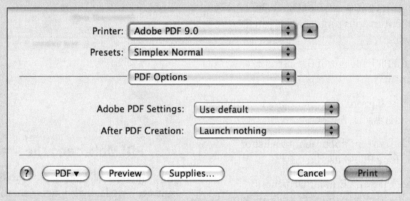

Figure 4.3 Some print options affect Adobe PDF's behavior. The default values work well.

Using PDFMaker in Microsoft Office (Windows)

The Windows version of Acrobat 9 automatically installs a set of tools into the Microsoft Office suite of software (**Figure 4.4**). These tools are known collectively as PDFMaker.

PDFMaker's appearance and abilities vary depending on your version of Office. In Office 2007, it installs tools that let you do the following:

◆ Create a PDF file out of the current document.

◆ Email the current document as a PDF file to an address of your choice.

◆ Send the current document to a list of people for a PDF-based review.

The Create PDF and Email PDF functions are available in all versions of Office, making it very simple to convert Word, Excel, and other Office documents to PDF.

The instructions below are for Office 2007. Earlier versions of Office have the same functions, but they reside in a PDFMaker toolbar, rather than an Acrobat "ribbon."

To create a PDF file in an Office application:

1. With your Office document active, select the Acrobat ribbon.

   The PDFMaker commands become visible, as in Figure 4.4.

2. Click the Create Adobe PDF button.

   Office presents you with the standard Save dialog box.

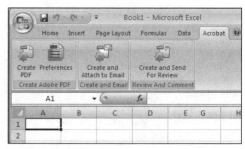

Figure 4.4 Acrobat 9 installs PDFMaker, a set of PDF-related controls into the Microsoft Office applications.

PDFMaker and the Mac

Even though PDFMaker is a Windows-only utility, Macintosh users shouldn't feel left out. The Mac doesn't really need PDFMaker, because Mac OS X provides similar functions to every Mac application. The Mac Print dialog box has a PDF drop-down menu in its lower-left corner that gives you access to a long series of PDF-related commands (**Figure 4.5**). Just select the function you want and Mac OS X does the rest.

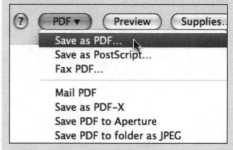

Figure 4.5 Mac OS X has a PDF menu in its standard Print dialog box that provides a variety of PDF-related commands.

Figure 4.6 The Convert to PDF and Email tool launches your mail client and opens a blank message that has the new PDF file attached to it.

3. Specify a name and location for your PDF file.

4. Click OK.

Acrobat creates the PDF file, displaying a progress bar while it works.

✔ Tip

■ PDFMaker uses the Adobe PDF virtual printer behind the scenes, so don't be alarmed if your Office application seems to be printing in the background when you use this toolbar.

To email an Office document as a PDF file:

1. With your Office document open, click the Create and Attach to Email button.

The standard Save dialog box opens.

2. Specify a name and location for your PDF file.

3. Click OK.

Acrobat creates the PDF file, displaying a progress bar while it works.

When it's finished, PDFMaker launches your email client software and opens a blank email window with the new PDF file already attached (**Figure 4.6**).

4. Fill out the destination address and subject in your email client.

5. Click your email client's Send button.

✔ Tip

■ Depending on your email client, PDFMaker may ask you for an email address and subject and send the PDF file directly, without launching your email client.

USING PDFMAKER IN MICROSOFT OFFICE

Converting Images and Other Files to PDF

Acrobat 9 can convert a variety of file types to PDF and then open them in a document window. The list of supported file types includes all the common vector and image formats (see the sidebar "Conversion File Types").

Converting these files to PDF is remarkably easy.

To convert a file to PDF:

1. In Acrobat, choose File > Create PDF > From File; or, on the Tasks toolbar, choose Create > PDF from File (**Figure 4.7**).

   Acrobat presents you with a standard pick-a-file dialog box.

2. Choose the file that you want to convert to PDF.

   Acrobat converts the file to PDF and opens it in a new document window.

3. If you want to save the document on your disk, choose File > Save As.

✔ Tip

- Acrobat's Preferences include a large collection of controls that determine how it converts files to PDF. The default values for these controls are sensible and should generally be left alone. However, as you gain experience, you may find it interesting to look at them. On the Mac go to Acrobat > Preferences, or in Windows choose Edit > Preferences, to get to the Convert to PDF options (**Figure 4.8**).

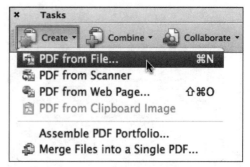

Figure 4.7 The Create menu on the Tasks toolbar lets you create a PDF file from a variety of sources.

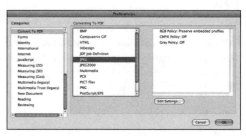

Figure 4.8 Acrobat 9's Preferences let you specify the details of how it converts the various file formats to PDF.

Conversion File Types

Acrobat 9 can convert the following types of files to PDF:

- BMP
- GIF
- HTML
- InDesign
- JPEG
- JPEG2000
- PCX
- PICT
- PNG
- PostScript/EPS
- Text
- TIFF

This list encompasses all the most common graphic, design, and image formats.

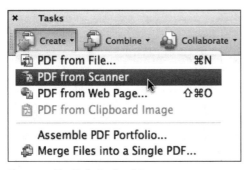

Figure 4.9 The Tasks toolbar lets you scan a paper document directly to PDF.

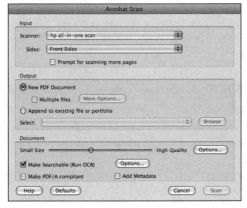

Figure 4.10 The Acrobat Scan dialog box lets you control how your scanned document is converted to PDF.

Scanning Directly to PDF

Using Acrobat, you can scan paper documents directly to PDF. Acrobat can operate any scanner with a TWAIN driver or, in Windows, a Windows Image Acquisition (WIA) driver. Most scanners install on a computer with one or both of these drivers.

Remember that if you scan a text document, the result is a *picture* of the text, not the text itself; the resulting document isn't searchable. Acrobat can use Optical Character Recognition (OCR) technology to convert the scanned text to real text; you'll see how to do this in Chapter 17.

To scan a page directly to PDF:

1. Choose File > Create PDF > From Scanner; or, on the Tasks toolbar, choose Create > PDF from Scanner (**Figure 4.9**).

   The Acrobat Scan dialog box opens (**Figure 4.10**).

2. From the Scanner pop-up menu, choose the scanner you want to use.

   This menu lists all the TWAIN and WIA scanners visible to your computer.

3. Choose the settings for the scan:

   ▲ If your scanner can do double-sided scans, choose Front Sides or Both Sides from the Sides menu.

   ▲ If you want to convert scanned text to searchable text, click the Make Searchable check box.

   The remaining controls in this dialog box are best left at their default settings. Check Acrobat Help for a description of these controls.

4. Click Scan.

   Acrobat scans your document and opens the resulting file in a new PDF document window.

5. Choose File > Save As to save your new PDF file on your disk.

✔ Tip

■ You can click the Append radio button in the Acrobat Scan dialog box to add your scanned page to the end of an existing PDF file. I use this sometimes when scanning receipts that need to be added to a PDF-format invoice.

Converting Web Pages to PDF

Acrobat can convert a Web page or an entire Web site into a single PDF file. The result is a self-contained PDF version of the original Web page, with all images and graphics intact and with functioning links.

I use this feature to convert online manuals and other documentation into a PDF file that I can keep, read, and search offline.

To convert a single Web page to PDF:

1. Choose File > Create PDF > From Web Page (**Figure 4.11**); or, on the Tasks toolbar, choose Create > PDF from Web Page.

   Acrobat presents you with the Create PDF from Web Page dialog box (**Figure 4.12**).

2. In the URL field, type the complete Web address of the Web page you want to convert to PDF.

3. If you want to capture part of the entire Web site (that is, not just a single Web page), click the Capture Multiple Levels button, which reveals some more controls (**Figure 4.13**):

   ▲ In the Get Only field, type the depth to which you want to convert the site. (See the sidebar "Web Site Conversion Settings.")

   ▲ Choose both "Stay on same path" and "Stay on same server."

4. Click Create.

   Acrobat displays the Download Status dialog box (**Figure 4.14**).

   When the conversion is finished, Acrobat displays the converted Web page or site in a document window. Note that there will be some differences in the text and graphics when they are converted. These changes are usually comparable to how a page's appearance changes from one Web browser to another.

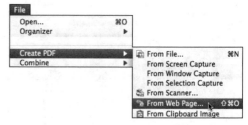

Figure 4.11 Acrobat lets you convert a Web page or an entire Web site into a PDF file.

Figure 4.12 The Create PDF from Web Page dialog box lets you specify the URL of a Web page you want to convert to PDF.

Figure 4.13 If you click the Capture Multiple Levels button, you get additional controls that limit the scope of the web page conversion.

Figure 4.14 As Acrobat converts the Web site to PDF, it shows you how the conversion is progressing.

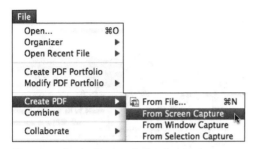

Figure 4.15 On the Macintosh, Acrobat can capture parts of your computer screen and convert the image to PDF.

Converting Screen Shots to PDF

This is a Macintosh-only feature. When it's selected, Acrobat lets you capture the contents of a window, a region, or an entire screen to a PDF file. This is convenient for people who write computer documentation.

To capture an entire screen to PDF:

1. Choose File > Create PDF > From Screen Capture (**Figure 4.15**).

   After a moment, Acrobat presents you with a document window containing an image of the entire screen.

2. Choose File > Save As to save this file to disk.

Web Site Conversion Settings

The controls in the Create PDF from Web Page dialog box (**Figure 4.12**) have the critical purpose of limiting the scope of your Web capture. At the extreme, they keep you from inadvertently trying to convert the entire World Wide Web into a single (large!) PDF file.

Get only *n* level(s). Here you specify the extent to which Acrobat should grab Web pages that are the target of links on your selected Web page. A value of 1 says to get only the Web page whose address you have specified. A value of 2 says to get that Web page and any pages linked to by that page. A value of 3 additionally captures pages linked to by *those* pages, and so forth.

Keep this number small. *Very* small. The larger the number of levels you specify, the exponentially longer the conversion will take.

Get entire site. As it says, this option converts the entire site to PDF. I strongly recommend against selecting this, since it can take an amazingly long time.

Stay on same path. Like all files, the HTML files that make up a Web site reside in a directory on a hard disk—in this case, the Web server's disk. This option prevents Acrobat from following links that reside outside the target Web page's location or its subdirectories. I recommend choosing this.

Stay on the same server. Acrobat won't follow links off your target page's server. I strongly recommend this option. Otherwise, for example, if the page you request has links to its sponsors, you may find yourself trying to convert all of Microsoft's Web site to a PDF file.

To capture a window to PDF:

1. Choose File > Create PDF > From Window Capture (Figure 4.15).

   The mouse pointer changes to a camera. As the pointer moves over the windows open on the screen, the current window turns blue.

2. Click the window whose contents you want to capture.

   A document opens, containing an image of the window you clicked.

3. Choose File > Save As to save this file to disk.

To capture a region of the desktop to PDF:

1. Choose File > Create PDF > From Selection Capture (Figure 4.15).

   The pointer changes to a crosshair.

2. Click and drag a rectangular marquee around the area you want to capture.

   Acrobat uses a nonstandard marquee with this tool: You drag out a light gray area on the screen (**Figure 4.16**).

   Acrobat presents you with a document containing the contents of the region you enclosed (**Figure 4.17**).

3. Choose File > Save As to save this file to disk.

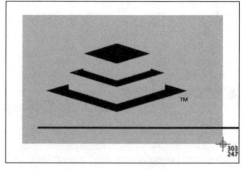

Figure 4.16 When capturing a part of the screen, you drag out a light gray rectangle that indicates the capture area.

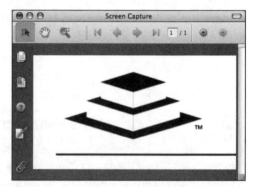

Figure 4.17 The area of the screen you selected turns into a PDF image.

CONVERTING SCREEN SHOTS TO PDF

Figure 4.18 Acrobat lets you combine several files into a single PDF file.

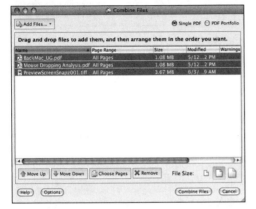

Figure 4.19 This dialog box lets you choose the files you want to merge.

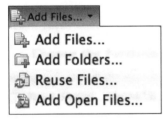

Figure 4.20 You may add files one at a time or a whole folder at once, or use previously merged files or currently open files.

Merging PDF Files

Acrobat can combine multiple files into a single PDF file. The component files may be PDF files, TIFF files, EPS files, or files of any format that Acrobat can convert to PDF. This is extremely useful for combining, say, all the files associated with an invoice—the invoice itself, an expense report, scanned receipts, justifications for your hourly rate, letters from your doctor—into a single file you can email.

To merge several PDF files into a single PDF file:

1. Choose Combine > Merge Files into a Single PDF (**Figure 4.18**); or, on the Tasks toolbar, choose Combine Files > Merge Files.

   The Combine Files dialog box opens (**Figure 4.19**). This dialog box lets you choose a list of files to combine.

2. Choose one of the following from the Add Files drop-down menu (**Figure 4.20**):

   ▲ **Add Files** lets you add individual files to the list.

   ▲ **Add Folders** lets you choose a folder, all of whose convertible contents will be added to the list.

   ▲ **Reuse Files** lets you choose files inside a PDF Portfolio. (We'll talk about PDF portfolios in the next chapter.)

   ▲ **Add Open Files** allows you to choose among the files currently open in Acrobat.

   No matter which option you choose, an Open dialog box appropriate to the task opens (**Figure 4.21**).

   The list of files currently selected is displayed in the Combine Multiple Files dialog box. You can click the Move Up and Move Down arrows beneath the list to alter the files' order.

MERGING PDF FILES

3. Click the Single PDF radio button in the upper right corner of the Combine Multiple Files dialog box.

We'll discuss the alternative, PDF Portfolio, in the next chapter.

4. Click Combine Files.

Acrobat merges the files together and presents you with a standard Save dialog box.

5. Specify a name for the new, merged PDF file and click OK.

Acrobat saves the new PDF file.

✔ Tips

■ In Figure 4.19, you see three File Size buttons in the lower-right corner of the dialog box; they let you choose a qualitative file size (small, medium, or large). These options mostly affect how images are stored in your PDF file. The smaller the file, the less image information Acrobat retains in the merged file. Note that if there are no images in your PDF files, you probably won't see much difference among these options.

■ Acrobat creates bookmarks in the merged file that take you to the start of each of the original documents. (See Chapter 2 for a reminder of how to use bookmarks.)

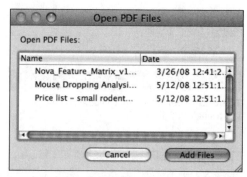

Figure 4.21 Each of the Add options presents you with an Open dialog box appropriate to the type of files.

PDF PORTFOLIOS

Figure 5.1 The initial view of an Acrobat 9 portfolio offers a representation of the files it contains.

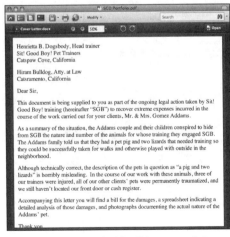

Figure 5.2 When you double-click on a portfolio member, Acrobat displays the contents of that file.

PDF portfolios are new to Acrobat 9, replacing the more-limited "packages" of Acrobat 8. A portfolio is a PDF file that contains one or more individual files bundled into a single container. The files within a portfolio can be any of a wide variety of types, including Microsoft Word documents, Microsoft Excel spreadsheets, Microsoft PowerPoint presentations, Apple QuickTime movies, JPEG images, Adobe Flash animations, and PDF documents. Each file within the portfolio retains its own identity; security settings and other characteristics of the document remain unchanged.

Portfolios let you bundle together a set of related documents for easy e-mailing, posting, or other distribution. Thus, a portfolio might contain all the files associated with an invoice: the cover letter, the invoice itself, the summary of expenses, the scanned receipts.

When you open a PDF portfolio in Acrobat 9, you see a display of its individual component files (**Figure 5.1**). Double-clicking a filename in the window displays that component file within the portfolio (**Figure 5.2**).

Continues on next page

Right-clicking a portfolio component lets you open the file in its original application or save it as a separate file (**Figure 5.3**). Furthermore, portfolios have a hierarchical structure; your portfolio may contain folders (**Figure 5.4**). Double-clicking one of these folder items displays the contents of that folder.

✔ Tip

■ If you open a portfolio file with an earlier version of Acrobat, you will see a window like that in **Figure 5.5**, in which the portfolio contents are presented as a simple list in the upper pane; clicking on an item in the list displays the contents of that item in the lower pane . This is not nearly as useful or slick as opening the file in Acrobat 9 or Adobe Reader 9, but you can at least see the file's contents.

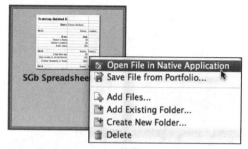

SGb Spreadshee

- Open File in Native Application
- Save File from Portfolio...
- Add Files...
- Add Existing Folder...
- Create New Folder...
- Delete

Figure 5.3 Right-clicking a portfolio member lets you open the file in its original application or save the original file to disk.

More Addams pets

Caution advised; some of these are feeding in a most disturbing way.

Figure 5.4 A portfolio may contain folders that contain additional files or folders.

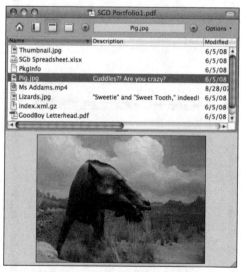

Figure 5.5 When you open a portfolio in Acrobat 8 or earlier, you get a bare list that lets you see the members' contents.

Creating a Portfolio

Creating a portfolio consists of the following steps, several of them optional:

1. Add files and folders to the portfolio.

2. Type in descriptions of the component files (optional).

3. Specify a layout for the portfolio, determining how the portfolio contents should be presented to the user.

4. Add a welcome page and header to the portfolio (optional).

5. Pick a color scheme (optional).

6. Save or publish the portfolio.

The portfolio user interface prompts you to carry out the steps in the above order, but you may actually do them in whatever order you wish.

To create a PDF portfolio:

1. Choose File > Create PDF Portfolio, or File > Combine > Assemble PDF Portfolio.

   A blank Edit PDF Portfolio window appears (**Figure 5.6**). This moderately complex window displays the files that comprise your portfolio and a series of controls that lets you insert files into the portfolio and specify the portfolio's appearance.

2. Do either of the following:

   ▲ Drag files from the Finder or Windows Explorer into the content area of the Portfolio window.

   ▲ Click the Add Files button and use the resulting pick-a-file dialog box to select one or more files or folders.

   Acrobat adds icons for the files and folders to the portfolio's Edit Portfolio window.

Continues on next page

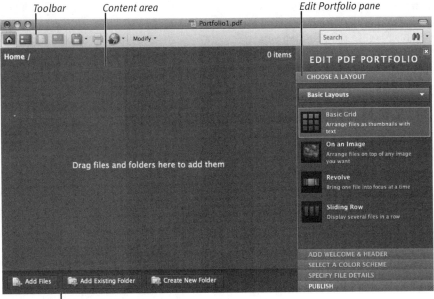

Figure 5.6 The Portfolio Editor window has all the tools you need to specify a portfolio's components, appearance, and behavior.

CREATING A PORTFOLIO

3. If you wish, add a description of each file by clicking in the big blank area beneath the file's name; you will see a prompt urging you to add a description (**Figure 5.7**). Click on this prompt and then type your description.

This text appears beneath the file's name in the portfolio; a couple of the files in the portfolio in Figure 5.1 have descriptions.

✔ Tips

■ Step 1 above lists the most convenient and common ways to make the initial, blank portfolio. As is generally true in Acrobat, you will find many other ways of creating the portfolio, including the following: choosing File > Create PDF > Assemble PDF Portfolio; choosing Create > Assemble PDF Portfolio from the Tasks toolbar; clicking the PDF Portfolio radio button in the Combine Files dialog (Figure 4.19).

■ The Add Folder button adds the selected folder to the portfolio, together with its contents. If the folder contains any other folders, they will also be added to the portfolio with all of their contents. Be careful with this: an excellent way to bring Acrobat to its knees is to drag your disk icon into the portfolio window; you can sit and watch the spinning beach ball or rotating hourglass for several hours while Acrobat tries to cram the entire contents of your hard disk into the portfolio.

■ On Mac OS X, many files are actually folders (called "packages") that are treated specially by the operating system. This is most commonly true of executable application files, but may be true of document files, as well; for example, files created by Pages and Numbers (Apple's word processing and spreadsheet software) are actually packages. If you import such a document into a portfolio, Acrobat treats it as a folder.

Figure 5.7 You can supply descriptive text for each member of the portfolio.

Figure 5.9 The list view is a very compact representation of all the member files of a portfolio.

The Portfolio Toolbar

The Portfolio window's toolbar provides a set of buttons that are available when editing or viewing the portfolio; these tools are as follows (**Figure 5.8**):

Home. This button returns you to the portfolio's initial view, which this may be a grid, a revolving set of icons, or a sliding row of icons, as determined by the portfolio's layout (discussed in the following section).

List View. This displays the portfolio's component files as a vertical, scrolling list (**Figure 5.9**). The list view is the most compact representation of files in a portfolio; I use it often when working with very large portfolios.

Preview Document. This displays the contents of one of the portfolio's component documents.

Show Welcome Page. This returns you to the portfolio's cover page, exactly as though you just opened the portfolio. (We'll discuss the welcome page later in the chapter.)

Save. This saves the portfolio to disk.

Print. This prints the currently selected component file. Unfortunately, this works only with PDF files.

Continues on next page

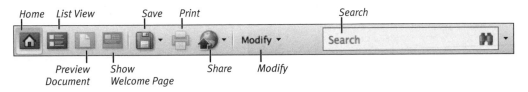

Figure 5.8 The Portfolio toolbar has controls that are available both when creating and when viewing a portfolio.

CREATING A PORTFOLIO

Share. This tool presents a drop-down menu that lets you e-mail the portfolio to someone or share it on Acrobat.com (**Figure 5.10**). We'll discuss Acrobat.com later in this chapter.

Modify. This drop-down menu contains commands that let you change the contents of the portfolio (**Figure 5.11**). Among other things, this lets you exit Edit mode (when you are finished creating a portfolio) and return to it (to make changes).

Search. This is a standard search field that lets you search for text within the portfolio's component documents.

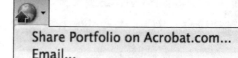

Figure 5.10 The Share button lets you e-mail the portfolio to someone or share the portfolio on Acrobat.com.

Figure 5.11 The Modify menu lets you, among other things, exit and reenter Edit mode.

Figure 5.12 The appearance controls determine the portfolio's appearance and behavior. Here we see the layout controls.

Figure 5.13 You may drag the portfolio members on top of a background image. They may be placed anywhere you like on that image.

Choosing a Layout

The portfolio layout specifies how the portfolio's component files will be presented to the user.

Along the right side of the Edit PDF Portfolio window is a pane containing a series of appearance controls (**Figure 5.12**). Each control appears as a horizontal strip that, when clicked, reveals a series of selections specific to a task; Figure 5.12 shows the set of selections under the Choose a Layout strip.

Acrobat 9 lets you select from four layouts for your portfolio:

Basic Grid. This presents the content files as a rectangular grid, as in Figure 5.1. This is the default layout.

On an Image. This lets you select an image to use as a background and then drag icons representing the portfolio's components on top of that image (**Figure 5.13**). These icons may be placed anywhere on the image.

Continues on next page

Revolve. The current file within the portfolio is large and in the center of the window, with the adjacent files fading off to either side (**Figure 5.14**).

Sliding Row. The portfolio's contents make up a single row of preview icons that the user can slide left or right to find a file of interest (**Figure 5.15**).

In all four layouts, double-clicking on the graphic representation of a component file displays the contents of that file.

Each layout has navigation controls appropriate to that layout. For example, the Revolve and Sliding Row layouts (Figures 5.14 and 5.15) have little arrowheads on the right and left sides of the window, allowing you to slide the file selection in those directions. Most of these controls are reasonably intuitive, so I shall let you experiment with them.

To select a portfolio layout:

1. Click the Choose a Layout strip in the Appearance Controls pane (Figure 5.12).

2. Select the layout you wish to use for your portfolio.

Figure 5.14 The Revolve layout provides a display similar to iTunes' cover flow.

Figure 5.15 The Sliding Row layout presents the portfolio's files as a row of icons that can slide left or right.

Figure 5.16 You can give your welcome page text, an image, text and an image, or a flash animation.

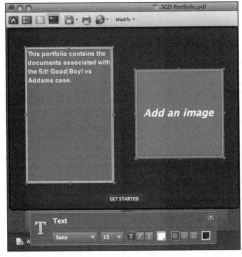

Figure 5.17 Once you select the type of welcome page you want, Acrobat presents you with content boxes for the items in that type.

Adding a Welcome Page

Acrobat displays a welcome page when the user first opens a portfolio. This lets you provide an introduction to the portfolio—perhaps describing its contents and purpose—or to display your corporate logo or other initial graphic.

The welcome page may contain text, an image, a combination of text and an image, or a flash animation.

To add a welcome page to a portfolio:

1. On the right side of the Edit PDF Portfolio window, click Add Welcome & Header (Figure 5.6).

   Acrobat reveals the controls for the welcome page (**Figure 5.16**).

2. Select the type of welcome page you want: none, text only, image only, and so on.

   Depending on the elements you choose, Acrobat displays in the portfolio's content area some combination of a text box, an image box, and a Flash animation box (**Figure 5.17**).

3. Click in each box and type in text or select a JPEG or SWF file, as appropriate, in the resulting pick-a-file dialog box.

   When you add content to a box, a toolbar that controls the appearance of that box's content appears (the text-appearance toolbar is visible in Figure 5.17).

4. Adjust whatever settings you wish in each box's appearance toolbar.

   The controls in these toolbars are pretty basic: font, size, and alignment for text; scale and opacity for images and Flash animations.

Continues on next page

5. Drag the text and graphics boxes to new locations and resize them as you wish.

   Each of the content boxes has a set of standard handles at the corners and sides, allowing you to easily change its size.

6. Click on the Home button in the toolbar to exit the welcome page.

Now, when users open your portfolio, they will be initially presented with your welcome page, as in **Figure 5.18**.

Note that, in addition to the usual Portfolio toolbar across the top of the window, the welcome screen provides a Get Started button, which dismisses the welcome screen and presents the user with the portfolio's home page (the initial view that presents a grid, list, or other representation of the portfolio's contents, as in Figure 5.15); it also provides a check box that lets the user specify that the welcome screen should be hidden the next time the user opens that portfolio.

✔ Tip

- Surprisingly, the only type of image you can use in the welcome page is JPEG; no TIFF, PNG, EPS, or (this is especially surprising) PDF graphics.

Figure 5.18 The welcome page is the first thing a user sees upon opening the portfolio.

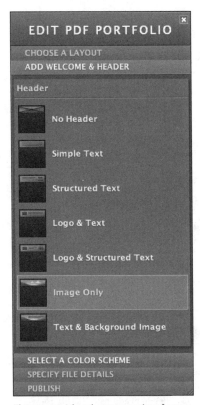

Figure 5.19 A header can consist of some combination of text and an image.

Figure 5.20 Acrobat provides a content box for each of the components of your header.

Adding a Header

A portfolio header is a combination of text and image that appears at the top of every page in the portfolio, including the welcome page.

You specify a header in a manner very similar to the way you create a welcome page.

To create a portfolio header:

1. On the right side of the Edit PDF Portfolio window, click Add Welcome & Header (Figure 5.6).

2. Click Header.

   Acrobat reveals the types of headers available to you (**Figure 5.19**).

3. Select the type of header you want: none, text only, image only, and so on.

   Acrobat displays in the portfolio's content area some combination of a text box and an image box, depending on your selection (**Figure 5.20**).

4. Click in each box and type text or select a JPEG file, as appropriate, from the pick-a-file dialog box.

   When you click in a box, a palette with appearance controls will appear; the Image Controls toolbar is visible in Figure 5.20.

5. Adjust whatever settings you wish for each box's Controls toolbar.

   The controls in these toolbars are again pretty basic: font, size, and alignment for text; scale and opacity for images and flash animations.

6. Resize the boxes as you wish by dragging the handles at the sides and corners.

   Continues on next page

ADDING A HEADER

7. Click on the Home button in the toolbar to exit the header editor.

The header will now appear at the top of every page in the portfolio (**Figure 5.21**).

✔ Tip

■ One particularly useful header layout is Logo and Structured Text. This gives you separate text boxes for your telephone number, e-mail address, and URL (**Figure 5.22**). Furthermore, the e-mail address and URL are clickable on the resulting portfolio page, linking to your e-mail software and your Web browser, respectively.

Figure 5.21 The header appears at the top of every page in the portfolio, including the welcome page.

Figure 5.22 A Logo and Structured Text header contains a clickable e-mail address and URL.

Figure 5.23 Clicking one of the color squares selects a standard color scheme for the portfolio.

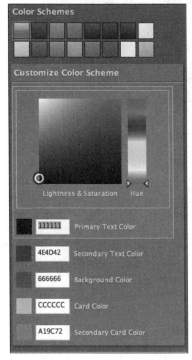

Figure 5.24 You can also create a custom color scheme, specifying the colors of all the components of a portfolio page.

Choosing a Color Scheme

By default, a portfolio's background, window frames, and so on are rendered in a set of soothing gray shades. You can change this by specifying a color scheme for your portfolio.

The color scheme affects the color of everything in the Portfolio window except the colors of the component documents. You may select from among predefined color schemes or create your own from scratch.

To choose a color scheme:

1. On the right side of the Edit PDF Portfolio window, click Select a Color Scheme (Figure 5.6).

   Acrobat displays the color scheme controls (**Figure 5.23**).

2. Do either of the following:

   ▲ Click on one of the colored squares to select a predefined color scheme.

   ▲ Click on the Customize Color Scheme link and then choose the colors you wish from the resulting color picker (**Figure 5.24**). You need to choose colors for all five parts that make up a portfolio page.

3. Click the Home button to end the process.

   You now return to the portfolio's home page, rendered with your new color scheme.

✔ Tips

■ The color picker in Figure 5.24 lets you specify each color either by using color-picker controls for Hue and Lightness & Saturation, or by typing a color value into a text box. For the record, the color value consists of a six-character hexadecimal RGB value. Personally, I'd as soon stick with the color picker controls.

■ Many companies have standard, corporate colors that you should use if you are creating a portfolio for use as marketing or other official materials.

Setting File Information

When a user clicks on the List View button in the Portfolio toolbar, Acrobat presents a scrolling list of the portfolio contents, as in Figure 5.9. Acrobat lets you control the information that is visible to the user in list view.

To specify list details:

1. On the right side of the Edit PDF Portfolio window, click the Specify File Details button (Figure 5.6).

   Acrobat switches to list view and displays a set of check boxes that determine what information is displayed for each of the portfolio's content files (**Figure 5.25**).

2. Click the check boxes for the information you want displayed in the list (**Figure 5.26**).

3. Click the Home button in the Portfolio toolbar to leave Specify File Details mode.

✔ Tips

- You can click a check box once to select a specific item and then click the up and down arrows, visible at the bottom of Figure 5.26, to change that item's location in the list. You can also click the adjacent Trash icon to remove that item from the list.

- The check boxes in Figure 5.26 include the somewhat mysterious X and Y controls. These refer to the x,y location of the document in the grid layout of the portfolio's home page.

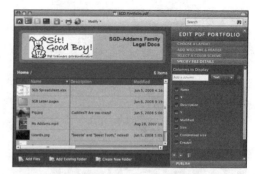

Figure 5.25 The portfolio details check boxes (in the right-hand panel) let you specify what information should appear in list view.

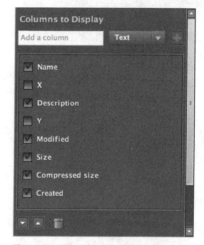

Figure 5.26 The check boxes toggle the visibility of the different information available to list view.

Figure 5.27 The Publish controls let you distribute your portfolio three ways: save to file, e-mail, or share on Acrobat.com.

Publishing Your Portfolio

Having created your portfolio, you now need to make it available to the people for whom you made it. The final control in the Edit Portfolio pane, Publish, lets you distribute your portfolio three ways: save it to disk; e-mail it to someone; share it on Acrobat.com.

To expose the publishing controls, simply click the Publish button in the Edit Portfolio pane; Acrobat displays three buttons, one for each publishing option (**Figure 5.27**).

Saving your portfolio to disk as a PDF file is the simplest of the Publish options. You may do anything with the saved portfolio that you could do with any other PDF file: view it, e-mail it, or archive it.

To save your portfolio to disk:

1. Click the Publish button in the Edit Portfolio pane to expose the Publish controls (Figure 5.27).

2. Click the Save button.
   Acrobat displays your system's standard save-a-file dialog box.

3. Specify a name for the portfolio's file and click OK.

✔ Tips

■ You can also save your portfolio the old-fashioned way: choose File > Save. Sounds crazy, I know, but it works.

If you want to e-mail your portfolio to someone immediately upon creating it, you can
conveniently do so from the Publish controls.

To e-mail your portfolio:

1. Click the Publish button in the Edit
   Portfolio pane to expose the publish
   controls (Figure 5.27).

2. Click the Email button.

   Acrobat launches your e-mail client and
   opens a blank e-mail message with the
   portfolio attached (**Figure 5.28**).

3. Fill in the destination address and subject, and send the message as you would
   normally with your e-mail client.

✔ Tip

■ Note in Figure 5.28 that the message body
   contains an image and text urging the
   reader to use Adobe Reader 9 to view the
   file; you can edit the message body as you
   wish, including removing the picture.

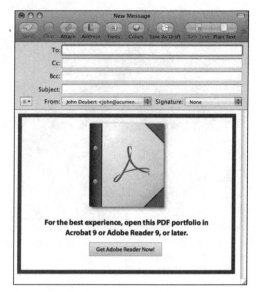

Figure 5.28 The Email button launches your mail
client and attaches the portfolio to a new message.

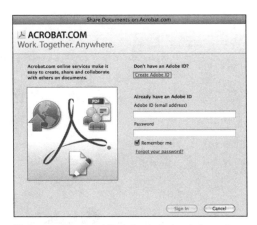

Figure 5.29 You must first sign in to Acrobat.com to share your files. Click on the Create Adobe ID link if you don't already have an ID with Adobe.

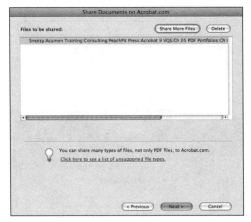

Figure 5.30 The Share Wizard first collects from you a list of the files you want to share on Acrobat.com.

Sharing with Acrobat.com

Finally, you can make your portfolio available through Adobe's new Acrobat.com service. Acrobat.com is a server-based service provided by Adobe to make it easy to share PDF files and comments among Acrobat users. Its introduction is arguably one of the most significant components of the Acrobat suite of software. I discuss Acrobat.com in some detail in Chapter 8.

When you share your portfolio on Acrobat.com, the file is uploaded to Adobe's server and Adobe assigns a URL to that file. The file may then be downloaded or viewed directly from Acrobat.com; you can decide if the file should be accessible to anyone who knows the URL or only to a specific list of people.

To share your portfolio on Acrobat.com:

1. Click the Publish button in the Edit Portfolio pane to expose the publish controls (Figure 5.27).

2. Click the Share on Acrobat.com button.
   Acrobat asks you for your Adobe ID and password (**Figure 5.29**).

3. Type in your Adobe ID and password, and click the Sign In button.
   Acrobat displays the first screen of the Share Wizard (**Figure 5.30**). This window lists all of the files you want to add to Acrobat.com for sharing, initially only your portfolio.

4. If you wish, click the Share More Files button to add files to the list.
   You are presented with a standard pick-a-file dialog box you may use to select additional files.

5. Click the Next button in Figure 5.30 to go to the second screen of the Share Wizard.

Continues on next page

6. Fill in the e-mail addresses of the people whom you want to notify of the file's availability, as well as the Subject and Message fields (**Figure 5.31**).

Acrobat will send e-mails to these people once the portfolio has been uploaded to Acrobat.com.

If you choose to edit the message body, make sure your don't remove the text in angle brackets (< >); in the received mail message, this will show the URL of your portfolio on Acrobat.com

7. In the Access menu, specify who will have access to this file (**Figure 5.32**).

You may choose Limited Access, in which case only the people whom you notify will have access to the file; or Open Access, which will allow anyone who knows the file's URL to read it.

8. Click the Send button.

Acrobat uploads the portfolio and then sends e-mail notices to the people you specified.

The people on your notification list will get an e-mail looking like the one in **Figure 5.33**. This provides them with a link that will let them download or view the file on Acrobat.com.

✔ Tip

■ You can share any kind of file you wish on Acrobat.com, not just portfolios. We shall see how to do this in Chapter 8.

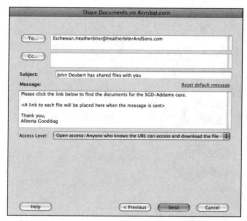

Figure 5.31 The Share Wizard gets from you the e-mail addresses of the people whom you want to notify of the portfolio's availability.

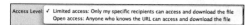

Figure 5.32 You can restrict access of the portfolio to only those people you notify, or you can make it available to anyone.

Figure 5.33 Acrobat sends an e-mail to the people on your notification list, providing the URL of the shared portfolio.

ADDING COMMENTS TO A DOCUMENT

One of the longest-standing features in Acrobat is the ability to add comments to a PDF document. Originally, these comments were simple, electronic sticky notes that a reader could attach to the page. The PDF annotation mechanism has since grown to include a broad set of highlighting, drawing, and other tools that you can use to do full-featured commentary on a document. Additionally, there are tools for reading and summarizing these comments, and even for conducting a document review involving your entire workgroup or company.

The annotation feature in Acrobat is so extensive and important that it occupies the next three chapters in this book, concentrating on adding comments to a PDF document, reading and managing those documents, and conducting a shared review of a document.

Examining Acrobat's Commenting Tools

Acrobat's commenting tools are accessible in three locations:

◆ The Tools menu and the Comments menu both have Comment & Markup submenus that contain items for all the comment tools (**Figure 6.1**).

◆ The Comment & Markup toolbar includes tools for the most commonly used comment tools (**Figure 6.2**).

You may add buttons to the Comment & Markup toolbar for the missing tools; see Chapter 1 for directions on how to add tools to a toolbar.

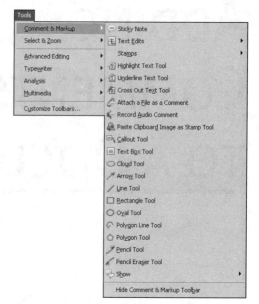

Figure 6.1 All of Acrobat's comment tools are available through the Tools menu (shown here) or the Comments menu.

Figure 6.2 The most commonly used comment tools are on the Comment & Markup toolbar.

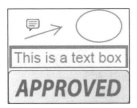

Figure 6.3 Every comment has an icon that indicates its position on the page.

Sticky Note 6/11/2008 2:57:56
John Deubert   Options ▾
No! No! No! No! No! No! No! No!
No! No! No! No!
Well, maybe...

Figure 6.4 Most comments have a pop-up window that holds the text for that comment.

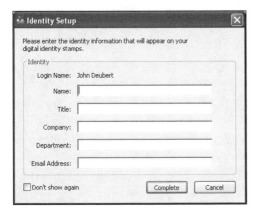

Figure 6.5 When you first use the comment tools, Acrobat may ask you for some information about yourself. This is strictly optional.

Comment icons and pop-ups

Every comment on a page has two visual parts.

A comment's *icon* is a graphic that indicates the position of the comment on the page (**Figure 6.3**). The icon differs for each comment type: a speech bubble for a Sticky Note, a piece of text for a Text Box, and a Sign Here pointer for a Stamp.

Most comments also have a *pop-up window* that displays the text associated with the comment (**Figure 6.4**). Double-clicking the comment's icon opens its pop-up, allowing you to read and edit the comment's text.

✔ Tips

- Acrobat's Preferences dialog box has a pane full of controls determining the behavior of comments. The default values for these options are sensible, so you can safely ignore them. However, once you've worked with comments for a while, you may want take a look at them. Choose Edit > Preferences, or Acrobat > Preferences on a Mac, to see Acrobat's preferences.

- The first time you use one of Acrobat's comment tools, it may present you with a dialog box that asks for your name, company, and so on (**Figure 6.5**). If you choose to provide this information, Acrobat uses it for some of the dynamic comments that add your name and other data to the comment on the fly.

EXAMINING ACROBAT'S COMMENTING TOOLS

Adding a Sticky Note Comment

The Sticky Note comment is Acrobat's oldest annotation type, dating back to Acrobat 1.0. This annotation type is the functional equivalent of the paper sticky note after which it's named; it holds a small amount of text attached to the page in a pop-up window.

To add a Sticky Note to a page:

1. Click the Sticky Note tool in the Comment & Markup toolbar.

   The pointer turns into crosshairs.

2. Click the page.

   Acrobat places the comment's icon on the page and opens the comment's pop-up window (**Figure 6.6**).

3. Type the text you want for the comment in the pop-up window.

✔ Tips

- To change the location of a comment's icon, click and drag it to a new location.

- You can change the text of an existing comment. To do so, double-click the icon to get to the pop-up, then click the text and edit it as usual. This works with any type of comment that has text.

A Sticky Note's default icon is a speech bubble. This is a perfectly serviceable icon, but Acrobat supplies a collection of other icons that may be used for Sticky Note comments (**Figure 6.7**).

Figure 6.6 When you place a Sticky Note on the page, Acrobat opens a pop-up window into which you can type your text.

Figure 6.7 Sticky Notes may be represented on the page by an assortment of icons.

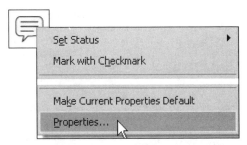

Figure 6.8 You change a Sticky Note's icon (and other characteristics) by modifying its properties.

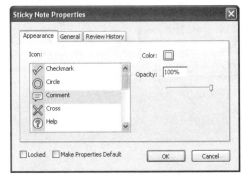

Figure 6.9 The Sticky Note Properties dialog box lets you modify a variety of Appearance settings.

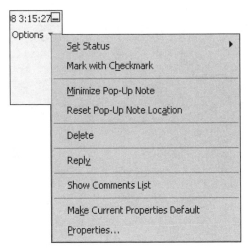

Figure 6.10 You can also get to a comment's properties by clicking the pop-up window's Options control.

To change a Sticky Note's icon:

1. Right-click the Sticky Note comment's icon to get a contextual menu.

2. Choose Properties in the contextual menu (**Figure 6.8**).

   Acrobat presents you with the Sticky Note Properties dialog box (**Figure 6.9**).

3. Choose a new icon from the list.

4. If you want this icon to become the default icon for future Sticky Note comments, click the Make Properties Default check box.

5. To change the note's color, click the square Color control and choose a new color from the resulting color picker.

6. To change the opacity of the note, drag the Opacity slider to the desired level or type a number in the Opacity percentage field.

7. Click OK.

✔ Tips

- You can prevent a comment from being edited by clicking the Locked check box shown in Figure 6.9.

- You can delete a comment the way you delete most everything else in the computer world: Select it, then press the Delete key.

- You can also get to the contextual menu by clicking the little Options arrow in a comment's pop-up window (**Figure 6.10**).

Adding a Text Box Comment

A Text Box comment is similar to a Sticky Note, but it has no pop-up window. Instead, the comment displays its text in a rectangular, editable field directly on the page (**Figure 6.11**).

This is the
last page,
not the first!

Figure 6.11 A Text Box comment presents a text annotation in a rectangular field placed directly on the page.

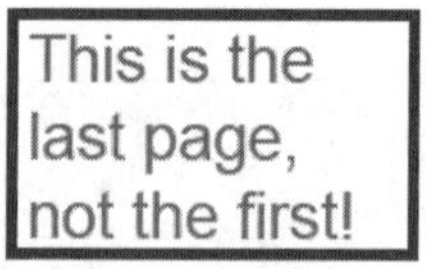

To place a Text Box on the page:

1. Click the Text Box tool in the Comment & Markup toolbar.
2. Click and drag a rectangle on the page.

   Acrobat places the Text Box at that location on the page.
3. Type your comment into the text box.

Having placed your Text Box on the page, you can move it around and resize it very easily.

To move and resize a Text Box:

1. Select the Hand or Selection tool, if necessary. These are on the Select & Zoom toolbar (**Figure 6.12**).

Select & Zoom

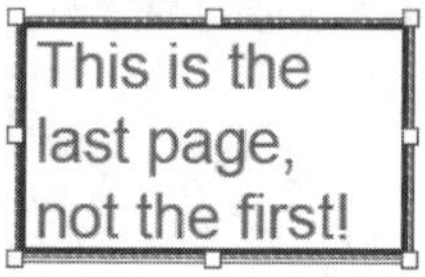

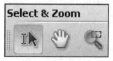

Figure 6.12 The Select & Zoom toolbar has the Selection tool and the Hand tool, which may both be used to move a comment's icon around on the page.

2. Click the Text Box.

   Handles appear at the sides and corners of the Text Box (**Figure 6.13**).

This is the
last page,
not the first!

Figure 6.13 When you select a comment's icon, handles appear at the corners and sides.

3. Click and drag the Text Box to change its position on the page.
4. Click and drag one of the handles to change the box's size.

Adding a Text Box Comment

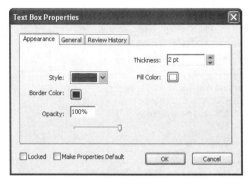

Figure 6.14 The Text Box Properties dialog box lets you change the appearance of the box that contains the text.

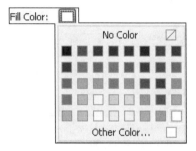

Figure 6.15 Clicking one of the color-well controls results in a standard color picker.

You can also control a Text Box's appearance to quite a large extent. Following are instructions for changing some of these characteristics.

To change a Text Box's colors:

1. With the Hand or Selection tool selected, right-click the Text Box to get a contextual menu.

2. Select Properties at the bottom of the contextual menu.

   Acrobat presents you with the Text Box Properties dialog box (**Figure 6.14**).

3. Click the square Border Color control.

   The color well drops down a standard color picker (**Figure 6.15**).

4. Choose the color you want for your border.

5. To choose a fill color, repeat Steps 3 and 4, clicking the square Fill Color control in Figure 6.14.

6. Click OK.

✔ Tip

- If you examine the Text Box Properties dialog box, you'll see that you can also change the style and thickness of the Text Box's border as well as the box's opacity. Feel free to experiment with these settings.

Finally, you can change the font and other characteristics of the text inside the Text Box. This takes a bit more effort, because you need to use the Properties toolbar (**Figure 6.16**).

Continues on next page

ADDING A TEXT BOX COMMENT

Figure 6.16 The Text Box Text Properties toolbar presents information on whatever is selected on the page. You can use it to change the characteristics of text.

To change a Text Box's font and text size:

1. Make the Properties toolbar visible, if necessary; to do so, choose View > Toolbars > Properties Bar.

2. Select the Hand or Selection tool in the Select & Zoom toolbar.

3. Double-click the text in the Text Box. A blinking cursor appears at the point where you double-clicked.

4. Choose the text in the Text Box whose font or size you want to change. The Properties toolbar reports the current font and size.

5. In the Properties toolbar, change the font and size to the values you want.

6. Click outside the Text Box to finish.

✔ Tips

- The Properties toolbar lets you change many characteristic of your Text Box text, including alignment, color, and placement above or below the baseline (**Figure 6.17**).

- You can also change the style of your text to some combination of bold and italic. Once you've selected text in the Text Box (Step 4 in the task above), right-click the text, and choose Text Style in the contextual menu (**Figure 6.18**).

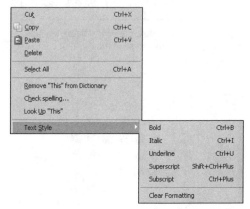

Figure 6.17 Using the Properties toolbar, you can change the font, size, and style of your Text Box text.

Cut	Ctrl+X
Copy	Ctrl+C
Paste	Ctrl+V
Delete	
Select All	Ctrl+A
Remove "This" from Dictionary	
Check spelling…	
Look Up "This"	
Text Style	▶

Bold	Ctrl+B
Italic	Ctrl+I
Underline	Ctrl+U
Superscript	Shift+Ctrl+Plus
Subscript	Ctrl+Plus
Clear Formatting	

Figure 6.18 You can also change the style of your Text Box text via the Text Style submenu.

ADDING A TEXT BOX COMMENT

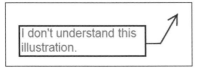

Figure 6.19 A Callout comment is just a Text Box with an arrow.

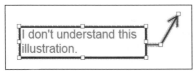

Figure 6.20 Clicking a Callout gives you handles you can use to position the box and its arrow.

Adding a Callout Comment

A Callout comment is a Text Box with an arrow attached (**Figure 6.19**). It lets you point to the page's object that your comment discusses.

To add a Callout to a page:

1. On the Comment & Markup toolbar, select the Callout tool .

2. Click and drag a rectangle on the page. Acrobat adds a Callout comment with a default arrow pointing at nothing in particular.

3. Type your comment into the text field.

4. Click the border of the comment to make handles appear (**Figure 6.20**).

5. Drag the handles to position the arrow as you want it.

A Callout comments has the same set of properties as a Text Box comment (font, point size, and so on). See the previous section for a discussion of these properties and instructions on how to change them.

Adding Lines and Arrows

Several of Acrobat's commenting tools let you add graphic items to your document's pages. The Line and Arrow tools let you add lines and arrows to the page (**Figure 6.21**).

To add a line or an arrow to the page:

1. Click the Line or Arrow tool on the Comment & Markup toolbar.

2. Click and hold on the page at one end of your line or arrow.

3. Click and drag to where you want the other end of the line or arrow to go.

4. Release the mouse button.

✔ Tips

- Lines can be turned into arrows and vice versa. In the Properties dialog box (right-click the item and select Properties in the resulting contextual menu), you can apply an End type to the line (**Figure 6.22**). A value of None turns an arrow into a line; a value of Open (for *open arrow*) turns a line into an arrow. You can choose from several other line ends.

- You can reverse an arrow by right-clicking it and selecting Flip Line in the contextual menu.

- Lines and arrows can have text comments associated with them. Double-click the line or arrow to see its pop-up window. Even when the pop-up window is closed, you can tell that an arrow or a line (or any graphic annotation) has a text comment because Acrobat adds a tiny speech bubble to it (**Figure 6.23**).

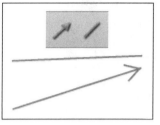
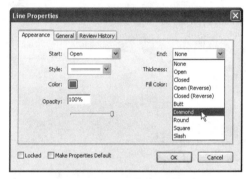

Figure 6.21 The Arrow and Line tools let you draw arrows and lines on the page. This explains their names.

Figure 6.22 The Line Properties dialog box lets you add an End to a line, converting it into an arrow, for example. Choosing None turns an arrow into a line.

Figure 6.23 A comment icon that has text associated with it displays a tiny speech bubble.

Figure 6.24 You can use the Oval tool to draw attention to items of interest on the page.

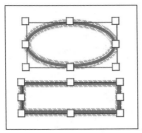

Figure 6.25 The Rectangle and Oval tools have icons on the Comment & Markup toolbar.

Figure 6.26 Clicking a Rectangle or an Oval icon produces handles you can use to resize that icon.

Drawing Ovals and Rectangles

The Oval and Rectangle comment tools let you call attention to items on the Acrobat page (**Figure 6.24**). These tools are on the Comment & Markup toolbar or from the Comments > Comment & Markup submenu.

To add an Oval or Rectangle comment to the page:

1. Click the Oval or Rectangle tool on the Comment & Markup toolbar (**Figure 6.25**).

   The pointer changes to crosshairs.

2. Click and drag the crosshairs on the page.

   Acrobat draws a rectangle or an oval as you drag.

3. Release the mouse button.

   Acrobat adds the oval or rectangle to the page.

4. Click the oval or rectangle.

   Acrobat adds handles to the sides and corners (**Figure 6.26**).

5. Reposition and resize the oval or rectangle as you wish.

✔ Tip

- You can get a perfect square or circle by holding down the Option/Alt key while clicking and dragging in Step 2.

Adding Polygons and Clouds

The polygon-related comment tools work the way similar tools work in most graphics software: you click sequentially on the vertices of the shape you want, and Acrobat connects the dots, making the polygon.

Acrobat supplies three polygon annotation tools (**Figure 6.27**):

Polygon tool. This tool creates a closed polygon. When you're finished clicking vertices, Acrobat adds a final side that connects the last point with the first.

Polygon Line tool. This is identical to the Polygon tool, except that Acrobat doesn't close the figure for you.

Cloud tool. This is identical to the Polygon tool, except that Acrobat draws the polygon as a cloud (Figure 6.27).

Unfortunately, only the Cloud tool is available by default on the Comment & Markup toolbar; you can add the other tools following the steps in Chapter 1.

Figure 6.27 There are three polygon-related comment tools: Polygon, Polygon Line, and Cloud.

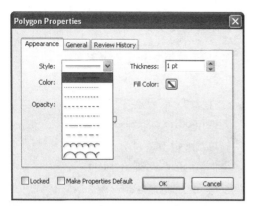

Figure 6.28 You can turn a polygon into a cloud by changing its line style.

To add a polygon or cloud to a page:

1. Do one of the following:
   - ▲ To add a cloud, click the Cloud tool on the Comment & Markup toolbar.
   - ▲ To add a closed polygon, choose Tools > Comment & Markup > Polygon Tool.
   - ▲ To add an open polygon, choose Tools > Comment & Markup > Polygon Line Tool.

2. Click the starting point of your polygon or cloud.

3. Click sequentially on all the corners in your polygon.

   Acrobat draws the line segments as you go so you can see how your polygon or cloud is looking.

4. Double-click the final point to finish the polygon.

✔ Tip

- ■ You can convert polygons to clouds and vice versa. Right-click the object, and look at its properties. One of the controls is a pop-up menu of line styles (**Figure 6.28**). Choose one of the cloud styles to convert your polygon to a cloud.

ADDING POLYGONS AND CLOUDS

Text Edits

Acrobat provides a complete set of tools for indicating changes that need to be made to text on a page. These include annotations to mark text for replacement and deletion, and to mark an insertion point for missing text.

The way you mark up text is a little counterintuitive at first, but it quickly becomes second nature with practice. Broadly, there are two steps to indicating a text change:

1. Indicate the position of the change.

   This entails placing the cursor at the location of an insertion or selecting the text that needs to be deleted or changed.

2. Apply the comment for the markup you want.

The tools you use to do this are most conveniently accessed through the Text Edits menu on the Comment & Markup toolbar (**Figure 6.29**).

The markup tools in Acrobat are as follows, from top to bottom in the illustration (**Figure 6.30**):

Highlight Selected Text adds a colored backdrop to the selected text to draw attention to it.

Insert Text at Cursor indicates that text should be inserted into the existing words. A little caret appears at the place you click in the text. The pop-up window associated with the annotation contains the new text.

Crossout Text for Deletion strikes through the selected text, indicating that it should be removed.

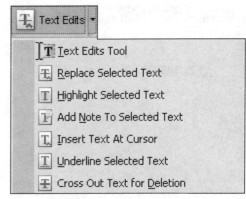

Figure 6.29 The text-markup tools reside in the Text Edits menu on the Comment & Markup toolbar.

Figure 6.30 Acrobat provides all the tools you need to do full text markup on an Acrobat file.

Figure 6.31 Acrobat provides short-cut tools for (from left) highlighting, underlining, and crossing out text. Unfortunately, only the highlighting tool exists in the Comment & Markup toolbar by default.

Replace Selected Text strikes through the selected text, indicating that it should be removed, and places an insert-text caret at the end, indicating that new text should be inserted. The pop-up window associated with the annotation contains the new text.

Add Note to Selected Text highlights the text. The pop-up window associated with the annotation contains a comment about the text. This seems to be in every way identical to the Highlight Text tool, except that Acrobat automatically opens the pop-up window so you can type your comment.

Underline Selected Text underlines the text for emphasis.

To add text markup to a page:

1. Click the Text Edit tool (not its drop-down menu) in the Comment & Markup toolbar.

   The pointer turns into an I-beam shape.

2. If you're indicating an insertion point, click a location in the text on the page.

   A blinking cursor appears at that point on the page.

3. For all other types of edits, select the text that you want to mark up.

   Acrobat highlights the text. You may use the Shift key to extend the selection, as is usual in word processors.

4. In the menu attached to the Text Edits tool (Figure 6.29), select the markup you want.

   Acrobat immediately applies the markup. If your markup requires insertion or notation text, a pop-up window opens so you can type your text.

✔ **Tip**

■ The Comment & Markup toolbar can contain tools that let you quickly highlight, underline, and cross out text (**Figure 6.31**). Unfortunately, only the Highlight Text tool is on the toolbar by default; see Chapter 1 for directions on adding the other two.

Adding a Stamp Comment

One of the most popular annotation types (well, *I* like it) is the Stamp. This comment type is modeled on the traditional rubber stamp once popular with banks and still popular with four-year-old children and me.

The Stamps are available from the Stamp drop-down menu on the Comment & Markup toolbar (**Figure 6.32**).

The Stamps are organized into categories: Dynamic, Sign Here, and Business are provided by default. You can also compile your own Favorites menu, containing Stamps you particularly like.

Note that some of the Stamps are dynamic, incorporating the identity data you may have supplied when you first started using the comment tools (**Figure 6.33**).

You can create your own Stamps and your own categories. The Acrobat version of a Stamp lets you use any PDF graphic—any combination of text, line art, and images—as your rubber stamp. You'll see how to do this in the next section.

Figure 6.32 Like a rubber stamp, the Stamp tool lets you place predefined graphics on the page.

Figure 6.33 Dynamic Stamps incorporate information from your system and personal identity data.

Figure 6.34 Having selected a Stamp in the Stamp menu, you move a ghostly version of it to the desired location on the page.

Figure 6.35 Clicking a Stamp yields handles you can use to resize and rotate it.

Figure 6.36 You rotate a stamp by dragging the "handle on a stick."

To apply a Stamp to the page:

1. In the Stamp menu (Figure 6.32), choose the category and Stamp you want.

   The pointer turns into a ghostly version of the Stamp you choose, like the Draft Stamp in **Figure 6.34**.

2. Click in the place on the page where you want your Stamp to go.

   Acrobat places the Stamp on the page in its default size.

3. Click the Stamp image on the page to select it.

   Handles appear at the corners of the Stamp (**Figure 6.35**).

4. Click and drag the handles to make the Stamp the size you want. You can also rotate the Stamp by dragging the handle-on-a-stick rising above it (**Figure 6.36**).

Creating Your Own Stamp

It is remarkably easy to create your own Stamp comment for use with the Stamp tool. You can take graphics, text, or images from any PDF file and turn them into a Stamp.

You can even create new categories for your Stamps.

To create a stamp:

1. From the Stamp tool's menu, choose Create Custom Stamp (**Figure 6.37**).

   Acrobat presents you with the Select Image for Custom Stamp dialog box (**Figure 6.38**).

2. Click the Browse button.

   The standard Open dialog box opens.

3. Choose the file that contains the artwork you want to use for your Stamp.

   This can be a PDF file or any type of file that Acrobat can convert to PDF. Acrobat displays the first page of the document in the dialog box.

4. Using the scroll bar, select the page in the document that you want to use as your Stamp.

5. Click OK.

   The Create Custom Stamp dialog box opens (**Figure 6.39**).

6. Choose a category to which to add your Stamp, or if you like, type the name of a new category.

7. Type a name for your new Stamp.

Figure 6.37 To create your own Stamp, choose Create Custom Stamp from the Stamp menu.

Figure 6.38 Select a file as the source for your Stamp's graphic.

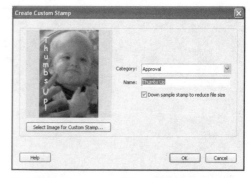

Figure 6.39 Give your new Stamp a name and assign it to a category. You may type a new category name if you wish.

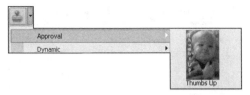

Figure 6.40 Your new category and Stamp appear in the Stamp menu.

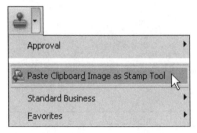

Figure 6.41 You can paste Clipboard contents onto the page as a Stamp.

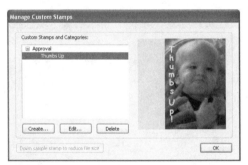

Figure 6.42 The Manage Custom Stamps dialog box lets you delete and edit existing custom Stamps and create new ones.

✔ Tip

- As you can see in Figure 6.42, you can also edit the selected Stamp (rename it and change its category) and create new Stamps.

8. Click OK.

Your new Stamp (and new category, if you made one) appears among the other Stamps in the Stamp tool menu (**Figure 6.40**).

✔ Tips

- If you never expect to use your Stamp at a large size on the page, you can save some space on your disk by checking the "Down sample stamp to reduce file size" check box in the Create Custom Stamp dialog box (Figure 6.39). This option can reduce your Stamp's size considerably, but it can also make your Stamp look chunky if you use the Stamp's handles to enlarge it.

- You can quickly create a one-off stamp by copying a graphic to the Clipboard (in whatever application you wish) and then choosing Paste Clipboard Image As Stamp Tool from the Stamp tool menu (**Figure 6.41**).

Having created a custom stamp, you can remove it using the Manage Custom Stamps dialog box (**Figure 6.42**).

To delete a custom Stamp:

1. In the Stamp tool's menu, select Manage Stamps.

Acrobat displays the Manage Custom Stamps dialog box.

2. In the list of Stamps, select the Stamp you want to delete.

Acrobat shows the Stamp's graphic in the dialog box.

3. Click Delete.

Acrobat deletes the custom Stamp.

4. Click OK.

CREATING YOUR OWN STAMP

Checking Spelling in Comments

Acrobat has a built-in spelling checker that looks for spelling errors in a document's comments and form fields. The only difficulty in using this feature is finding it; it's located in a submenu that's otherwise unrelated to forms or commenting.

To check spelling in your comments:

1. Choose Edit > Spelling > In Comments, Fields, & Editable Text.

   The Check Spelling dialog box opens (**Figure 6.43**).

2. Click the Start button.

   Acrobat examines all the comments and form text fields in your document, looking for spelling errors. When it finds a misspelling, Acrobat presents the error in context and shows you a list of replacements (**Figure 6.44**).

3. For each misspelled word, do one of the following:

   ▲ Click Ignore to ignore that instance of the misspelled word.

   ▲ Click Ignore All to ignore all instances of that word.

   ▲ Choose a replacement in the list, and click either Change or Change All.

   ▲ Click Add to add the word to Acrobat's dictionary of known words.

   After you change, ignore, or add the misspelled word, Acrobat goes on to the next.

4. When there are no more misspellings, click Done.

Figure 6.43 Use the Check Spelling dialog box to check the spelling in your document's comments and form fields.

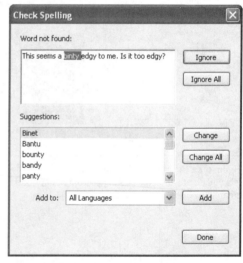

Figure 6.44 When Acrobat finds a misspelled word, it presents you with a list of alternatives.

Exporting and Importing Comments

The data associated with a document's comments is much smaller than the document itself. A 10 MB PDF file may have less than 1 KB of comment data.

If someone sends you that 10 MB file for comment and you want to return the annotated file, it's more efficient to send just the comment data than it is to send the entire PDF file.

You do this by exporting the comments to a Form Data Format (FDF) file (**Figure 6.45**). This file contains only the text, images, position, and other data associated with your comments. You can e-mail this relatively tiny file to another person; they can then import the FDF data into their copy of the same PDF file.

When Acrobat imports an FDF file, it places the comments into the new document in their original locations. This is a much more efficient way of sending comments from one location to another.

✔ Tip

- If you import an FDF file into a document that is *not* the same as the one you originally annotated, the imported comments won't correspond to any particular text or graphic in the new document.

Figure 6.45 Exporting comments results in an FDF file that contains only the document's comment data.

To export your comments to an FDF file:

1. Choose Comments > Export Comments to Data File (**Figure 6.46**).

   Acrobat presents you with a standard Save dialog box.

2. Specify a name and location for your FDF file.

3. Click OK.

   Acrobat creates the FDF file.

✔ Tip

- If you examine Figure 6.46, you'll see that you can also export PDF comments to a Microsoft Word or Autodesk AutoCAD document. In this case, the PDF file you've annotated must have been originally created in Word or AutoCAD. The resulting file contains comments that may be imported into the original Word or AutoCAD document.

To import comments from an FDF file:

1. With the PDF file open, choose Comments > Import Comments.

   An Open dialog box appears.

2. Choose the FDF file that contains the comments.

   Acrobat reads the file and places the comments it contains into the current document.

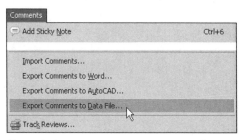

Figure 6.46 To export your comments to an FDF file, choose Comments > Export Comments to Data File. In Windows, you can also export to Microsoft Word and Autodesk AutoCAD.

Enabling Commenting in Adobe Reader

Acrobat Pro Only: By default, PDF documents cannot be modified in any way with the free Adobe Reader. Unfortunately, this ban includes attaching comments to a file. If you want people to be able to review your document in Adobe Reader, you must explicitly turn on that capability for the document.

Once your PDF document has been enabled for commenting in Reader, you're restricted in what you can do to that document. Even if you're examining the file in Acrobat Standard or Pro, you can no longer shuffle pages, edit page contents, add form fields or links, or otherwise modify the document. This will be true until you disable Acrobat's ability to annotate the document in Reader.

To enable a document for commenting in Adobe Reader:

1. Choose Document > Enable for Commenting and Analysis in Adobe Reader (**Figure 6.47**).

   Acrobat presents you with a dialog box warning you that file editing will be restricted (**Figure 6.48**). Then a Save dialog box opens, because Acrobat insists that you resave the Reader-enabled file.

2. Save the Reader-enabled file with a new name and new location on your disk.

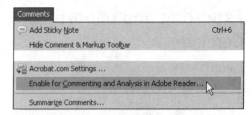

Figure 6.47 You must explicitly enable the use of Adobe Reader to comment on a document.

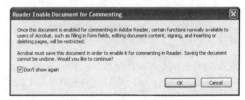

Figure 6.48 Acrobat warns you that once a document is enabled for commenting in Adobe Reader, editing capabilities are limited, even in Acrobat Pro.

READING COMMENTED DOCUMENTS

The previous chapter described how to annotate a PDF file with Sticky Notes, circles, arrows, and paragraphs of explanatory text. We covered how to mark up the text in your PDF files to indicate insertions, deletions, and replacements.

In this chapter, we discuss what to do when you receive such a marked-up document. Of course, you can always just double-click an annotation and read the text in the resulting pop-up window. However, Acrobat gives you several more-efficient ways of examining a document's annotations.

Let's see what they are.

Examining the Comments List

The Comments List is a navigation pane you can view by clicking the appropriate icon to the left of your document page (**Figure 7.1**). Unlike the other navigation panes, the Comments List displays across the bottom of the document window.

The Comments List itemizes all the comments in your document. It also has a toolbar across the top that provides easy access to a variety of tasks common to working with comments. This pane is invaluable when you're working with a document that has more than just a few comments.

Like all navigation panes, the Comments List pane can be dragged off the left edge of the document window to become a stand-alone palette (**Figure 7.2**).

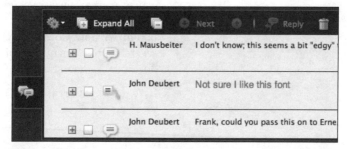

Figure 7.1 The Comments List itemizes all the comments in your document.

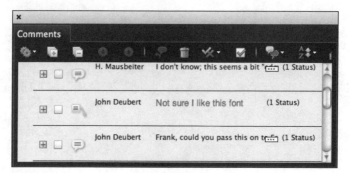

Figure 7.2 When you drag the Comments List away from the document window, it becomes a stand-alone floating palette.

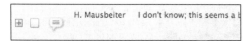

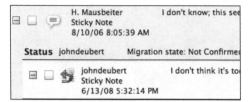

Figure 7.3 When collapsed, an entry in the Comments List shows only the comment's author and text.

Figure 7.4 An expanded entry displays all the information for a comment, including any replies.

Expand All

Figure 7.5 The Expand All and Collapse All buttons do just what their names imply.

Each entry in the Comments List has two states. Initially, the entry is collapsed, showing only the comment's author and text (**Figure 7.3**).

The collapsed item has a Expand button, the boxed plus sign in Figure 7.3. When you click it, you see additional information associated with the comment. This can include the comment's status and any replies that have been made to that comment (**Figure 7.4**). Note in the figure that the Expand button becomes a Collapse button—a minus sign in a box.

✔ Tip

- I find it useful to use the Comments List as a palette. When it's docked to the bottom of the window, the list obscures too much of the document's page for my liking.

To expand and collapse entries in the Comments List:

1. Select the comment in which you're interested.

2. Click the Expand button to display that comment's additional information.

3. Click the Collapse button to hide the additional information.

The Comments List toolbar also has a pair of buttons that expand and collapse all the entries in the list (**Figure 7.5**).

To expand and collapse all entries in the Comments List:

1. Click the Expand All button to expand all the comments in the list.

2. Click the Collapse All button to collapse all the comments in the list.

Replying to a Comment

Having read a comment, you may want to reply to it—answer a question posed in the comment, deny any wrongdoing implied by the comment, and so on.

To reply to a comment in the Comments List:

1. Select the comment you want to reply to.

2. Select the Reply to Comment icon on the toolbar (**Figure 7.6**).

   Acrobat expands the comment entry and adds a new line with a text box for your reply (**Figure 7.7**).

3. Type the text of your reply.

✔ Tip

■ You can also reply to a comment by right-clicking the comment's icon and choosing Reply in the contextual menu.

Figure 7.6 Select the toolbar's Reply to Comment icon to, well, reply to a comment.

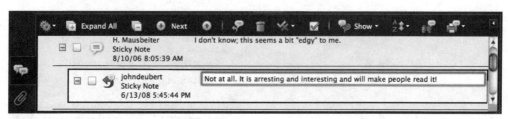

Figure 7.7 When you select the Reply to Comment icon, Acrobat expands the comment entry and gives you space to type your reply.

REPLYING TO A COMMENT

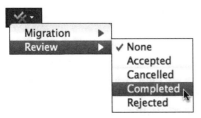

Figure 7.8 The Review submenu of the Set Status tool lets you assign a status state to a comment.

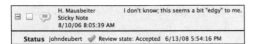

Figure 7.9 A comment's status state is among the information displayed when you expand a comment's entry.

Figure 7.10 You can also set a comment's status state from the Options menu in its pop-up window.

Figure 7.11 Each comment entry has a check box whose significance is up to you.

✔ Tip

- You can also check-mark a comment by right-clicking the comment's icon and selecting Mark with Checkmark in the contextual menu. This menu item becomes Remove Checkmark if the comment is already checked.

Marking Comments

The Comments List toolbar lets you indicate that you have reviewed a comment. Setting a comment's review status indicates that you have come to some decision about that comment, such as accepting it as true or rejecting it as an outright lie.

To set the review status of a comment:

1. Choose the comment in the Comments List.

2. In the Comments List toolbar, select the Set Status tool (**Figure 7.8**).

   A menu drops down from the tool.

3. In the Review submenu, choose the status you want for this comment.

   The comment's new status appears in the Comments List (**Figure 7.9**).

✔ Tips

- You can also set the review status of a comment from the Options menu in the comment's pop-up window (**Figure 7.10**), or by right-clicking the comment's icon.

- Acrobat provides five review status values: None, Accepted, Cancelled, Completed, and Rejected. The precise meaning of these status values is up to the reviewer. Acrobat doesn't define the difference between, for example, Cancelled and Rejected.

Each comment in the Comments List has a check box whose significance is up to the reviewer (**Figure 7.11**). If, for example, you were keeping track of which comments mentioned bunnies, you could set each comment's check mark as you encountered a *bunny* reference.

To set or clear a comment's check mark:

- Click the comment's check box.

   This action toggles the checked state; it turns on if it was off and vice versa.

Managing the Comments List

The Comments List toolbar gives you considerable control over which comments it displays and how it displays them. In this section you'll see how to modify the visibility of items in the Comments List.

The Show tool lets you choose which comments you want to appear on the PDF page and in the Comments List. The menu attached to the Show tool consists of a series of submenus that let you choose visible comments by type, reviewer, status, and whether the comment is checked (**Figure 7.12**).

Each submenu lets you choose among the available comment types, reviewers, and so on. Note in Figure 7.12 that you can have multiple selections scattered among the submenus. You can choose to see all the Notes and Text Editing Markups from reviewer Quentin P. Fonebotham, for example.

To choose which comments should be visible:

1. In the Comments List toolbar, click the Show tool (Figure 7.12).

2. Choose the type, reviewer, status, or checked state you want to make visible in the Comments List.

If you want to make all the comments visible again, there is a bit of a trick to it. The Show All Comments item in the Show tool's menu is not available unless all the document's comments are hidden. So, to make all comments visible, you must first choose Hide All Comments. Go figure.

To make all comments visible:

1. In the Show menu, select Hide All Comments.

   All the comments in the document disappear, and the Show All Comments item appears in the Show tool menu.

2. In the Show tool menu, select Show All Comments.

   All the document's comments become visible.

The Comments List toolbar lets you sort the comments in the list by a variety of criteria, including type, page number, and author.

To sort the items in the Comments List:

1. In the Comments List toolbar, click the Sort By tool (**Figure 7.13**).

   A menu drops down from the tool button.

2. Select the criterion by which you want to sort the comments.

   The list immediately redraws itself in the new order.

Figure 7.12 You may choose among a variety of criteria to determine which comments are displayed on the page and in the Comments List.

Figure 7.13 You can sort the Comments List several ways.

MANAGING THE COMMENTS LIST

Figure 7.14 The Search tool lets you look for a word or phrase in a document's comments.

Searching for Text in Comments

The Comments List allows you to search for words or phrases in the document's comments. The process is much like searching for text in the PDF file as a whole.

To search for a word among a document's comments:

1. In the Comments List toolbar, click the Search tool (**Figure 7.14**).

   Acrobat resizes your document window and opens the Search window next to it (**Figure 7.15**). The two windows together take up the entire screen. (This can be disconcerting the first time you see it.)

2. In the Search window, type the word or phrase you want to find.

   Continues on next page

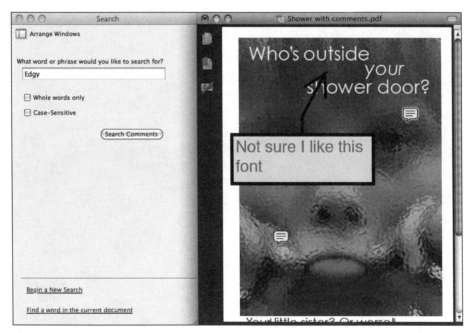

Figure 7.15 When you click the Search tool, Acrobat resizes your document window and displays the Search window.

SEARCHING FOR TEXT IN COMMENTS

3. Click the Search Comments button.

Acrobat searches through your comments and returns a list of results in the Search window (**Figure 7.16**).

4. To view one of the found comments, click its entry in the Results list.

Acrobat highlights that comment in the document window, changing pages as needed.

5. To do another search, click the New Search button in the Search dialog box and then repeat Steps 2–4.

6. To finish searching, click the Search window's standard Close control (the red button on the Mac or the X button in Windows).

Acrobat closes the Search window and returns the document window to its original size and position on the screen.

Figure 7.16 The Search window displays all the comments in your document that contain the target phrase.

Printing Comments

You can print the comments in a document two ways:

- ◆ Print the PDF file as usual, with the comments in place on the printed pages.

- ◆ Print a summary of the comments, printing the comment text and, optionally, a reduced image of each document page showing where the comment occurs in the document.

To print a PDF file with comments in place:

1. Choose File > Print.

Acrobat presents you with the Print dialog (**Figure 7.17**).

Continues on next page

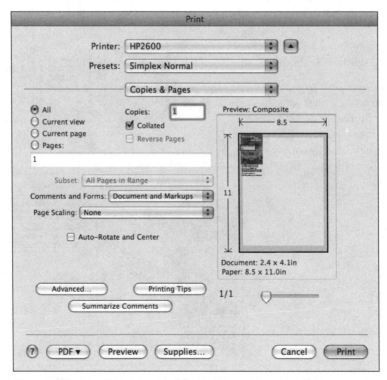

Figure 7.17 The Print dialog lets you print your document together with its comments.

PRINTING COMMENTS

2. In the Comments and Forms pop-up menu (**Figure 7.18**), select one of the following:

   ▲ To print the document and annotations other than Stamps, choose Document and Markups.

   ▲ To print the document and Stamps, choose Document and Stamps.

   You can't print both markups and Stamps; I don't know why.

3. Click Print.

   Acrobat prints the document and annotations.

Summarizing comments

Acrobat can also print a summary of all the comments in the document. It can print the summary in one of four formats (**Figure 7.19**):

◆ Each document page alternating with a page of comment text. Lines connect the comment text to the corresponding place on the document page when the pages are placed side by side (**Figure 7.20**).

◆ A thumbnail of each page printed side-by-side on a single page with the comment text for that page. Lines connect each comment with the corresponding position on the document page.

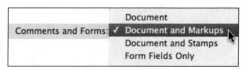

Figure 7.18 You can print the document and either its markups or its stamps.

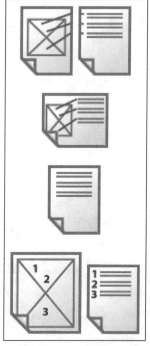

Figure 7.19 Acrobat offers four formats for printing a summary of a document's comments.

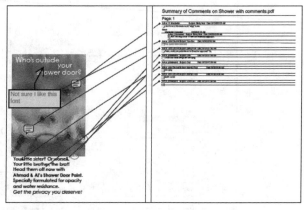

Figure 7.20 Most of the summary formats print each comment's text and indicate its position on the document page.

PRINTING COMMENTS

Figure 7.21 You can print a comment summary on paper or save it as a PDF file.

◆ A list of all the comment text, sorted by page number.

◆ Each document page alternating with a page of comment text. Each comment is numbered, and a corresponding number is placed at the comment's position on the document page.

To print a summary of a document's comments:

1. In the Comments List toolbar, click the Print Comments tool.

   A menu drops down from the tool (**Figure 7.21**).

2. Choose Print Comments Summary.

   The Summarize Options dialog opens (**Figure 7.22**).

3. Click the radio button corresponding to the type of summary you want.

4. Click the Print Comment Summary button.

   Acrobat prints the comment summary.

✔ Tip

■ If you select Create PDF of Comments Summary in the Print Comments menu, Acrobat creates a PDF file of the summary in the format you've chosen, rather than printing the summary on the page.

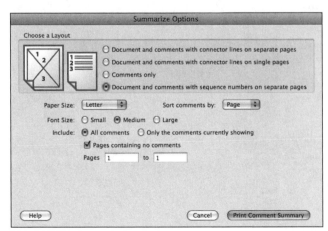

Figure 7.22 The Summarize Options dialog lets you select the format you want for the summary.

Migrating Comments

In the previous chapter, we discussed importing comments from an FDF file into a PDF document. The imported comments are placed onto the document's pages in their original locations—the same x and y coordinates as in the reviewer's copy of the file.

Unfortunately, if the PDF file has been revised since the review so it's no longer identical to the reviewer's copy, the imported comments may no longer line up with the text or graphic elements to which they pertain (**Figures 7.23** and **7.24**).

Migrating comments into the revised document, instead of importing them, solves this problem. With migration, Acrobat attempts to place each comment in the same position relative to the page's contents. Even if text has been reflowed, illustrations have moved to different pages, and images have been repositioned, the comments pertaining to those items still find their proper targets.

To migrate comments into a modified PDF file:

Start with both files open in Acrobat and the revised document in the foreground.

1. Choose Comments > Migrate Comments.

    The Migrate Comments dialog opens (**Figure 7.25**).

2. Select the file to be tagged from the drop-down menu.

    This menu contains the names of all currently open files.

3. Click OK.

    Acrobat reads the comments in the file you selected, placing them in the appropriate places on the current document's pages.

> You~~ù~~ little sister? Or worse!. ⌐
> Your little brother, the brat!
> Head them off ~~now~~ with

Figure 7.23 This text has a variety of markups added to it.

> You∧bratty little sister? Or~~worse~~!
> Your little brother, the brat!
> Frustrate their ~~fun~~ ~~now~~ with

Figure 7.24 Importing the markups from Figure 7.23 into a revised version of the PDF file results in many of the markups no longer lining up with the original text.

Figure 7.25 You migrate comments from the reviewer's copy of the PDF file.

REVIEWING PDF DOCUMENTS

In previous chapters we discussed Acrobat's tools for placing and reading comments on a PDF page. The techniques those chapters covered are excellent for soliciting comments from two or three other people.

However, what if you're conducting a company-wide review of a document? You may be sending the PDF file to a dozen people to get comments and critiques. How do you keep track of the people to whom you have sent the document for review? And once you start receiving the annotated files back from the reviewers, how do you handle all the comments? Read them side by side? Import them into a single PDF file so you can look at them all at once?

Acrobat 9 makes it relatively easy to conduct a broadly distributed review of a document. Acrobat manages the process for you, sending copies of the document to reviewers and then collecting all their comments into a single copy of the file.

Acrobat can deliver copies to reviewers in two ways: e-mailing the document to all the reviewers (an *e-mail–based review*) or arranging a server-based distribution across a corporate network (a *shared review*).

Let's see how to do both of these.

Starting an E-mail–Based Review

In an e-mail–based review, Acrobat e-mails copies of your document to a group of reviewers you designate. When they open the document, they comment on it using the standard Acrobat annotation tools and then return the document by e-mail. When you open the returned, annotated copy, Acrobat merges the comments into your original PDF file. Eventually, the original file contains the comments returned by all the reviewers.

To start an e-mail–based review:

1. On the Tasks toolbar, choose Comment > Attach for Email Review (**Figure 8.1**).

   Acrobat displays the first step in the Email-Based Review Wizard, in which you choose the review file (**Figure 8.2**).

2. Click the Choose button, and choose the PDF file to be reviewed in the pick-a-file dialog.

   As a convenience, you may choose an open PDF document in the pop-up menu.

3. Click Next.

   Acrobat displays the second step in the Email-Based Review Wizard, which allows you to invite reviewers (**Figure 8.3**).

4. Type the e-mail addresses of your reviewers into the text box.

   You can separate reviewers' e-mail addresses with spaces, semicolons, or new lines.

   You may instead click the Address Book button and choose people in your system's address book.

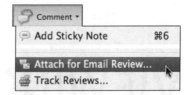

Figure 8.1 You initiate an e-mail–based review by choosing Comment > Attach for Email Review on the Tasks toolbar.

Figure 8.2 The first step in the Email-Based Review Wizard specifies the file that is to be reviewed.

Figure 8.3 The second step in the Wizard collects the e-mail addresses of all your reviewers.

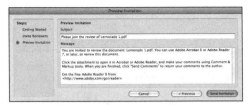

Figure 8.4 You finish by editing the subject and message text of the notification e-mails.

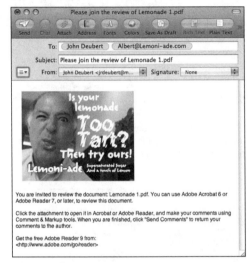

Figure 8.5 When you're invited to review a document, the PDF file is attached to the e-mailed notification.

5. Click Next.

Acrobat displays the final step in the Wizard (**Figure 8.4**), which lets you read and modify the e-mail the reviewers will see.

6. Type the text you want for your e-mail's subject in the Preview Invitation's Subject field.

7. Modify or replace the email's message text as you wish in the Preview Invitation's Message field.

In most cases, you should leave the message text as is, because it provides detailed directions to the reviewers on what to do.

8. Click the Send Invitation button.

Acrobat launches your e-mail client and displays the outbound message with the PDF file attached (**Figure 8.5**).

9. Click your e-mail client's Send button or otherwise send the e-mail message on its way.

✔ Tip

■ Depending on your computer setup, you may not see your e-mail client. In particular, the Windows version of Acrobat may send the e-mail messages directly.

Reviewing an E-mailed Document

When you receive a document for review, you get an e-mail with the PDF file attached. When you open that PDF file, Acrobat recognizes that it's part of a review and automatically does three things that make it easy to review the document (**Figure 8.6**):

◆ It makes the Comment & Markup toolbar visible.

◆ It adds a Send Comments button to the toolbar.

◆ It offers instructions on what to do with the document.

To review a PDF document:

1. Open the PDF file attached to the notification e-mail.

   If another reviewer sent you this e-mail, the Merge Comments dialog box asks if you want to see the other people's comments (**Figure 8.7**).

2. If you are presented with the Merge Comments dialog, click Yes or No, according to whether you want to see other people's comments.

   Acrobat displays the document in a window with the review instructions, as in Figure 8.6.

3. Make your comments on the document, as described in Chapter 6.

4. When you're finished, click the Send Comments button to display the Send Comments dialog box (**Figure 8.8**).

5. Click the Send button.

   Acrobat launches your e-mail client and displays the outbound message with the PDF file attached.

6. Click your e-mail client's Send button or otherwise send the e-mail message on its way.

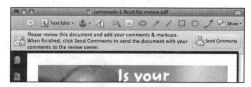

Figure 8.6 Acrobat presents the reviewer with instructions on how to review the e-mailed document and adds a Send Comments button.

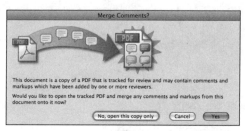

Figure 8.7 When a reviewer opens the e-mail attachment, Acrobat offers to display any comments placed in the file by other reviewers.

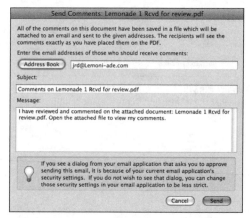

Figure 8.8 When the reviewer clicks Send Comments, Acrobat provides a chance to alter the return e-mail's subject and message texts.

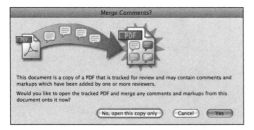

Figure 8.9 When the author opens a reviewed copy of the document, Acrobat offers to merge the comments into the original PDF file.

Receiving E-mail–Reviewed Documents

When you receive a reviewed copy of your document, the annotated version of the PDF file is attached to the notification e-mail. Open this attached document, and Acrobat merges the comments it contains into your original copy.

To receive a reviewed document:

1. In your e-mail software, open the attached PDF file.

   Acrobat presents you with the Merge Comments dialog box (**Figure 8.9**), which asks if you want to merge the comments into your copy of the document.

2. Click the Yes button.

   Acrobat opens the original PDF document and imports the comments from the attached PDF file into your original.

3. Read the comments as described in Chapter 7.

Starting a Shared Review

A shared review is technically more efficient than an e-mail–based review, because all the comments are stored in a single location rather than being shuttled around attached to different copies of the document. A shared review may also be more appropriate if the file being reviewed is very large, because many e-mail servers won't send or accept attachments that exceed some maximum size (5 MB is a typical limit).

The disadvantage of a shared review is that it's server-based, so someone must set up and maintain a location on your corporate server to serve as a repository for the PDF file, its comments, and the associated bookkeeping.

Happily, Adobe will do this for you as part of a new service called Acrobat.com. Acrobat's server maintains all the information associated with your shared review. This makes doing a shared review just as easy as an e-mailed review.

Arguably, Acrobat.com is one of the most significant components in the Acrobat 9 suite of software. Since Adobe takes upon itself the maintenance of a server available directly within the Acrobat application, a lot of tricky tasks suddenly become very easy. Many people found the benefits of shared reviews to be only barely worth the effort of creating and maintaining the server-based resources; now there is no effort at all associated with these reviews. See the sidebar on Acrobat.com, later in this chapter, to see what other services are available through this new Adobe product.

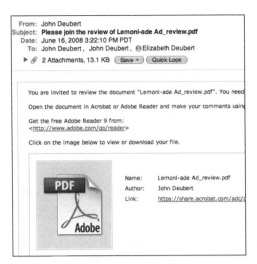

Figure 8.10 When invited to a shared review, reviewers are e-mailed a link to the PDF document, which is stored on the Acrobat.com server.

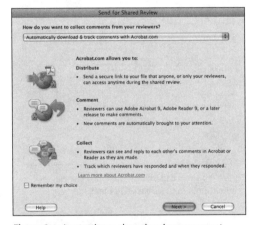

Figure 8.11 In starting a shared review, you must first decide where to store the review document and comments.

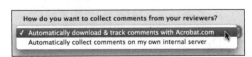

Figure 8.12 The review document and comments may be stored on Acrobat.com or on a Web- or SMB-based server of your choice. Pick Acrobat.com; you'll be happier.

Shared reviews on Acrobat.com

When you use Acrobat.com for your shared review, Acrobat automatically uploads your PDF file to the Acrobat.com server; Acrobat then e-mails to all of your reviewers a link to that file on the server (**Figure 8.10**). When your reviewers click the link, their copies of Acrobat automatically download the file and open it for review (very much like what happens with files e-mailed for review).

Each reviewer can then add comments to the file as usual. When finished, he or she clicks on a Publish Comments button that tells Acrobat to upload the comments to Acrobat.com.

To start a shared review:

1. On the Tasks toolbar, choose Comment > Send for Shared Review.

   Acrobat displays the first pane of the Send PDF for Shared Review Wizard, which records server information (**Figure 8.11**).

2. In the pop-up menu, choose "Automatically download & track comments with Acrobat.com" (**Figure 8.12**), then click Next.

   The pop-up menu also lets you use your own server to collect people's comments; however, someone will need to set up space on a Web- or SMB-based server volume to do this. In this book, we assume you'll be using Acrobat.com, because it's easy and free.

Continues on next page

STARTING A SHARED REVIEW

3. If you are not already logged into Acrobat. com, you are presented with a dialog box that lets you do so (**Figure 8.13**). Supply your e-mail address and password, and click the Sign In button.

Note this dialog box also lets you create a new Acrobat.com account if you don't already have one. Trust me, you want one of these accounts; the benefits are many and the disadvantages are nil.

Once you are logged in, Acrobat presents you with the next pane of the Send for Shared Review Wizard (**Figure 8.14**), which lets you invite reviewers.

4. Type the e-mail addresses of the reviewers into the text box.

You can separate reviewers' e-mail addresses with spaces, semicolons, or new lines. As a convenience, you may instead click the Address Book button and choose people in your system's address book.

5. Specify an access level for the reviewed document, using the pop-up menu (**Figure 8.15**). You may specify that only the people you notify may access the file, or that the file may be reviewed by anyone who knows its URL.

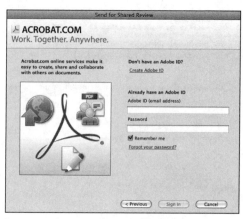

Figure 8.13 If you are not already logged onto Acrobat.com, you'll be prompted to do so.

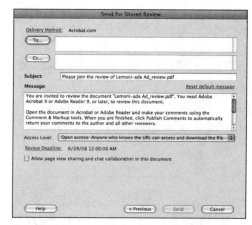

Figure 8.14 You can edit the text of the reviewer-notification e-mail subject and message.

Access Level: ✓ Limited access: Only my specific recipients can access and download the file
            Open access: Anyone who knows the URL can access and download the file

Figure 8.15 You can decide who should have access to the review document: anyone who knows the address or only people you have specifically notified.

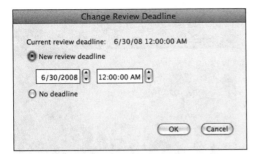

Figure 8.16 You may set a deadline for the review; Acrobat.com will no longer accept comments on the document after this date.

Figure 8.17 Acrobat creates a review copy of the original PDF file; this is the file you will open to see comments sent by reviewers.

6. If you wish to set a deadline for the review, click the Set Deadline link and enter a date in the resulting dialog box (**Figure 8.16**).

7. If you want to use page sharing and chat collaboration with this file, click the check box labeled "Allow page view sharing and chat collaboration in this document."

   We'll talk about this feature later in the chapter; it's very, very nifty.

8. Click Send.

   Acrobat posts the PDF file to the server folder and notifies the reviewers by e-mail.

When you are done setting up the shared review, you will find a new copy of your PDF file in the same folder as the original. This new version will have the same name as the old, with _review added (**Figure 8.17**). This is the copy of the file that you will use to view reviewers' comments.

Reviewing a Shared Document

If you are on the reviewers' list for a shared review, you receive an e-mail that contains a link to the PDF file stored on Acrobat.com (Figure 8.10). In brief, you retrieve the PDF file from Acrobat.com, add your comments to the file, then post the comments back to Acrobat.com. All very easy.

To review a server-based document:

1. In your e-mail software, click on the link to the PDF file.

    Acrobat launches your Web browser, taking you to Acrobat.com (**Figure 8.18**).

2. Click the Downloads link in the Acrobat.com window.

    Acrobat downloads the review copy of the document to your hard disk.

3. Open the document and add your comments, using the comment tools as usual.

4. Click the Publish Comments button at the top of the document window (**Figure 8.19**).

    Acrobat stores your comments on the Acrobat.com server.

Figure 8.18 The link in the notification e-mail leads the reviewer to Acrobat.com, where he or she can download the file and then open it in Acrobat.

Figure 8.19 After reviewers have opened a document for shared review and added comments, they can publish those comments back to Acrobat.com.

Figure 8.20 You display the Tracker window by choosing Comment > Track Reviews on the Tasks toolbar.

Figure 8.21 Clicking a shared review in the Tracker window displays a list of reviewers and other information about that review.

■ There are many other things you can do through the Review Tracker, including starting a new review using the same set of reviewers and sending an e-mail to one or all the reviewers.

Receiving Server-Based Reviews

The best way to collect comments from a shared review is to use the Acrobat Review Tracker. This tool lists all the reviews you've initiated and lets you conveniently see the current state of all their comments.

To read comments from a server-based review:

1. On the Tasks toolbar, choose Comment > Track Reviews (**Figure 8.20**).

   Acrobat presents you with the Tracker window (**Figure 8.21**). This window lets you track all current e-mail–based and shared reviews, as well as the results returned from people filling out PDF-format forms.

2. In the left-hand pane, click the review you want to examine ("Lemonade 1" in Figure 8.21).

   The right side of the window shows information about that review, such as when it was initiated, who the reviewers are, and so on.

3. Click the View Comments link (near the top of the right-hand pane).

   Acrobat opens the review copy of the PDF file, displaying all the comments made by the various reviewers.

4. View the comments in the document as discussed in Chapter 7.

✔ Tips

■ The review copy of the document has a Publish Comments button, like that in Figure 8.19. This allows you to respond to comments and push the responses up to the server for others to see.

Real-Time Collaborative Reviews

Real-time live collaboration is a feature new to Acrobat 9, and a stunning one it is, too. If you enable this feature for a particular shared review, any number of reviewers may participate in a live chat within Acrobat, discussing the document online. It is even possible for one of the reviewers to share his or her screen with the other online reviewers, so that everyone is looking at the same document view as the discussion proceeds.

This is very cool stuff, particularly because it is available to anyone reviewing the document with any version of Acrobat 9 and Adobe Reader 9.

Enabling live collaboration

Live collaboration is enabled on a review-by-review basis. You do this by initiating the shared review exactly as we did earlier: you choose Comment > Send for Shared Review on the Tasks toolbar, then supply the information requested by the resulting wizard (**Figure 8.22**).

To allow a mundane shared review to become a live collaborative review, you simply click the check box labeled "Allow page view sharing and chat collaboration in this document" in the wizard's second panel (Figure 8.22). That's it; real-time collaboration is available to all the reviewers of this document.

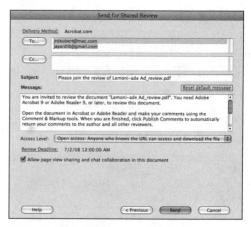

Figure 8.22 You allow a review document to be used in live collaboration by clicking the check box "Allow page view sharing and chat collaboration."

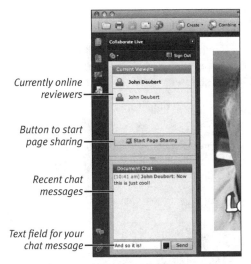

Currently online reviewers

Button to start page sharing

Recent chat messages

Text field for your chat message

Figure 8.23 The Collaborate Live navigation pane has a list of online reviewers, a simple but effective chat interface, and a button that starts live page sharing.

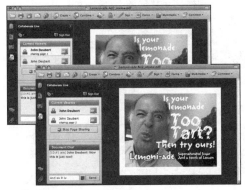

Figure 8.24 When page sharing is turned on, all the online reviewers see the same view of the document as you do.

Figure 8.25 All the reviewers' pointers are visible when page sharing is turned on, each identified with the reviewer's name.

Using live collaboration

When you open a document that has been enabled for live collaboration, Acrobat displays the Collaborative Live navigation pane (**Figure 8.23**). This pane contains a list of currently online reviewers and a basic e-chat facility.

Simply type text in the Document Chat field at the bottom of the left pane and press the Return key or click Send. Your text immediately appears in the other reviewers' Collaborative Live panes.

Page sharing

Anyone who has collaborated on a document with someone who lives or works in a different location knows what a nuisance it can be to discuss that document over the telephone. Trying to get the other person to understand what item on the page it is that bothers you can take years off your life in frustration.

Enter page sharing.

If your document is enabled for live collaboration, you can simply click the Start Page Sharing button (Figure 8.23), and every online reviewer sees exactly what you see: their copies of Acrobat display the same document page as yours; when you change pages, so automatically do they. As long as page sharing is enabled, their view of the document will be slaved to yours (**Figure 8.24**).

Everyone even gets to see where everyone else's pointers are on the page; each reviewer's pointer appears as a small arrow, identified by the reviewer's name (**Figure 8.25**).

I cannot adequately tell you how exciting this is for those of us who have worked on documents with other people!

REAL-TIME COLLABORATIVE REVIEWS

Acrobat.com

Acrobat.com is a new online service provided free by Adobe Systems. Although it is not properly part of Adobe Acrobat, that software uses Acrobat.com for many of its features, such as the live collaboration and page sharing discussed in this chapter.

Acrobat.com allows easy access to a remarkably large collection of features, including the following (**Figure 8.26**):

Word processing. Adobe Buzzword is an online word processor that lets you create, edit, store, and print sophisticated word processing documents anywhere you have access to a web browser (**Figure 8.27**).

Figure 8.26 Acrobat.com is a free service from Adobe Systems that provides file sharing, word processing, and other tools.

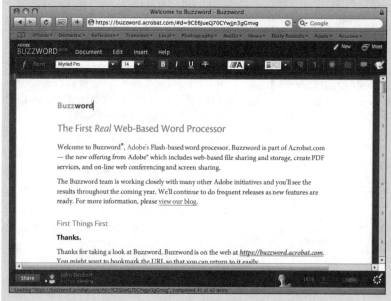

Figure 8.27 Adobe Buzzword is Acrobat.com's free, online word processor.

Acrobat.com *(continued)*

Online conferencing. Acrobat.com's ConnectNow feature lets you conduct an online conference with one or more people. This may include any combination of video, audio, or text chatting (**Figure 8.28**). The people with whom you are conferring don't even need to have Acrobat.com accounts.

File sharing. You can share any kind of files—zip files, photos, whatever—with one or more people of your choosing. Just place the files on Acrobat.com, and anyone who knows the URL can download them to his own computer.

Creating PDF files. Acrobat.com converts files of a wide variety of types (including Word documents, TIFF images, and Excel spreadsheets) to PDF without requiring any Acrobat software. This may be done only five times; after that you must either purchase Acrobat 9 or subscribe to Adobe's Create Online PDF service.

Continues on next page

Figure 8.28 ConnectNow provides real-time conferencing using any combination of text, audio, and video.

ACROBAT.COM

Acrobat.com *(continued)*

Joining Acrobat.com is free and easy: just point your Web browser to Acrobat.com and click the Sign Up link (**Figure 8.29**).

Trust me—there's no good reason not to do this.

Figure 8.29 When you access Acrobat.com, you are invited to sign in and, if necessary, sign up. You want to sign up!

MANIPULATING PAGES

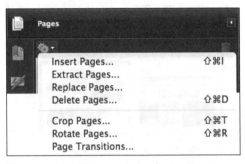

Figure 9.1 You have access to Acrobat's page-manipulation commands in the Pages pane's Action menu, identified by a gear icon.

Document		
Header & Footer	▶	
Background	▶	
Watermark	▶	
Insert Pages...	⇧⌘I	
Extract Pages...		
Replace Pages...		
Delete Pages...	⇧⌘D	
Split Document...		
Crop Pages...	⇧⌘T	
Rotate Pages...	⇧⌘R	

Figure 9.2 The page-manipulation commands are also available in the Document menu.

Acrobat 9 provides tools that make it easy to insert, delete, rearrange, and otherwise change the order of pages within a PDF document.

You can get to these features in three ways:

◆ Click the Action button (identified by a gear icon) at the top of the Pages navigation pane (**Figure 9.1**). Acrobat displays a menu that contains all the page-manipulation commands.

◆ Right-click a thumbnail in the Pages navigation pane. The resulting contextual menu is identical to the Action menu described above.

◆ Go to Acrobat's Document menu (**Figure 9.2**), which contains many of the same commands.

I tend to find it most convenient to use the Action button in the Pages navigation pane. You may prefer the other methods, and you have my permission to use them.

Rearranging Pages

You can move pages around in a PDF file using the Pages navigation pane; simply drag pages from their original locations to the places you want them.

To move a page from one location to another:

1. Click the Pages tab to open the Pages navigation pane.

   Acrobat displays thumbnails of all the document pages.

2. Click the thumbnail of the page you want to move.

   Acrobat creates a highlight around the thumbnail, indicating that the page is selected (**Figure 9.3**).

3. Drag the selected thumbnail to its new position in the document.

   As you drag the page, Acrobat places a light-colored vertical line between existing thumbnails, indicating where the page will be placed (see pointer in **Figure 9.4**).

4. Release the mouse button.

   Acrobat moves the selected page to its new location.

✔ Tip

- You can select more than one thumbnail in the Pages pane. Acrobat follows the conventional mouse-click rules in this pane: Shift-click selects a contiguous range of thumbnails; Command-click/ Ctrl-click selects a noncontiguous set of pages.

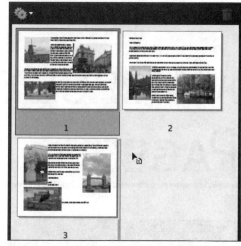

Figure 9.3 When you select a thumbnail in the Pages pane, Acrobat highlights the thumbnail with a red outline.

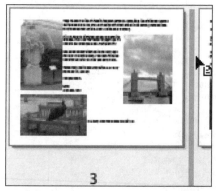

Figure 9.4 As you drag a page in the Pages pane, a vertical line indicates the page's new location.

Figure 9.5 In the Extract Pages dialog, you specify the range of pages you want to extract.

Extracting Pages

You can extract a range of pages from a PDF file and create a new PDF file from those pages. You can place all the extracted pages into a single PDF file or have Acrobat create a separate PDF file for each page.

To extract a range of pages from a document:

1. With the document open, click the Pages tab to open the Pages navigation pane.

2. In the Pages pane's Action menu, choose Extract Pages (Figure 9.1).

   Acrobat presents you with the Extract Pages dialog box (**Figure 9.5**).

3. In the From and To fields, indicate the beginning and ending page numbers of the pages you want to extract.

4. If you want to remove those pages from the original document, click the check box "Delete Pages After Extracting."

5. If you want each extracted page to become a separate, one-page PDF document, click the check box "Extract Pages As Separate Files."

6. Click OK.

   Acrobat extracts the pages as you've specified. The extracted pages appear in a new window named "Pages from [*original document*].pdf."

✔ Tip

- As an alternative, you can select a set of thumbnails in the Pages navigation pane, right-click one of the selected thumbnails, and select Extract Pages from the contextual menu. The Extract Pages dialog box opens with the page range already set to the pages you selected.

Inserting One File into Another

Acrobat makes it easy to insert the contents of another PDF file into your current document.

To insert pages from another file into a document:

1. With the document open, click the Pages tab to open the Pages navigation pane.

2. In the Pages pane's Action menu, select Insert Pages.

   The standard Open dialog box opens.

3. Choose the file that contains the pages you want to insert, and click OK.

   Acrobat presents you with the Insert Pages dialog box (**Figure 9.6**).

4. Specify where in your document you want the new pages to be inserted.

   Using the Location pop-up menu and the radio buttons, you may select before or after the first page or last page, or a specific page number.

5. Click OK.

   Acrobat inserts the contents of the other file into your current document.

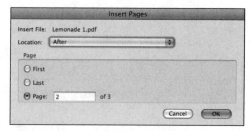

Figure 9.6 The Insert Pages dialog boxlets you specify where the inserted pages should be placed.

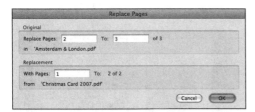

Figure 9.7 In the Replace Pages dialog, you indicate which pages should be replaced and which page in the other document should replace them.

Replacing Pages

Acrobat lets you replace a range of pages in the current document with pages taken from another PDF file.

To replace pages in your document:

1. With the document open, click the Pages tab to open the Pages navigation pane.

2. In the Pages pane's Action menu, select Replace Pages.

    The standard Open dialog box opens.

3. Select the file that contains the replacement pages, and click OK.

    The Replace Pages dialog box opens (**Figure 9.7**).

4. In the Original section, specify the range of pages that should be replaced.

5. In the Replacement section, specify the starting page number of the replacement pages in the other PDF file.

    Note that you don't need to specify an ending page number; the length of the replacement page range matches the number of pages you're replacing.

6. Click OK.

    Acrobat replaces the specified pages with pages taken from the other document.

✔ Tip

■ Interestingly, when you replace a range of pages in a document, this does not replace any links, comments, or form fields on the original pages. Those remain in place, resting on top of the new pages. Note that these active elements will probably not align with the appropriate text in the replacement pages.

REPLACING PAGES

Rotating Pages

When you export a landscape-oriented document from page-layout software or a word processor, Acrobat often displays the resulting pages sideways (**Figure 9.8**). The page is laid out in landscape, but Acrobat displays it in portrait orientation.

This is easily fixed by having Acrobat rotate the pages in your document. Acrobat can rotate all the pages or a specified range of pages.

The pages retain their new orientation in future viewings.

To rotate pages in the current document:

1. With the document open, click the Pages tab to open the Pages navigation pane.

2. In the Pages pane's Action menu, select Rotate Pages.

   The Rotate Pages dialog box opens (**Figure 9.9**).

   In the Direction pop-up menu (**Figure 9.10**), choose whether the pages should be rotated 90 degrees clockwise or counterclockwise, or a full 180 degrees.

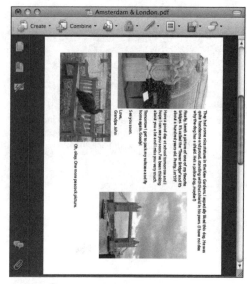

Figure 9.8 Many applications produce landscape pages that Acrobat displays in portrait orientation.

Figure 9.9 The Rotate Pages dialog box lets you specify which pages should be rotated and in what direction they should rotate.

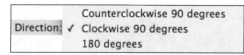

Figure 9.10 You may rotate pages 90 degrees clockwise or counterclockwise or a full 180 degrees.

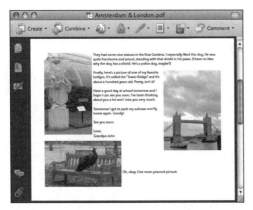

Figure 9.11 In Acrobat you can rotate your pages so they are oriented the way you want.

3. Click the appropriate radio button to choose the range of pages you want to rotate (Figure 9.9):

   ▲ To rotate the entire document, click All.

   ▲ To rotate pages you've selected in the Pages pane, click Selection.

   ▲ To rotate a specific range of page numbers, click Pages, and specify the beginning and ending page numbers.

4. In the Rotate pop-up menu, choose whether you want to rotate even pages, odd pages, or both.

5. In the unnamed pop-up menu below the Rotate pop-up menu, choose whether to rotate landscape pages, portrait pages, or both.

6. Click OK.

   Acrobat rotates the pages you specified (**Figure 9.11**).

✔ Tip

■ Acrobat often uses the orientation of text on a page to determine whether that page is landscape or portrait. If you select a specific orientation in Step 5, pages with no text on them may not be rotated, regardless of the actual orientation of the page.

ROTATING PAGES

Cropping Pages

Graphics applications often create PDF files whose pages have a lot of white space around the pages' contents (**Figure 9.12**). Acrobat lets you pare down the document page, cropping it so it contains only the content you want (**Figure 9.13**). You can also change the page dimensions to a standard size, such as Letter or A4.

To crop a page in a document:

1. With the document open to the page you want to crop, choose Document > Crop Pages.

   Acrobat presents you with the Crop Pages dialog box(**Figure 9.14**). In addition to the page-cropping controls, this dialog box has a preview that shows the border of the cropped document.

Figure 9.12 Many graphics applications produce PDF pages with a lot of white space around the graphic.

Figure 9.13 You can crop pages so they contain only the part that is useful.

CROPPING PAGES

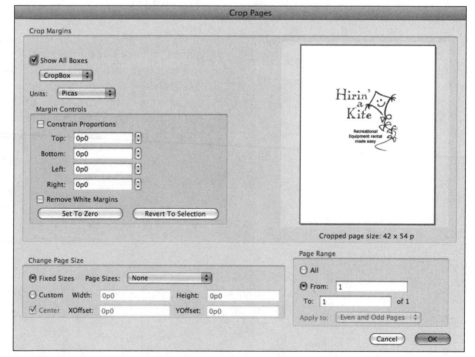

Figure 9.14 The Crop Pages dialog boxlets you specify how much of the page should be trimmed from the top, bottom, left, and right of the page.

2. In the Margin Controls section, either enter values for the top, bottom, left, and right margins or click the up and down arrows to increase or decrease the values of these margins (**Figure 9.15**).

As you do so, Acrobat draws a rectangle showing you the present size of the page.

3. In the Page Range section, indicate the range of pages whose size you want to change.

You can select a range of pages or click All to crop all the pages. By default, the page range is set to include only the current page.

4. Click the OK button.

Acrobat reduces the page size.

Continues on next page

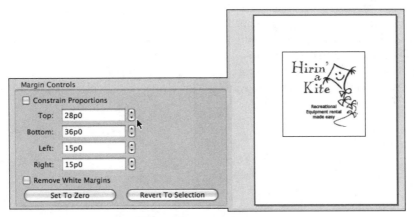

Figure 9.15 As you increase the margin sizes, Acrobat displays a rectangle in the preview picture, indicating the new page boundaries.

✔ Tips

■ Acrobat doesn't discard any content data when it crops a page. If you select the cropped page and return to the Crop Pages dialog, you can click the Set to Zero button to recover the original page size. This is true even after you have saved, closed, and later reopened the file.

■ You can choose whatever unit of measure you wish from the Units pop-up menu. It offers points, picas, millimeters, centimeters, and inches. No furlongs, I'm afraid.

■ You can indicate units of measure for the margins by using abbreviations (pt, p, mm, cm, in) in the margin size boxes, as in Figure 9.15.

■ You can use the Crop Pages dialog box to change the paper size of your document. Select the paper size (Letter, Legal, A4, and so on) from the Page Sizes pop-up menu. I often use this with scanned document pages, which never seem to come out exactly 8 by 11 inches. I choose Letter for the page size and all my pages are resized.

Adding and Changing Text and Graphics

10

PDF isn't intended to be an editable document format. Adobe meant a PDF file to be a snapshot of a document as it was at a particular time.

Nonetheless, Acrobat breaks with that vision by providing extremely useful tools for *touching up* a document—making common changes that are convenient to some people and absolutely vital to others. This includes fixing typos, adding page numbers, and even modifying images using Adobe Photoshop or another editor of your choice.

In this chapter, we'll look at the most routinely useful tools for modifying a PDF document in Acrobat 9.

Touching Up Text

One of the first—and most requested—editing capabilities Adobe included in Acrobat was the ability to make minor changes to the text in a PDF file. This capability isn't intended for wholesale rewriting of text; rather, it lets you make small changes like fixing a wrong telephone number or adding a missing comma. Before Adobe added this feature, even a minor typo would send you back to your original word-processor file, where you'd have to make the change and regenerate the PDF file.

When you select the TouchUp Text tool in the Advanced Editing toolbar (**Figure 10.1**), the pointer becomes a text-editing I-beam whenever it roams over text (**Figure 10.2**). You edit text using the same techniques you use in a text editor: click the text you want to change, and type your addition or replacement.

To change text in a document:

1. Click the TouchUp Text tool in the Advanced Editing toolbar (Figure 10.1).

2. Either click the text to insert a change or select text that you want to delete or replace.

   Acrobat inserts a blinking cursor at the place you clicked or highlights the text you selected (Figure 10.2).

3. Type the text you want to insert into the PDF file.

✔ Tips

■ Acrobat implements all the standard key commands for moving the blinking cursor to the next word, the end of the line, and so on.

■ To replace or add text, that text's font must be installed in your computer system.

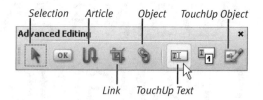

Selection   Article   Object   TouchUp Object

Link   TouchUp Text

Figure 10.1 The Advanced Editing toolbar contains tools for manipulating and modifying documents.

Figure 10.2 With the TouchUp Text tool, you can select text on your PDF page.

Figure 10.3 Right-clicking text with the TouchUp Text tool yields a contextual menu with access to text properties.

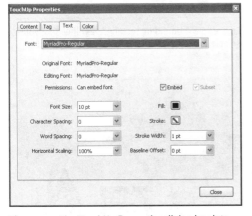

Figure 10.4 The TouchUp Properties dialog box lets you change the font, size, and other characteristics of the selected text.

In addition to inserting and deleting text, the TouchUp Text tool lets you change the font, size, alignment, and other properties of text in your PDF file.

To change text properties:

1. Select the TouchUp Text tool in the Advanced Editing toolbar.

2. Select the text whose properties you want to change.

   Right-click the text to display a contextual menu (**Figure 10.3**).

3. Choose Properties.

   Acrobat presents you with the TouchUp Properties dialog box (**Figure 10.4**).

4. Choose a font from the pop-up menu.

5. If you select a font, also choose the Embed and Subset check boxes.

   These options embed the font in the PDF file, ensuring that the text will look the same on other computers.

6. Type a font size into the Font Size field, or click the tiny up and down arrows to increase or decrease the font size.

7. Click Close.

✔ Tip

■ The TouchUp properties dialog box lets you change a number of other properties, including word spacing and horizontal offset. These can be occasionally useful for adjusting the appearance of your text.

Modifying Line Art

There are two ways you can change lines, rectangles, and other line art on an Acrobat page. Acrobat provides a TouchUp Object tool that lets you change the position and orientation of graphic objects on the page. For extensive changes, Acrobat lets you edit page contents in Adobe Illustrator (the default) or another graphics editor.

Keep in mind we're talking about graphic objects that are part of the page content, not the lines, rectangles, and other graphics that can be associated with a comment.

Let's start by looking at the Acrobat tools.

Changing an object's position and size:

1. Click the TouchUp Object tool in the Advanced Editing toolbar (**Figure 10.5**).

2. Click a graphic object on the document page.

   Acrobat draws a rectangle around the object to indicate that it's selected (**Figure 10.6**).

3. To change the object's size, click and drag one of the handles at the square's corners.

4. To reposition the object, click and drag it to the desired position (**Figure 10.7**).

✔ Tips

- Holding down the Shift key as you drag an object constrains your motion to angles of 90 degrees from the original position.

- In contrast, when you resize an object, Acrobat normally preserves the object's original shape, scaling the object identically in the horizontal and vertical directions. To release this constraint, hold down the Shift key while you drag the object's handles; Acrobat lets you drag that handle anywhere you wish, scaling the horizontal and vertical dimensions separately.

Figure 10.5 The TouchUp Object tool lets you modify line art and images in your PDF document.

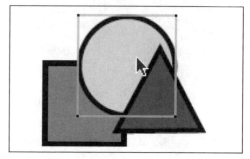

Figure 10.6 A bounding rectangle signifies that you've selected an object with the TouchUp Object tool.

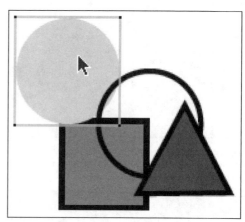

Figure 10.7 You can drag objects around the page with the TouchUp Objects tool. Note that the fill and border of an object are often separate.

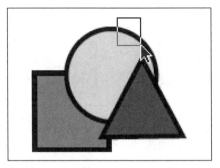

Figure 10.8 To choose both the fill and border of an object, with the TouchUp Object tool drag a marquee that intersects the object's border.

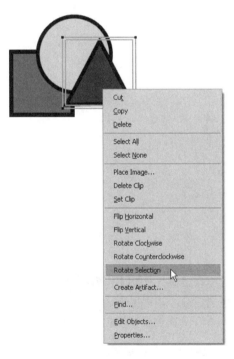

Figure 10.9 To rotate artwork on the PDF page, right-click an object and choose Rotate Selection. Note there are a variety of other commands available.

Fill, Border and Rotate

A graphic object may reside in a PDF file as two objects, one each for the fill and the border. In that case, the TouchUp Object tool may choose only one of the two objects.

If that is the case for the object you're editing, you need to either move the two objects separately or choose both at once by dragging out a marquee with the TouchUp Object tool (**Figure 10.8**). This marquee must touch the outline of the object to choose both the fill and border; it doesn't need to completely enclose the object. Then you can move or resize both the fill and the border of the object.

Right-clicking a graphic object with the TouchUp Object tool yields a contextual menu (**Figure 10.9**) that lets you flip or rotate objects. Simply choose the appropriate command from the menu. The menu commands are generally straightforward; one item that may be tricky is rotating by an arbitrary amount.

To rotate an object by an arbitrary amount:

1. Click the TouchUp Object tool in the Advanced Editing toolbar.

2. Click a graphic object to select it.

   Note that if the object consists of separate fill and border objects, you need to select both by dragging a marquee.

3. Right-click the object to get to its contextual menu.

4. Choose Rotate Selection.

5. Click and drag the selection rectangle's corners to rotate the object (**Figure 10.10**).

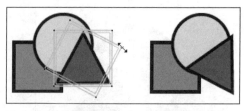

Figure 10.10 Having chosen Rotate Selection, you can drag one of the handles at the bounding box's corners to rotate the object.

Editing in Adobe Illustrator

Acrobat also lets you edit graphics in Adobe Illustrator. This capability opens up a vast array of editing possibilities. The cool part is that when you save the modified graphic in Illustrator, it's inserted back into the PDF file. I get excited about this feature! (Yes, I do lead a simple life.)

To edit artwork in Illustrator:

1. Click the TouchUp Object tool in the Advanced Editing toolbar.

2. Do either of the following:
   - ▲ While holding down the Alt/Option key, double-click the artwork.
   - ▲ Right-click the object, and choose Edit Object from the contextual menu.

   Acrobat launches Illustrator and opens the artwork in a new Illustrator window.

Editing Images

The TouchUp Object tool works with pixel-based images exactly as it does with line art. Right-clicking an image provides a contextual menu with the commands we discussed, which you use exactly the same way.

Option/Alt double-clicking an image opens that image in Adobe Photoshop, allowing you to make any change you wish to that image. Saving the image from Photoshop inserts the modified image back into the original PDF file.

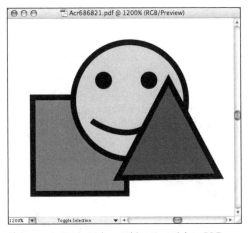

Figure 10.11 You can do anything you wish to PDF artwork you've opened in Illustrator; here we've added eyes and a smile to the circle.

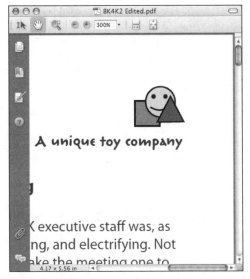

Figure 10.12 When you save the artwork from Illustrator, the modified objects are inserted into the original PDF file.

3. Edit the artwork using usual Illustrator tools.

You may do anything that is valid in Illustrator, including adding new artwork or text. (The eyes and smile in **Figure 10.11** were added in Illustrator.)

4. In Illustrator, choose File > Save.

Illustrator saves the artwork directly into the original PDF file (**Figure 10.12**).

✔ Tip

■ Acrobat's Preferences allow you to use alternative editors, instead of Illustrator and Photoshop. Go to the Preferences dialog box, and choose the Touch Up category. You'll see a pair of controls that let you choose editing software for graphics and images.

MODIFYING LINE ART

Adding Headers and Footers

Acrobat lets you add headers and footers to a PDF file. This new text can be in any font and point size, and can include page numbers and the current date.

The Add Header and Footer dialog box, although complex, isn't as confusing as it may seem at first (**Figure 10.13**).

Note that the header and footer each have three text fields, corresponding to left justified, centered, and right justified. You may supply up to three pieces of text for both the header and the footer, one snippet of text for each of the three positions.

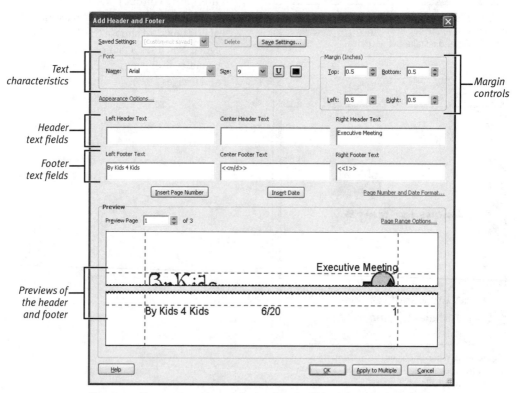

Figure 10.13 Here are the main sets of controls in the Add Header and Footer dialog box.

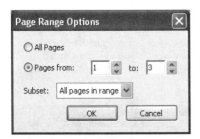

Figure 10.14 Clicking the Page Range Options link yields this dialog box, which lets you specify the pages to which your headers and footers should be applied.

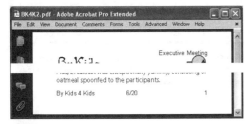

Figure 10.15 When you close the Add Header and Footer dialog box, your new text appears at the top and bottom of your PDF pages.

To add a header or footer to a document:

1. Choose Document > Header & Footer > Add.

   The Add Header and Footer dialog box opens (Figure 10.13).

2. Choose the font and size you want for your header and footer text.

   The controls to the right of the Size combo box let you turn on underlining and specify a text color.

3. In the Margin fields, type the values you want for the top, bottom, left, and right margins.

   The top margin is the baseline for the header; the footer is placed just below the bottom margin.

4. In the six text fields running across the center of the dialog box, type the left-justified, centered, and right-justified text for the header and/or footer.

   The preview across the bottom of the dialog box shows what your text will look like in place on your document page.

   At any time while typing text, you can click the Insert Page Number button or the Insert Date button to insert the respective value into your text.

5. If you want your header and footer to apply only to certain pages in your document, click the Page Range Options link.

   Acrobat opens a dialog that lets you specify the pages to which the header and footer should be applied (**Figure 10.14**).

6. Click OK.

   Acrobat adds the header and footer to your document (**Figure 10.15**).

ADDING HEADERS AND FOOTERS

✔ Tips

- If you have a header and footer combina-tion that you use frequently, you can save your settings by clicking the Save Settings button in the Add Header and Footer dia-log (**Figure 10.16**). You're asked to name the collection of settings; that name will appear in the Saved Settings pop-up menu.

- You can control the appearance of the page number and date inserted into your text. Click the Page Number and Date Format link to the right of the Insert Date button. Acrobat opens a dialog that lets you select from a set of predefined formats (**Figure 10.17**).

- You can modify your header and footer settings by choosing Document > Header & Footer > Update. The Add Header and Footer dialog box opens, filled in with your current settings. Make whatever changes you want, and click OK.

- You can delete your header and footer by selecting Document > Header & Footer > Remove.

Figure 10.16 The Save Settings button lets you add the current set of control settings to the Saved Settings pop-up menu.

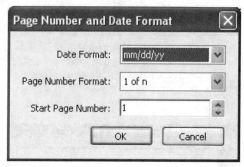

Figure 10.17 Clicking the Page Number and Date Format link lets you specify how the page numbers and date will appear on the page.

Adding a Background

Acrobat can add a background to the pages in your document. That background can be either a solid color or page contents taken from another PDF or image file. In the latter case, depending on the type of file you choose, the page contents can be any combination of text or graphics.

To add a background to your document pages:

1. Choose Document > Background > Add/Replace.

   The Add Background dialog opens (**Figure 10.18**).

2. If you want to use a page from another PDF file as your background, click the File radio button.

Continues on next page

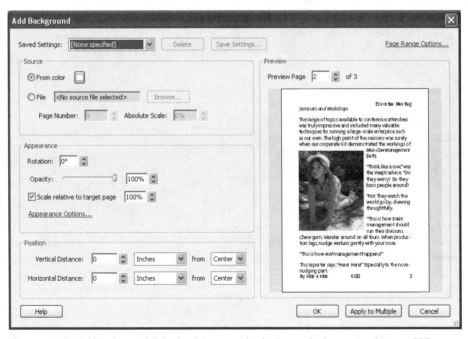

Figure 10.18 The Add Background dialog box lets you apply a background color or artwork to your PDF pages.

ADDING A BACKGROUND

3. Click the Browse (Windows) or Choose (Mac) button, and choose the file that you want to use as the source of your background.

4. In the Page Number field, specify the page within the file you want to use.

5. In the Absolute Scale field, type the zoom percentage value you want to apply to the imported page.

The preview reflects your choice of background (**Figure 10.19**).

6. Choose an opacity value for the background by either using the slider control or typing a percentage into the text field.

Reducing the opacity is important because it can keep the new background from overpowering the original page contents.

7. If you want your background to apply only to certain pages in your document, click the Page Range Options link (at the upper right in Figure 10.18), as described in Step 5 of the task "To add a header or footer to a document."

8. Click OK.

✔ Tips

- If you want a solid color for your background, click the From Color radio button, and then click the color-well control and choose a color from the resulting color palette (**Figure 10.20**).

- You can save common background settings by clicking the Save Settings button. Acrobat lets you specify a name that will appear in the Saved Settings pop-up menu.

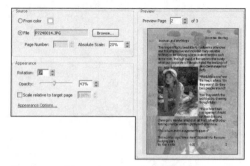

Figure 10.19 if you choose artwork taken from another PDF file, your background can be any combination of text, line art, and images.

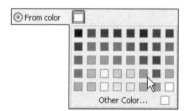

Figure 10.20 To apply a color as a background, choose the color from the color-well control.

ADDING A BACKGROUND

Adding a Watermark

A *watermark* is text or graphics that are placed on a page either in front of or behind the page's contents. The watermark may be text, a logo, or other page contents taken from another PDF, Illustrator, or image file.

To add a watermark to a document:

1. Choose Document > Watermark > Add. Acrobat presents you with the Add Watermark dialog (**Figure 10.21**).

2. If you want a text watermark, click the Text radio button.

3. Type the text you want for your watermark.

4. Choose a font and size for the watermark text.

5. Click one of the text-alignment buttons.

Continues on next page

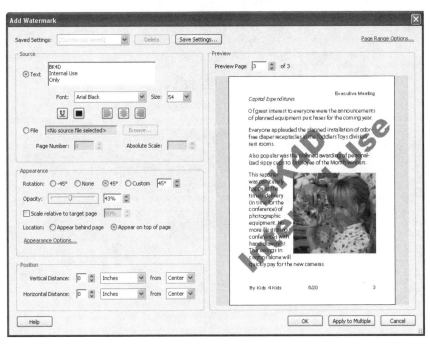

Figure 10.21 The Add Watermark dialog box lets you add text or artwork from another PDF file to your pages.

ADDING A WATERMARK

6. Choose an opacity value for the watermark by either using the Opacity slider or typing a percentage into the text field.

It's important to reduce the watermark's opacity so that your original page contents remain readable.

7. Specify whether you want the watermark in front of or behind the page contents by clicking the appropriate Location radio button.

8. If you want your watermark to apply to only certain pages in your document, click the Page Range Options link, as described in Step 5 of the task "To add a header or footer to a document."

9. Click OK.

✔ Tip

■ If you want to use a page in another PDF file as your watermark, click the File radio button, and then follow the directions in the previous task, "To add a background to a document."

Figure 10.22 Redacted items in your PDF file are covered with opaque redaction overlays. (*Exp. Del.* Is short for *Expletive Deleted*, if you were curious.)

Figure 10.23 The Redaction toolbar has the tools you use to carry out redaction.

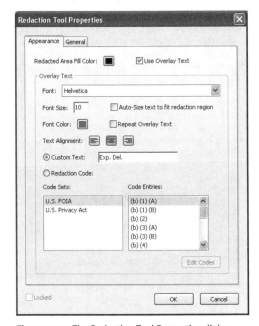

Figure 10.24 The Redaction Tool Properties dialog box lets you specify the appearance of the redaction overlays.

Redacting a Document

Acrobat Pro Only: *Redaction* refers to marking out or otherwise rendering unreadable sensitive parts of a document, usually to preserve information secrecy. This may be done to protect legal or trade secrets or to prevent someone's personal information from being broadcast.

In Acrobat 9, redaction is a three-step process. First you set the redaction properties, specifying how redacted items appear on the page. Next, you go through the document and choose the text and graphics that should be redacted. Finally, you apply redaction to the marked items. Acrobat replaces each redacted item with a colored block (a *redaction overlay*), optionally containing a text message (**Figure 10.22**).

Once redacted, the items are permanently unreadable; the process cannot be undone. (It wouldn't be worth much if it could be undone, now would it?)

You can most conveniently carry out the redaction process using the Redaction toolbar (**Figure 10.23**).

To set redaction properties:

1. In the Redaction toolbar, click Redaction Properties (Figure 10.23).

   The Redaction Tool Properties dialog opens (**Figure 10.24**).

2. Choose the color you want for the redaction overlays by clicking in the color well and selecting a color from the resulting color picker.

3. If you want to have text placed into the redaction overlays, click the Use Overlay Text check box.

4. Choose your text characteristics: font, size, color, and alignment.

   Remember that the text color must be readable against the fill color you chose in Step 2.

Continues on next page

5. If you want to supply your own text for the overlay, type the text in the Custom Text field.

6. If you want to use a standard code to indicate the reason for the redaction, choose one from among the code sets.

   Acrobat provides codes for the U.S. Freedom of Information Act and the U.S. Privacy Act. You can add your own sets of codes, if you wish; consult the Acrobat 9 Help to see how to do this.

7. Click OK.

✔ Tips

- I always click the "Auto-size text to fit redaction region" check box. Acrobat picks a font size for each redacted item that makes the overlay text exactly fit the overlay.

- Although you technically don't have to reset the redaction properties for each document you redact, I find I usually do, since I want a different label for the overlay.

To redact items in a document:

1. In the Redaction toolbar, click Mark for Redaction (Figure 10.23).

   The pointer turns into an I-beam when it's over text, and a crosshairs when it's over white space in your document.

2. With the I-beam pointer, select all the text that needs to be hidden.

3. With the crosshairs, drag enclosing rectangles around artwork or other items that need to be obscured.

   Acrobat draws a thick rectangle around the marked text and artwork (**Figure 10.25**). When the pointer moves over it, the rectangle changes to show the redaction overlay that will be placed there when the redaction is applied (**Figure 10.26**).

Also popular was the planned awarding of personalized sippy cups to Employee of the Month winners.

This reporter was particularly happy at the timely delivery (in time for the conference) of photographic equipment. No more illustrating conferences with hand drawings! The savings in crayons alone will quickly pay for the new cameras.

Figure 10.25 Items you've selected for redaction are outlined with a thick border.

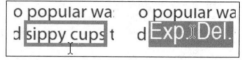

Figure 10.26 When the Select for Redaction pointer moves over a redaction marker, the rectangle changes to show how the final redaction overlay will look.

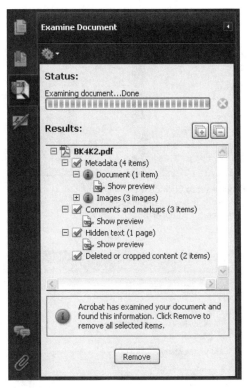

Figure 10.27 Having redacted the items you selected, Acrobat searches the document for other, hidden items you may want to remove.

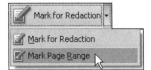

Figure 10.28 The Mark for Redaction tool lets you redact the entire contents of one or more pages.

4. In the Redaction toolbar, click the Apply Redactions button.

   Acrobat hides all the redacted items with redaction overlays.

   Acrobat then examines your document, looking for other internal information that you may also want to remove for security's sake. Acrobat optionally presents you with the Examine Document pane (**Figure 10.27**), which lists all the comments, bookmarks, electronic signatures, and other data it found in the file.

5. Click the Remove button, if you wish.

   Acrobat removes the internal objects from the document and returns you to your now-redacted document page.

   Acrobat marks the newly redacted document as Save-As Only. When you close the document, the standard Save dialog box opens, prompting you to save the document with a new name.

✔ Tips

- While you are marking items for redaction, you can change your mind and remove the mark from an item. To do so, click its marking rectangle, and press the Delete or Backspace key. You need to do this before you apply the redaction.

- You can also redact entire pages in the document. Click on the little down-arrow next to the Mark for Redaction button in the Redaction toolbar; Acrobat will display a drop-down menu (**Figure 10.28**). Choose Mark Page Range from this menu and specify a range of pages to be redacted. Every page of the range you specify will have its entire contents marked for redaction.

Search and Redact

As a great convenience, Acrobat searches for words and phrases in your document's text and redacts all instances of that text. The process is similar to searching for text, as discussed in Chapter 2.

Acrobat can search out and redact three types of text in your document:

◆ All instances of a particular word or phrase.

◆ All instances of a list of words or phrases.

◆ All instances of a particular text pattern (such as social security numbers or telephone numbers).

To redact all instances of a phrase in a document:

1. In the Redaction toolbar, click Search and Redact (Figure 10.23).

   Acrobat opens the Search dialog box and zooms your document page out so the two windows (Search and Document) together fill your screen (**Figure 10.29**). The Search window defaults to searching for a particular phrase.

2. Type in the Search dialog box's text field the phrase or word you want to redact.

3. Click the Search and Redact button.

   The Search dialog box opens and presents you with a list of instances of the search phrase found in the document (**Figure 10.30**). Each item in this list has a check box next to it, indicating that that instance should be redacted.

4. Click the check boxes for all the instances in the list that you want to redact.

   You can also click the Check All button to choose all items in the list.

Figure 10.29 Clicking the Search and Redact tool lets you specify a word or phrase that should be redacted throughout your document.

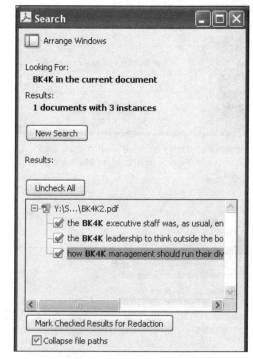

Figure 10.30 The Search window presents a list of all the instances of the found text. Clicking an item's check box marks the item for redaction.

The 2006 meeting of the BK4K executive staff was, as usual, entertaining, enlightening, and electrifying. Not one expense was spared to make the meeting one to remember, if only through the mists of a major sugar buzz.

The event started off with our President's traditional motivational breakfast address, exhorting the BK4K leadership to think outside the box and work smarter, not harder.

Figure 10.31 Clicking the Search window's "Mark Checked Results for Redaction" button causes all the selected items to be marked for redaction.

Figure 10.32 If you opt to redact multiple words or phrases, Acrobat makes visible a button labeled Select Words.

5. Click the "Mark Checked Results for Redaction" button.

Acrobat marks for redaction all selected instances of the text in the document (**Figure 10.31**).

6. In the Redaction toolbar, click Apply Redactions.

To redact all instances of a list of phrases in a document:

1. In the Redaction toolbar, click Search and Redact (Figure 23).

2. In the Search window, click the "Multiple words or phrase" radio button.

The window rearranges itself, among other things making visible a Select Words button (**Figure 10.32**).

3. Click the Select Words button.

Acrobat presents you with a dialog box that lets you create a list of words or phrases that should be redacted (**Figure 10.33**).

4. Repeatedly type a phrase into the "New word or phrase" field and then click the Add button.

Acrobat adds the words and phrases to the redaction list. The dialog box gives you buttons that let you export and import a list of words and to remove words from the redaction list.

5. Click OK when you have completed your list.

Acrobat immediately marks for redaction all instances of any of the words or phrases in your list.

6. In the Redaction toolbar, click Apply Redactions.

To redact all instances of a text pattern in a document:

1. In the Redaction toolbar, click Search and Redact (Figure 10.23).

2. In the Search window, click the Patterns radio button.

The window rearranges itself, presenting a drop-down menu of standard text patterns (**Figure 10.34**).

3. Select a pattern from the drop-down menu (**Figure 10.35**).

4. Click the Search and Redact button.

Acrobat immediately marks for redaction all instances of text matching the pattern you selected.

5. In the Redaction toolbar, click Apply Redactions.

Figure 10.33 The Words and Phrases dialog box lets you specify a list of, well, words and phrases that should be redacted in your document.

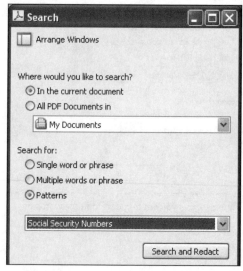

Figure 10.34 You may choose to redact all text that fits a particular pattern.

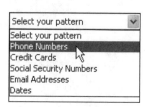

Figure 10.35 Acrobat gives you a small but useful set of text patterns from which you may choose.

ADDING SIMPLE NAVIGATION FEATURES

11

If you intend for your PDF document to be read onscreen, you'll make life much easier for your reader if you provide some minimal tools for navigating the document. The easiest—and most consistently useful—navigation tools you can add to your document are bookmarks, links, and articles. These tools are the topics of this chapter.

Adding Bookmarks

Bookmarks constitute a clickable table of contents that reside in the Bookmarks navigation pane (**Figure 11.1**). Clicking a bookmark takes you to the corresponding view in the document.

A *view* in Acrobat is a combination of a page, a position on that page, and a zoom value (**Figure 11.2**).

To add a bookmark to a document, you set the document window to reflect the page, position, and zoom you want for that bookmark; then you create the bookmark, which records that view as its destination.

To create a bookmark in a document:

1. Using the Acrobat's standard navigation tools, set the document window to display the view you want as the bookmark's target.

2. Open the Bookmark pane by clicking the Bookmark icon.

3. Click the New Bookmark icon at the top of the bookmark list (**Figure 11.3**).

   Acrobat inserts a new bookmark named Untitled into the Bookmarks pane. *Untitled* is already selected so you can type over it.

4. Type the name you want for the new bookmark.

5. Click outside the Bookmarks pane or press Enter or Return to make the new name permanent.

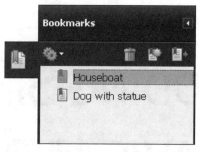

Figure 11.1 Bookmarks make up a clickable table of contents that resides in the Bookmarks pane.

Figure 11.2 A bookmark's destination is a *view:* a combination of a page, a location on the page, and a zoom level.

Figure 11.3 Clicking the New Bookmark icon creates a new bookmark named Untitled.

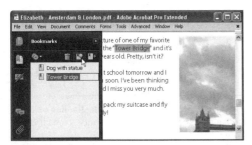

Figure 11.4 If you select text and then create a new bookmark, the selected text becomes the bookmark's title.

Figure 11.5 You can drag a bookmark to a new location in the Bookmarks list.

Figure 11.6 The Bookmark Properties dialog box lets you change the style and color of your bookmark's text in the Bookmarks list.

✔ Tips

- Clicking a bookmark selects that bookmark in the list. When you create a new bookmark, it is inserted into the list immediately after the currently selected bookmark.

- If you select text on your document page with the Select tool (**Figure 11.4**) and then create a bookmark, the selected text becomes the new bookmark's name.

- You can easily rearrange bookmarks by dragging them to a new location in the list. A bit less obvious is the fact that you can drag a bookmark to be a descendent of another (**Figure 11.5**). Once child bookmarks have been moved into another bookmark, you can display or hide them using the disclosure control to the left of the parent bookmark; this control is a plus sign in Windows and a triangle on the Macintosh, as usual.

- You can select and move multiple bookmarks at one time. To do so, hold down the Command or Control key to select individual bookmarks, or the Shift key to select a contiguous range of bookmarks in the list.

You can make a bookmark stand out in the list by changing its color or its text style.

To change a bookmark's color and text style:

1. Open the Bookmarks pane, if necessary.

2. Right-click the bookmark whose properties you want to change.

3. In the resulting contextual menu, choose Properties.

   The Bookmark Properties dialog box opens (**Figure 11.6**).

Continues on next page

ADDING BOOKMARKS

4. Choose a text style from the drop-down menu.

You can choose from the standard styles: bold, italic, and bold italic.

5. Click the color well, and choose a color from the resulting palette.

6. Click OK.

✔ Tip

■ I often use style to accentuate a document's structure. Bolding the bookmarks associated with chapter titles makes them stand out; in some documents, I'll make the bookmarks of the very important topics red.

Sometimes you need to change the destination of a bookmark, often because you have changed the document—inserted new pages, perhaps—and the new contents are a better destination for the bookmark. Changing a bookmark's target is very easy to do.

To change a bookmark's destination:

1. Using the Acrobat's standard navigation and zoom tools, set the document window so it displays the new destination you want for the bookmark.

2. Open the Bookmarks pane, if necessary.

3. Right-click the bookmark whose destination you want to change.

4. In the contextual menu choose Set Destination.

Acrobat opens a dialog box asking if you're sure you want to change the bookmark's destination (**Figure 11.7**).

5. Click Yes.

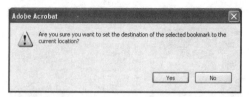

Figure 11.7 When you change the destination of a bookmark, Acrobat gives you a chance to change your mind.

Selection tool

Article tool

Link tool

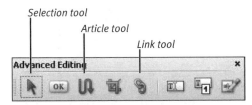

Figure 11.8 The Advanced Editing toolbar contains three tools you use in this chapter.

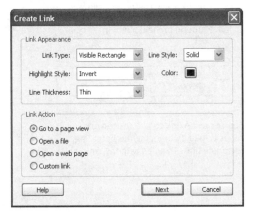

Figure 11.9 The Create Link dialog box lets you specify the appearance and behavior of a link.

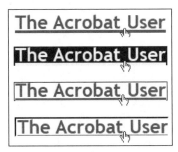

Figure 11.10 The highlight style specifies how a link changes when you click it. From top to bottom, they are None (boring), Invert, Outline, and Inset.

Creating Links

Links are the easiest way to make a PDF file a dynamic online document. They are, in effect, bookmarks that reside on your document page rather than in a navigation pane. They behave exactly like the links familiar to you on Web sites: you click the "hot" area of the link, and something happens—usually, the link sends you to another view in the document.

Links can have a visible border, but otherwise no icons or labels are associated with them. If you want such artwork, it must already be part of the contents of the PDF page; you lay the link on top of the existing graphics or text on the page.

You create links with the Link tool in the Advanced Editing toolbar (**Figure 11.8**).

To create a link on a page:

1. On the Advanced Editing toolbar, click the Link tool.
   The pointer changes to a crosshairs cursor.

2. Click and drag a rectangle on the PDF page where you want the link to be.
   Acrobat displays the Create Link dialog box (**Figure 11.9**).

3. Using the standard navigation and zoom tools, set the view in the document window to the destination of the new link.

4. If you want a visible rectangle around the link, choose Visible Rectangle in the Link Type drop-down menu; otherwise, choose Invisible Rectangle.

5. If you chose a visible rectangle for your link, specify the style, color, and thickness you want for the rectangle.

6. Choose a highlight style for the link (**Figure 11.10**).

Continues on next page

CREATING LINKS

7. Among the Link Action radio buttons, click "Go to a page view."

See the sidebar "Link Actions" for a discussion of the other actions.

8. Click Next.

The Create Go to View dialog box opens (**Figure 11.11**). This dialog box behaves like a palette, in that your Acrobat document is still active in the background; you can still use the navigation and zoom tools to move around in the document.

9. Use the navigation and zoom tools to set the document view to the link's destination.

10. Click the Set Link button.

Acrobat returns your document window to the link's page. Your new link is visible as a bounding rectangle (**Figure 11.12**); when you roll the pointer over this rectangle, handles appear at its sides and corners, as in the figure.

11. Adjust the position of the link by dragging its bounding rectangle.

12. Adjust the size of the link by dragging the handles at the sides and corners of its bounding rectangle.

13. To make another link, repeat Steps 2–12.

14. When you're finished making links, click Acrobat's Hand tool.

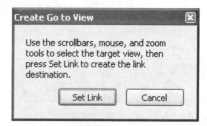

Figure 11.11 While the Create Go to View dialog box is open, the document window is active in the background; you can use the arrow keys and other navigation tools to move around in the document.

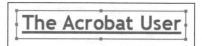

Figure 11.12 A link can be resized and repositioned by dragging the bounding rectangle or its handles with the Link tool.

Link Actions

The Create Link dialog box (Figure 11.9) has four radio buttons you can choose from to specify what your link should do. The default action is "Go to a page view," which displays a new view in the document window when you click the link.

The other three radio buttons have the following meanings:

Open a file creates a link that opens a spreadsheet, word-processing, or other file on your computer. Clicking the finished link opens the file in whatever application is associated with that type of file.

▲ When you click the Next button in the Create Link dialog box, Acrobat lets you specify the file to be opened.

Open a Web page tells the link to launch your default Web browser with a particular Web page. When you click the dialog box's Next button, Acrobat opens a dialog box in which you can type the URL of the Web page (**Figure 11.13**).

Custom link provides access to more than a dozen advanced actions available to a link. Clicking Next takes you to the

Actions tab in the Link Properties dialog box (**Figure 11.14**), whose Select Action menu lets you choose the action you want. This can be anything from playing a sound to executing an Acrobat menu item.

We'll talk about some of these actions in the next chapter. However, most of them are beyond the scope of this book. See the Acrobat Help files for more information.

Interestingly, the advanced actions are also available to your bookmarks. If you right-click a bookmark and choose Properties from the contextual menu, you get a dialog box with the same Actions tab shown in Figure 11.14.

Figure 11.13 The Edit URL dialog box lets you specify a Web address to associate with a link.

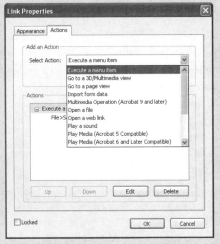

Figure 11.14 The Actions tab of the Link Properties dialog box lets you assign one of a variety of advanced actions to a link.

Modifying Existing Links

Whenever the Link tool is selected, all the links in your document appear as black bounding rectangles on the page. Clicking one of these rectangles selects that link; the bounding rectangle changes color, and handles appear whenever you move the pointer over the rectangle (Figure 11.12).

You can make a number of changes to a link when it's selected with the Link tool.

To modify an existing link:

1. Click the Link tool in the Advanced Editing toolbar.

2. Click the link you want to modify.

3. To change the position of the link, drag its bounding rectangle to the new location.

4. To change the size of the link, drag the handles at the sides and corners of the rectangle.

5. To change the appearance of the link, right-click the link and choose Properties from the contextual menu.

    Acrobat displays the Appearance controls of the Link Properties dialog box, allowing you to reset the visibility, thickness, color, and other visual properties of the link (**Figure 11.15**).

6. To delete the link, press the Delete key.

✔ Tips

- You can change multiple links at one time. To do so, hold down the Shift or Command/Ctrl key, and click the links you want to modify. Any changes you make apply to all the selected links.

Figure 11.15 The Appearance tab of the Link Properties dialog box lets you specify the visual characteristics of a link.

- You can nudge the position and size of a selected link. Pressing an arrow key moves the selected link one pixel in the corresponding direction. Holding down the Shift key and pressing an arrow key moves the link 10 pixels. Finally, holding the Control key increases or decreases the size of the link by one pixel.

- You can delete all the links in your document by choosing Advanced > Document Processing > Remove All Links. Acrobat lets you select the pages from which to remove all the links.

- You can also double-click a link with the Link tool to obtain the Link Properties dialog box (Figure 11.15).

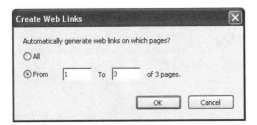

Figure 11.16 The Create Web Links dialog box lets you specify the pages that should be searched for URLs.

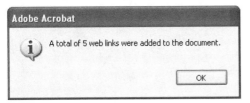

Figure 11.17 Acrobat tells you how many Web links it added to your file.

Making Automatic Web Links

The "Link Actions" sidebar discusses making a link to a Web page; when the reader clicks on this link, Acrobat launches the default Web browser and opens the Web page tied to that link. Acrobat sensibly refers to such links as *Web links*.

Acrobat can automatically make Web links throughout your document. The Create Web Links command searches the text in your PDF file and places links over any Web or e-mail addresses it finds. Web addresses in the text receive links to that URL; e-mail addresses get links that open the default mail client with a blank message addressed to the target e-mail address.

To add Web links to your document:

1. With the document open to any page, choose Advanced > Document Processing > Create Links from URLs.

   Acrobat presents you with the Create Web Links dialog box (**Figure 11.16**).

2. Enter the beginning and ending page numbers of the range that should be scanned for URLs, or click All to select all pages.

3. Click OK.

   Acrobat scans your PDF file, adding links to all the URLs it finds. When it's finished, Acrobat reports on the number of links it added (**Figure 11.17**).

Creating Articles

An *article* in Acrobat is a set of rectangular regions scattered throughout your document that, taken together, represent a single thread of text. It's similar to an article in a newspaper, which may start on the front page, continue on pages 13 and 14, and finish up on page 27.

Articles are extremely useful for taking documents that were originally laid out for print—usually with a small point size, often with multiple columns—and making them readable online. I've used articles a lot in my documents and tend to get unreasonably enthusiastic about them!

When your pointer moves over an article on a page, the pointer turns into a hand with a downward-pointing arrow (**Figure 11.18**). When you click the article, Acrobat zooms in until the article exactly fits across the width of the document window (**Figure 11.19**). This makes the text easy to read.

Figure 11.18 When the pointer moves over an article, it becomes a hand with a downward arrow.

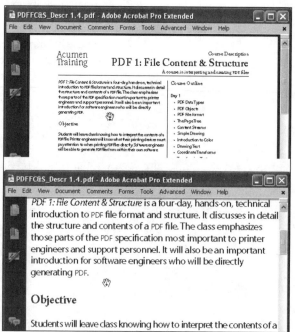

Figure 11.19 When you click an article (top), Acrobat zooms in until the article fills the width of the document window (bottom).

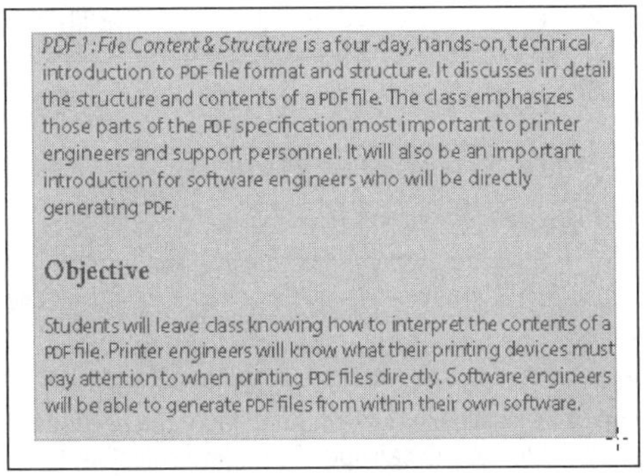

> PDF 1:File Content & Structure is a four-day, hands-on, technical introduction to PDF file format and structure. It discusses in detail the structure and contents of a PDF file. The class emphasizes those parts of the PDF specification most important to printer engineers and support personnel. It will also be an important introduction for software engineers who will be directly generating PDF.
>
> Objective
>
> Students will leave class knowing how to interpret the contents of a PDF file. Printer engineers will know what their printing devices must pay attention to when printing PDF files directly. Software engineers will be able to generate PDF files from within their own software.

Figure 11.20 With the Article tool, you drag out a series of rectangles that will be the sections of your article text.

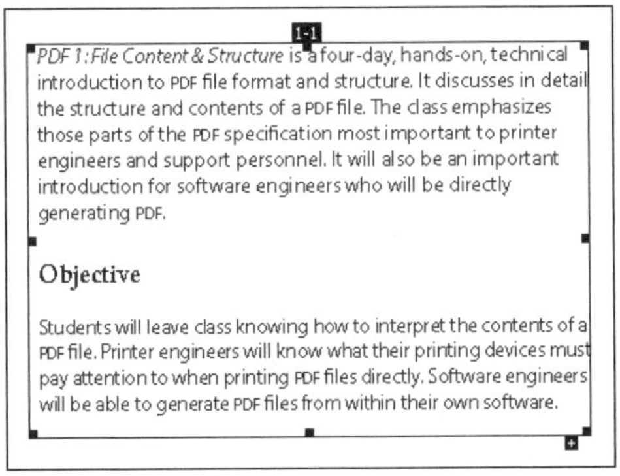

> 1-1
> PDF 1:File Content & Structure is a four-day, hands-on, technical introduction to PDF file format and structure. It discusses in detail the structure and contents of a PDF file. The class emphasizes those parts of the PDF specification most important to printer engineers and support personnel. It will also be an important introduction for software engineers who will be directly generating PDF.
>
> Objective
>
> Students will leave class knowing how to interpret the contents of a PDF file. Printer engineers will know what their printing devices must pay attention to when printing PDF files directly. Software engineers will be able to generate PDF files from within their own software.

Figure 11.21 Each section of your article is identified by an article number and a section number within that article. Each rectangle's handles let you resize the section.

While you're reading an article, each click of the mouse button takes you down one screen in the article, changing from one column to another as needed. No scrolling, dragging, or fussing with navigation buttons is required.

When you reach the end of the article, a final click reverts the view to what it was before you entered the article.

To create an article in a document:

1. In the Advanced Editing toolbar, click the Article tool.

   The pointer turns into a crosshair.

2. Click and drag a rectangle, indicating the first segment in the article (**Figure 11.20**).

   While you're dragging out the rectangle, the pointer becomes a crosshair.

3. Continue to click and drag additional rectangles in the order you want the reader to see them.

   When you are finished, each of your article segments is surrounded by a black rectangle labeled with an article number and a segment number (**Figure 11.21**). Note that if you click a segment with the Article tool, Acrobat provides you with the handles visible in Figure 11.21, which allow you to resize the article.

Continues on next page

CREATING ARTICLES

4. When you've dragged out all the article segments, click the Article tool again (or any other tool, for that matter) to indicate you're finished constructing your article.

Acrobat presents you with the Article Properties dialog box (**Figure 11.22**). The information this dialog box requests is all optional, but it will make your article more useful to the reader.

5. Type in some combination of title, subject, author, and searchable keywords.

6. Click OK.

You've now created your article, which will behave properly as soon as you click the Hand tool.

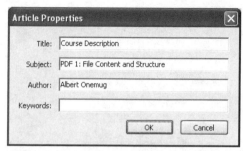

Figure 11.22 When you've defined all of the sections of your article, you can specify a title, subject, author, and searchable keywords for the article.

✔ Tips

■ Acrobat has an Article navigation pane (hidden by default) that lists all the articles in the current document. You can make this pane visible, as usual, by choosing View > Navigation Panels > Articles.

■ I sometimes use the Article tool to create a "linked list" of illustrations within my document. I create an article, each of whose segments encloses one of the document's illustrations. In the final distributed document, the reader can click on an illustration to enter the article and then click repeatedly to be taken from one illustration to the next.

CREATING AN ACROBAT PRESENTATION

12

Acrobat provides a range of features that makes it easy to use a PDF document as a presentation for a variety of situations:

◆ A group presentation, in which you're displaying the PDF pages using a computer projector. In this case, the PDF file replaces the more common (though not as graphically sophisticated) Microsoft PowerPoint file.

◆ A distributed presentation file that is intended to be viewed by readers on their own computers. This may be an electronic brochure, distributed on the Web.

◆ An interactive kiosk presentation, in which the PDF document is viewed in a public place on a dedicated computer. A "Where to Go" kiosk in an airport is a good example.

PDF documents can be viewed full-screen with all the transitions and navigational control offered by any other presentation software. Furthermore, graphic and typographic control in Acrobat documents is much better than in other presentation software.

This chapter covers the features that allow you to turn an Acrobat document into a presentation file.

✔ Tip

■ Note that this chapter does not discuss the Adobe Presenter tool that is part of Adobe Acrobat Pro Extended. That tool turns a PowerPoint presentation into a stand-alone Flash- or PDF-based presentation. It's a very impressive tool, but beyond the scope of this book.

Setting Open Options

In a presentation, the Acrobat toolbars and navigation panes are a distraction. You want readers to see only your document and just enough of an interface to let them move around in the document.

Acrobat gives you the ability to control what should be displayed when a document is opened. These *open options* are stored with the PDF file, so whenever readers open that document, you control exactly what they see.

To set a document's open options:

1. Choose File > Properties.

   The Document Properties dialog box opens.

2. Click the Initial View tab to see the controls that determine how the document will be presented to the user (**Figure 12.1**).

3. In the "Navigation tab" pop-up menu, choose Page Only.

   This option specifies that all the navigation panes should be hidden.

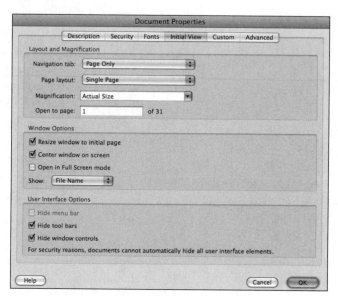

Figure 12.1 The Initial View pane in the Document Properties dialog box lets you specify what readers see when they first open your document.

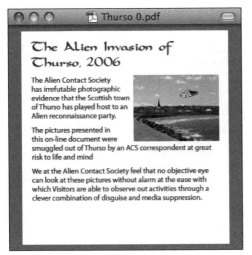

Figure 12.2 You can minimize the distractions in an Acrobat presentation by hiding the toolbars and other user interface elements.

4. In the "Page layout" pop-up menu, choose Single Page.

   The alternatives, which display multiple pages side-by-side or vertically, aren't good for a presentation.

5. In the Magnification pop-up menu, choose Actual Size.

6. Click the "Resize window to initial page" check box.

   The document will open in a window that exactly matches the page size. There won't be a gray border around the page in the document window.

7. Click the "Center window on screen" check box.

8. If you want your presentation to take over the entire computer screen, click the "Open in Full Screen mode" check box.

9. Click the "Hide tool bars" check box.

   The toolbars are distracting in a presentation.

10. Click the "Hide window controls" check box.

    This option hides the navigation pane icons, which are also distracting during a presentation.

    ▲ Steps 9 and 10 leave your document window displaying only page content, as in **Figure 12.2**.

✔ Tip

- Full Screen mode is useful for corporate presentations or for kiosk documents. I recommend against it if you'll be distributing your PDF document to other readers; most people find it annoying when a document covers everything else on their computers. We'll talk more about Full Screen documents in the next section.

SETTING OPEN OPTIONS

Creating a Full-Screen Slide Show

If you're using a PDF file for a group presentation, you will often want Acrobat to show your document as a full-screen display, masking all user-interface items. This eliminates distractions and makes the document's contents large and legible. In effect, you're presenting a slide show to your audience.

If your document will only be used full-screen, then you can set its Initial View properties to automatically display the document full screen, as described in the previous section.

On the other hand, if this is a document you use in a variety of circumstances—or you just don't like having full-screen display invoked automatically—then you should turn on Full Screen mode only as needed.

To turn Full Screen mode on and off:

◆ To turn Full Screen mode on, choose View > Full Screen Mode (**Figure 12.3**).

Acrobat displays your document zoomed so it fills the entire screen.

◆ To turn Full Screen mode off, press the Escape key.

Acrobat returns you to viewing the document in a window.

Navigating in Full Screen mode

Full Screen mode hides the entire Acrobat user interface, leaving you no buttons or other visual controls you can use to navigate through the document. How do you move through your full-screen presentation?

In fact, there are several ways you can navigate a full-screen document:

◆ To move to the next page, click anywhere on the screen or press the right arrow key or the down arrow key.

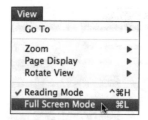

Figure 12.3 You can manually open a document in Full Screen mode from the View menu.

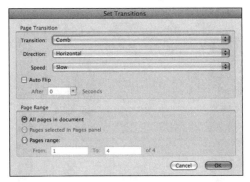

Figure 12.4 The Set Transitions dialog box lets you apply special effects that are used when you move from one page to another in your Full Screen document.

Figure 12.5 You can choose from a variety of transitions built into Acrobat.

◆ To move to the previous page, Shift-click anywhere on the page, right-click anywhere on the page, or press the left arrow key or the up arrow key.

◆ To go to the beginning of the document, press the Home key.

◆ To go to the end of the document, press the End key.

Adding transitions

Acrobat supplies a number of transition effects you can use when moving from one page to another in Full Screen mode. These have names evocative of what they look like, such as Dissolve, Fade, and Split. They're next to impossible to describe, so I recommend you experiment with them to see what they do.

To specify a transition for Full Screen mode:

1. With your document open, choose Advanced > Document Processing > Page Transitions.

   Acrobat displays the Set Transitions dialog box (**Figure 12.4**).

2. Choose the transition you want from the Transition pop-up menu (**Figure 12.5**).

3. Choose a direction (horizontal or vertical) for the transition, if appropriate.

   Not all transitions have a direction.

4. Choose a transition speed (slow, medium, or fast) from the Speed pop-up menu.

5. If you want the document to turn the page automatically, click the Auto Flip check box and specify a duration.

6. Use the Page Range controls to choose the pages to which the transition should apply.

7. Click OK.

Keep in mind that these settings do not affect viewing the document unless you're in Full Screen mode.

CREATING A FULL-SCREEN SLIDE SHOW

Creating a Next Page Button

Acrobat provides a variety of keys and clicks that let you go from one page to the next in Full Screen mode or in a presentation whose toolbars are hidden. However, most people find it comforting to have visible controls to navigate within the document (**Figure 12.6**). Here you'll see how to add Next Page and Previous Page buttons to your document.

The easiest way to create a Next Page button is to make the button artwork part of the original page design, as in Figure 12.6, and then lay on top of the button a link that does the work.

The following task steps through the creation of a Next Page button. You can use nearly the same steps to create a Previous Page button.

These steps assume the button artwork is already on the page.

To create a Next Page button:

1. Click the Link tool on the Advanced Editing toolbar.

2. Click and drag a link rectangle around the Next Page button's artwork.

   The Create Link dialog box opens (**Figure 12.7**).

3. Choose the following settings:
   - ▲ For Link Type, choose Invisible Rectangle.
   - ▲ For Highlight Style, choose Inset.
   - ▲ For Link Action, choose Custom link.

4. Click Next.

   The Link Properties dialog box opens (**Figure 12.8**).

5. Click the Actions tab.

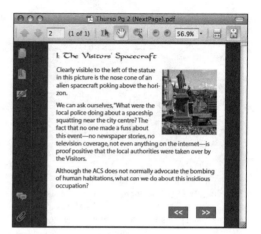

Figure 12.6 If you intend a document to be read in Full Screen mode, you should provide buttons that the reader can use to move within the document.

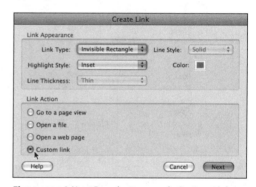

Figure 12.7 A Next Page button needs Custom Link as its action.

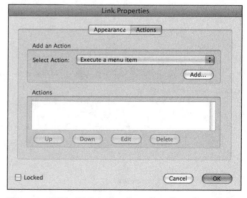

Figure 12.8 The Link Action for a Next Page button is "Execute a menu item."

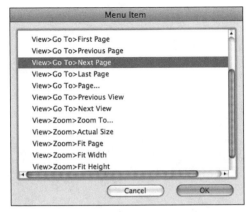

Figure 12.9 The menu item your link should execute is View > Go To > Next Page.

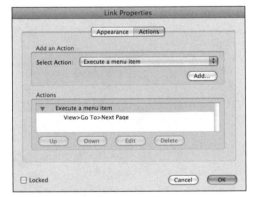

Figure 12.10 When you return to the Link Properties dialog box, the menu item appears in the Actions list.

Figure 12.11 With the Link tool still active, a rectangle surrounds the link that lets you position and resize the link so it fits the button artwork.

6. In the Select Action pop-up menu, choose "Execute a menu item."

7. Click Add.

   The Menu Item dialog box opens (**Figure 12.9**). This dialog box lists all the menu items in all of Acrobat's menus.

8. From the list in the Menu Item dialog box, choose View > Go To > Next Page.

   For a Previous Page button, you would choose View > Go To > Previous Page.

9. Click OK.

   Acrobat returns to the Link Properties dialog box, now showing your chosen menu item in its list of Actions (**Figure 12.10**).

10. Click OK.

    Acrobat returns you to your document page. The Next Page artwork is now surrounded by a link's blue border rectangle and handles, as in **Figure 12.11**.

11. Reposition and resize the link as necessary by dragging the rectangle and its handles.

12. Click the Hand tool (or any other tool) to indicate that you're finished creating the link.

    When you click the Next Page button, Acrobat moves the document view to the next page.

✔ Tip

■ You can easily reproduce the Next Page link by copying it and then pasting it on other pages. Select the link with the Link tool, then choose Edit > Copy (or use whatever technique you prefer to do a copy). Now, go to each page that has a Next Page button and paste the link onto the page.

Creating a Self-Running Presentation

Acrobat lets you turn your document into a self-running slide show that moves from page to page without human intervention. This is extremely useful in retail situations, where a computer can run a presentation for passers-by to watch.

To turn a file into a self-running presentation, you must do two things, both of which apply to Full Screen mode: auto-flip the pages, so the document automatically moves from one page to the next; and tell Acrobat to loop the last page back to the first, so that the document plays itself indefinitely.

To create a self-running presentation:

1. Choose Advanced > Document Processing > Page Transitions.

   Acrobat displays the Set Transitions dialog box (Figure 12.4).

2. Click the Auto Flip check box, and specify a duration.

   Each page will be visible for the number of seconds you specify.

3. Set the other Page Transition controls as described in the task "To specify a transition for Full Screen mode," earlier in this chapter.

4. Click OK.

5. Choose Edit > Preferences in Windows or Acrobat > Preferences on the Mac.

   The Preferences dialog box opens.

6. Choose Full Screen in the Categories list (**Figure 12.12**).

   Acrobat displays the Full Screen controls.

7. In the Full Screen Navigation section, click the "Loop after last page" check box.

   All your full-screen documents will wrap from the last page to the first. Unfortunately, there is no way to set this option for just a single document.

8. Click OK.

This document will always play as a self-running presentation when you put it into Full Screen mode.

✔ Tips

■ If you want the current document to always act as a full-screen presentation, remember that the Document Properties dialog box has an "Open in Full Screen mode" check box among its Initial View options (Figure 12.1).

■ The Preferences dialog box also lets you specify a transition and auto-flip. If you select these as preferences, then every time you enter Full Screen mode, Acrobat applies the transition and automatically flips the page. I recommend against this unless you are creating a kiosk or have another situation in which you always want the same transition and the same auto-flip setting.

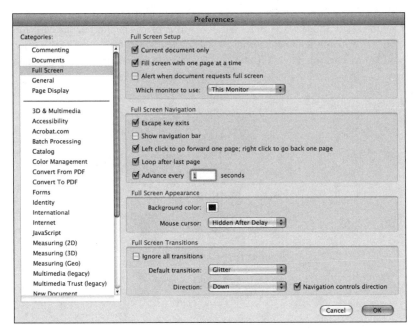

Figure 12.12 About halfway down the set of check boxes in the Full Screen controls is "Loop after last page," which is important for self-running presentations.

Placing a Movie on a Page

Acrobat Pro Only: Multimedia is becoming increasingly common in presentations. Marketing presentations and stand-alone kiosk displays often feature an animated walk-through or demonstration of a product.

Acrobat supports this marketing need by letting you place movies on your PDF pages. Movies may be embedded and played in a PDF file two ways: as a Flash animation or as a legacy animation.

Flash multimedia files and movies that are H.264 compliant can be embedded on the page as Flash animations and played by Adobe Reader 9 and Acrobat 9 (and later). H.264 is a video standard that is both compact and high-quality, and can be implemented by a broad range of movie file types (including MOV and MP4).

Note that Acrobat 9 can play Flash animations itself, without any external software. As a result, the animation is guaranteed to play and you get a consistent appearance on all platforms. You also automatically get some very nice-looking navigation controls that the reader may use to control the video.

On the other hand, these animations will play *only* with Acrobat 9 or Adobe Reader 9. Older versions of Acrobat will not be able to play them. (You'll get a warning immediately upon trying to open the file with an earlier version of Acrobat.)

You can also embed movies in a format that may be played by Acrobat 5 or later. You can do this with any type of movie file compatible with QuickTime, including MPEG and most AVI files, and (in Windows) movies playable by Windows Media Player or RealPlayer.

Acrobat uses an external player (QuickTime, Windows Media Player, and so on) to play these movies, so the appropriate software must be installed on the computer. The player software Acrobat looks for is pretty common on most computer systems, so this is generally not a very big problem.

You place movies on a PDF page using the Multimedia toolbar or the Multimedia tool on the Tasks toolbar. The directions below assume we are using the Multimedia toolbar (**Figure 12.13**).

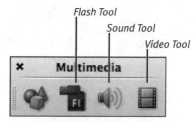

Figure 12.13 The Multimedia toolbar has three tools that are important for creating an Acrobat-based presentation.

Figure 12.14 The Insert Video dialog box lets you specify the movie you want to place on the page.

Figure 12.15 If the movie file you pick is neither a Flash animation nor an H.264-compatible movie, Acrobat warns you and lets you place the movie as a legacy animation, if you wish.

Figure 12.16 The placed movie appears on the page as a "poster" with a small Play icon in its lower left corner.

To place a movie on a PDF page as a Flash animation:

1. Click the Video tool on the Multimedia toolbar.

   The pointer turns into a crosshair.

2. Click and drag a rectangle on the page where you want the movie to go.

   Acrobat presents you with the Insert Video dialog box (**Figure 12.14**).

3. Click the Choose button and select the movie file in the resulting pick-a-file dialog box.

   This file must be either a Flash animation document or an H.264-compatible movie file. If it is not, then Acrobat tells you that it can't convert the file to Flash (**Figure 12.15**) and then presents you with the Add Movie dialog box (Figure 12.20, below); we shall discuss the controls in this dialog box in the next section.

4. Click OK.

   Acrobat places the movie on the page. The placed movie appears as a *poster frame* (usually the first frame in the movie; see Tips below) with a Play button superimposed in its lower left corner, as in **Figure 12.16**.

To play the movie, simply click the movie's image on the page.

Continues on next page

PLACING A MOVIE ON A PAGE

When the pointer is over the movie, a set of translucent controls appears over the movie, allowing the user to pause, rewind, and otherwise control the movie (**Figure 12.17**).

✔ Tips

- If you select the Video tool on the Multimedia toolbar and then click on a placed movie, Acrobat displays a rectangle around the movie together with a set of standard handles (**Figure 12.18**). You can now resize and reposition the movie on the page in the usual fashion.

- Note that the Insert Video dialog box (Figure 12.14) has a check box labeled Show Advanced Options. If you click this, Acrobat makes visible a large collection of controls that allow you to tailor the appearance and behavior of your movie (**Figure 12.19**). The default values for these controls are completely reasonable, so you can ignore these controls most of the time. Nonetheless, you may want to experiment.

- You can access the movie controls in Figure 12.19 at any time by right-clicking on a movie and choosing Properties in the contextual menu.

- The picture visible on the page when the movie isn't playing is called its poster frame; by default, this is the movie's first frame. Some movie files have a poster picture embedded in them, which Acrobat can use. If you wish, you can also click the "Create poster from file" check box in the Insert Video dialog box, click Choose, and pick a JPEG or other image file to use as the poster.

Figure 12.17 Moving the pointer over a playing movie reveals a set of controls for pausing, scrolling, and otherwise controlling the movie's playback.

Figure 12.18 Clicking a placed movie with the Video tool active yields a border and a set of handles that let you move and resize the movie on the page.

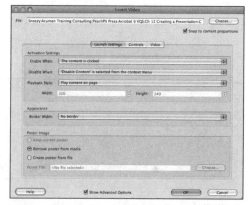

Figure 12.19 The Advanced Options in the Insert Video dialog box lets you set a variety of properties that control the movie's appearance and behavior.

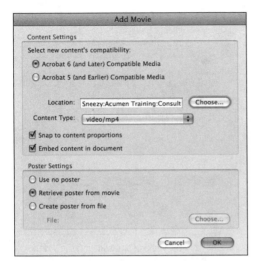

Figure 12.20 When you place a movie as a legacy animation, you get the Add Movie dialog box, which lets you specify the details of the movie placement.

Again, keep in mind that movies you place in the PDF file as Flash animations will be playable only with Adobe Reader 9 and Acrobat 9 (and later, of course). To place a movie in a PDF file so that it may be played on any reasonably recent version of Acrobat, you need to embed it as a "legacy" animation; typically, this is just the raw movie file itself, which Acrobat can play using whatever application your system associates with that file type.

To place a movie on a PDF page as a legacy animation:

1. Click the Video tool on the Multimedia toolbar.

   The pointer turns into a crosshair.

2. Click and drag a rectangle on the page where you want the movie to go.

   The size of the rectangle doesn't matter, since Acrobat will resize it to match the movie's native size.

   Acrobat presents you with the Insert Video dialog box (Figure 12.14).

3. Click the "Create legacy multimedia content" link.

   Acrobat presents you with the Add Movie dialog box (**Figure 12.20**).

4. Click the Choose button and select the movie file in the resulting pick-a-file dialog box.

5. Choose "Embed content in document."

   This is the safest choice, but see the sidebar "To Embed or Not to Embed," below, for a discussion of why you want to embed your movie (or not).

   The other settings in this dialog box default to reasonable values and should usually be left alone.

   Continues on next page

6. Click OK.

Acrobat places the movie on the page, displaying the movie's poster frame. Note that in this case, Acrobat does not automatically give you controls to pause or otherwise affect the playback of the movie. You will very likely want to supply your own controls, as we shall discuss in the next section.

7. Drag the movie to its correct place on the page, and resize it by dragging the handles.

The handles become visible only when the pointer is over the movie. You can retain the rectangle's original proportions when resizing it by holding down the Shift key as you drag its handles.

8. Click the Hand tool to finish placing the movie.

✔ Tip

- If you right-click on a placed movie with the Video tool selected on the Multimedia toolbar, the Multimedia Properties dialog box opens, with a variety of controls (**Figure 12.21**). These controls default to reasonable values so may be largely ignored; however, as with all such controls, you'll be a better person if you look them over sometime.

Figure 12.21 Right-clicking a movie with the Video tool and then selecting Properties displays a dialog box with a set of controls that let you change the movie's details.

Movie File Compatibility

There are two types of compatibility you need to bear in mind when placing a movie on a PDF page as a legacy animation:

Acrobat 5 compatibility. Adobe added a great deal of movie capability with Acrobat 6. Acrobat 5 could play only QuickTime-compatible movies, even in Windows. Acrobat 6 and later give you Windows support for the additional file types.

I suggest that you not worry too much about Acrobat 5 compatibility; that was a *long* time ago.

Cross-platform compatibility. The only movie formats that work on both Mac and Windows are those that are playable with QuickTime.

To Embed or Not to Embed

One of the choices you make in the Add Movie dialog box (Figure 12.20) is whether to embed the movie in the PDF document.

Generally, you should embed placed movies in your PDF file. Doing so makes the PDF file self-contained—you never have to worry about the movie getting lost.

Note that embedding or not is a choice only when placing a movie as a legacy animation. Flash animations are always embedded in the PDF file.

There are two problems with embedding the movie: The PDF file becomes larger—potentially much larger—which puts a strain on bandwidth and storage. More important, an embedded movie requires Acrobat 6 or later to play; it can't be viewed by people using older versions of Acrobat.

If you don't embed the movie, it can be played by all versions of Acrobat or Adobe Reader. However, the movie data remains in the separate movie file, which must be available to Acrobat when the movie is played. When you move the PDF file to another disk or server, the movie file must travel with it. Furthermore, the movie must remain in the same location, relative to the PDF file; if the movie file was originally in the same folder as the PDF file, it must remain in the PDF file's folder when you move them both.

I recommend embedding movies in the PDF file; it guarantees that the movie will play, unless the reader has an astonishingly old version of Acrobat (in which case they should be encouraged to upgrade, anyway).

Playing a Movie

Once a movie has been placed, you can play it by clicking it with the Hand tool. This is obvious if the movie has been embedded as a Flash animation; Acrobat places a Play icon on the movie's poster art, as in Figure 12.16.

If the movie is a legacy animation, you get no prompts that indicate this is a clickable movie, and a reader may conceivably not realize the "picture" on the page can move. For legacy animations, you should give the reader some visible Play/Pause/Stop controls. That's easily done with links.

The easiest way to create a Play Movie button is to place the button artwork on the page in the original document design (**Figure 12.22**). You can then lay links on top of the button graphic to do the actual work.

The following task steps through the creation of a Play button. Making buttons for Stop, Pause, and other commands is done virtually the same way. The steps presume the Play button's artwork is already on the PDF page.

To create a Play button:

1. Follow Steps 1–5 in the task "To create a Next Page button," earlier in this chapter.

2. In the Select Action pop-up menu of the Link Properties dialog box, choose either Play Media (Acrobat 6 and Later Compatible), Play Media (Acrobat 5 Compatible), or Multimedia Operation (Acrobat 9 and later), according to the way you placed your movie (**Figure 12.23**).

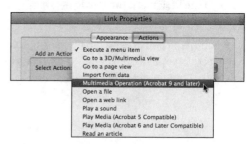

Figure 12.22 Movies placed as legacy animations don't automatically get playback controls; you should add your own.

Figure 12.23 In the Link Properties dialog box, specify that the link should play media or perform a multimedia operation.

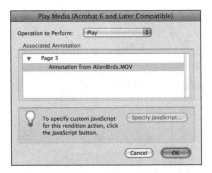

Figure 12.24 The Play Media (for Acrobat 8 and earlier) and Multimedia Operations (Acrobat 9) dialog boxes let you specify which movie the link should control.

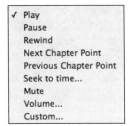

Figure 12.25 A link may perform many useful operations on a movie. Some of these are not available for legacy animations.

Figure 12.26 Having placed your link over the button artwork, you can use the link's handles to get the fit just right.

3. Click Add.

Acrobat presents you with either the Play Media (for legacy animations) or the Multimedia Operations (for Flash) dialog box (**Figure 12.24**).

These dialog boxes are functionally identical for our purposes; they differ only in the set of movie-related actions each makes available to the link. They both have all the actions we discuss here.

4. Select in the appropriate list the movie that you want the link to the control.

5. In the Action pop-up menu, choose Play.

This pop-up menu has all the other actions you might perform with a movie: Pause, Rewind, and so on (**Figure 12.25**).

6. Click OK.

Acrobat returns you to the Link Properties dialog box (Figure 12.8), which now shows Play Media or Multimedia Operation in its Actions list.

7. Click OK.

Acrobat returns you to your page, which now has a link rectangle with handles that you can use to reposition and resize the link as needed (**Figure 12.26**).

8. Click the Hand tool to finalize the link.

When you click the Play button, Acrobat plays the movie.

In some cases, you might want the movie to automatically play when the reader opens its page. You do this by creating a Page Action that Acrobat carries out when the reader enters a particular page. Our page action will play our movie.

To automatically play a movie when a page opens:

1. With your document open, display the Pages navigation pane by clicking the Pages icon.

2. Right-click the thumbnail of the page that has your movie.

3. Choose Page Properties from the contextual menu (**Figure 12.27**).

    The Page Properties dialog box opens (**Figure 12.28**).

4. Click the Actions tab.

5. In the Select Trigger pop-up menu, choose Page Open.

    This option tells Acrobat to play the movie when the reader opens the page, rather than when the reader closes it.

6. Follow Steps 2–8 in the task "To create a Play button," above, but choose Play Media (Figure 12.28) or Multimedia Operation in the Select Action pop-up menu.

    Acrobat will now play the movie every time the page is opened.

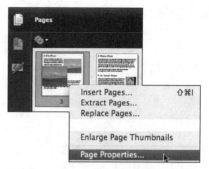

Figure 12.27 The first step in having a movie or sound automatically play when a page opens is to access the Page Properties from the Pages navigation pane.

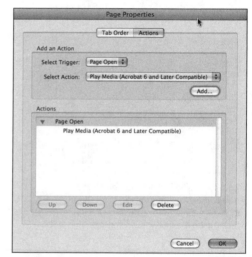

Figure 12.28 The Page Properties dialog box lets you specify a sound or movie that will play when the page opens.

Placing a Flash Animation on the Page

Acrobat Pro only: The Flash tool on the Multimedia toolbar allows you to add a Flash file, with the file type swf, to a PDF page. The process is identical to adding movies to the page and, indeed, Flash files may be placed with the Video tool, as well. Keep in mind that Flash animations will work only in Acrobat 9 or Adobe Reader 9.

You get a whole lot of bang for your nickel when you use Flash animations in your PDF file.

For example, while a Flash animation is playing, all of its interactive parts—links, buttons, sliders, and the like—are active; if the Flash file has a slider that controls the speed of the animation, that slider works exactly as it should.

The instructions below are very brief, for the dialog boxes and controls are virtually identical to those in our previous discussion of placing movies in your PDF file.

To place a Flash animation on the page:

1. Click the Flash tool on the Multimedia toolbar.

   The pointer turns into a crosshair.

2. Click and drag a rectangle on the page where you want the movie to go.

   Acrobat presents you with the Insert Flash dialog box (**Figure 12.29**).

3. Click the Choose button and select the SWF file in the resulting pick-a-file dialog box.

4. Click OK.

   Acrobat places the Flash animation on the page. The placed movie appears as a poster frame (usually the first frame in the movie) with a Play button superimposed in its lower left corner, as in Figure 12.16.

Users can play the Flash animation by clicking on it. Curiously, once started, an animation can be stopped again only by right-clicking it and choosing (not very obviously) Disable Content from the resulting contextual menu.

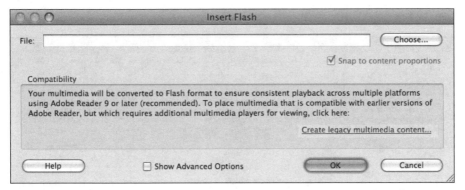

Figure 12.29 The Insert Flash dialog box is nearly identical in appearance and behavior to the Insert Video dialog box.

Adding Sound to a PDF Page

Acrobat Pro Only: The Sound tool on the Advanced Editing toolbar lets you attach a sound to a page in your PDF file. This can be any sound playable by QuickTime (including AIFF and MOV), Flash, and—in Windows—sounds playable by Windows Media Player and RealPlayer. Furthermore, if the sound file is an MP3, then Acrobat will play the sound directly, without using an external utility (such as QuickTime Player or Windows Movie Player); this ensures that the sound will play correctly on all systems.

Embedding a sound on a PDF page is identical to embedding a movie, except you start with the Sound tool rather than the Movie tool.

To place a sound on a document page:

1. Click the Sound tool on the Advanced Editing toolbar.

2. Click and drag a rectangle on the page. The Insert Sound dialog box opens (**Figure 12.30**).

3. Follow the steps in the task "To place a movie on a PDF page."

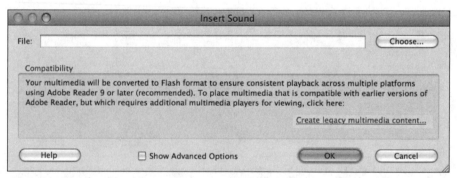

Figure 12.30 The Insert Sound dialog box is identical to the Insert Video dialog box and is used exactly the same way.

Figure 12.31 An MP3 file placed on the page will display a set of tiny controls so you can pause, stop, and restart the sound.

When you're finished, your sound will appear in one of two ways, depending on what type of sound it is:

◆ If the sound is an MP3, you get a visible rectangle with a little Play icon in it, exactly as you got when embedding a movie. Furthermore, when you click the rectangle, Acrobat plays the sound and displays some (very tiny) controls that let you pause, adjust the volume, and so on (**Figure 12.31**).

◆ If you embed any sound file other than an MP3, your sound is on the page, but no visible cue indicates that it is there. (Unlike videos, there is no first frame that Acrobat can use as a poster on the page.) You should provide a Play button on the page so a reader can play the sound. You do this the same way you made the Play button for your placed movie.

✔ Tips

■ Although non-MP3 sounds don't automatically get a poster, you can provide a picture to use as a marker on the page. In the Add Sound dialog box, choose "Create poster from file," and select a TIFF, JPEG, or other picture file to use as a poster.

■ As with videos, you can have Acrobat automatically play a sound (a bugle fanfare, perhaps) when the user opens the page. Follow the directions for attaching a movie to a page (see "Placing a Movie on a Page," earlier in this chapter), but choose a sound file instead of a movie file.

■ Use automatic sounds with restraint. A sound that plays every single time a reader passes through a page can get really annoying after the first hundred repetitions.

ORGANIZING DOCUMENTS

The Organizer has been a feature in Acrobat since version 7 and yet remains surprisingly underused. This astonishingly handy tool provides lists of your PDF files categorized a variety of ways for convenient access:

- ◆ You can find files according to when you last looked at them—yesterday, last week, and so on.

- ◆ You can find files in any location on your hard disk.

- ◆ You can create a list of favorite folders on your hard disk, which can be examined with a single click.

- ◆ You can create collections of PDF files pertaining to a particular task or topic. A collection's files can be scattered throughout your hard disk but are all accessible in the same list.

I find I use this tool all the time, particularly when I'm working on a project that requires repeated reference to a number of PDF-format reference documents.

Examining the Organizer

Opening the Organizer involves a single menu selection: File > Organizer > Open Organizer. As a shortcut, you can press Shift-Command/Control-1. You're now looking at the Organizer window (**Figure 13.1**).

This window has three columns. From left to right, they are as follows:

Places. This column has three panes presenting collections of PDF files. Some of these collections are created for you, such as the collection of all files viewed yesterday; you can create other collections for convenient access to your files.

Files. When you choose a container in the left-hand column, the Files column lists PDF files in that container.

Pages. When you choose a PDF file in the Files column, the Pages column shows you thumbnails of the pages in the document.

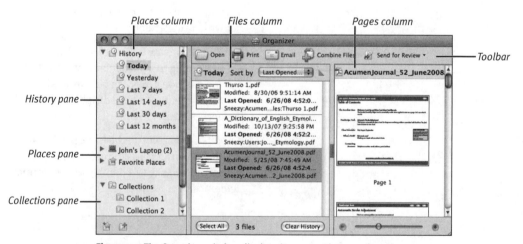

Figure 13.1 The Organizer window displays its content in several sections.

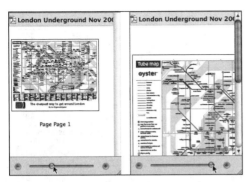

Figure 13.2 The slider beneath the Pages column zooms the page preview.

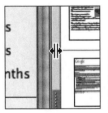

Figure 13.3 The Organizer window's toolbar gives you quick access to commonly used features.

Figure 13.4 You can resize any of the columns by dragging the divider separating one column from the next.

✔ Tip

■ You can zoom the thumbnails displayed in the Pages column by dragging the slider beneath the thumbnail pane or clicking the + or – button (**Figure 13.2**).

Running along the top of the Files and Pages columns is a set of tool buttons that perform various actions on files you select in the Files column (**Figure 13.3**). These tools are duplicates of tools that exist in the Acrobat toolbars; we've discussed them elsewhere in this book. For the record, the tool buttons are as follows:

Open opens the file selected in the Files column.

Print prints the file selected in the Files column.

Email uses your e-mail client to send the selected file as an e-mail attachment.

Combine Files combines two or more selected files into a single PDF file or Portfolio. (We described this in Chapter 5.

Send for Review starts the review process for the select file. We discuss reviewing PDF files in Chapters 6–8.

✔ Tips

■ You can easily change the width of the columns in the Organizer window by dragging the dividers between the columns (**Figure 13.4**).

■ You can open a file by either selecting it in the Files column and then clicking the Open button, or double-clicking it in the Files column. I recommend double-clicking; it's faster.

EXAMINING THE ORGANIZER

Using the History Pane

The purpose of the History pane in the Places column (**Figure 13.5**) is to allow easy access to files you've looked at before.

In this pane you can choose from a useful variety of time periods: Today, Yesterday, "Last 7 days," and so on.

Without any intervention on your part, Acrobat keeps track of all the documents you view and adds them to the appropriate time category.

To examine the files from a time period:

◆ Click the desired time period.

The Files column lists all the files you viewed in that time period. For each file, Acrobat lists the name of the file, the date it was last modified and viewed, and the location of the file on the hard disk.

✔ Tip

■ You can sort the files in the Files column a variety of ways, including by filename, file size, and author. Choose the criterion from the "Sort by" pop-up menu.

Sometimes you may want to clear out Acrobat's internal list of files you've viewed. This may be for security purposes or just to simplify the list—for example, the "Last 12 months" list can be so long that it isn't practical to find a particular file.

When you clear out Acrobat's history records, all the history categories become empty. Be certain you really want to do this, because it isn't undoable.

To clear the history:

◆ Click the Clear History button at the bottom of the Files column.

Having cleared the history, Acrobat again starts accumulating files into the history categories.

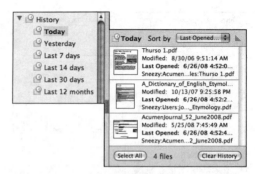

Figure 13.5 The History pane (top left) lets you see files according to when they were last viewed.

Figure 13.6 The Places pane (left) lets you view files according to where they're located on your computer.

Figure 13.7 You can add a new folder to the Places pane by clicking the New Favorites icon, located below the Places column.

Figure 13.8 To delete a folder from the Favorite Places folder, right-click the folder and choose Remove from the contextual menu.

Using the Places Pane

The Places pane (**Figure 13.6**) lets you view places on your hard disk and server volumes that hold PDF files. Initially, this pane contains two folders:

◆ Your computer's disk, which may be opened to examine folders anywhere on your disk.

Opening this item gives you access to your entire hard disk's folder hierarchy.

◆ Favorite Places, where you can put folders that you frequently visit for PDF documents. This initially contains your Documents folder and your computer's Desktop.

The Favorite Places category is extremely useful if you have folders that contain libraries of PDF files. Add one of those folders to your favorites, and you can get to any of the files in that folder without having to work your way through your disk's file hierarchy.

To add a folder to the Favorite Places folder:

1. Click the New Favorites icon, beneath the Categories column, in the lower-left corner of the Organizer dialog box (**Figure 13.7**).

Your system's standard pick-a-folder dialog box opens.

2. Choose the folder on your disk that you want to add to your favorites.

Acrobat adds that folder to your favorites. From now on, you can access the contents of that folder by clicking the folder in the Favorite Places category.

To remove a folder from the Favorite Places folder:

1. Right-click the folder in the Favorite Places list to get to the contextual menu (**Figure 13.8**).

2. Choose the Remove item in the menu.

Acrobat removes the folder from your favorites.

Using the Collections Category

This is my favorite part of the Organizer. The Collections pane (**Figure 13.9**) lets you create collections of PDF documents that reside anywhere on your hard disk. If you have PDF files scattered here and there that pertain to a particular subject, you can place them all in a collection and access them from this virtual folder.

Initially, the Collections category has three "starter" collections, all of them empty, named Collection 1, Collection 2, and Collection 3. You can add files to these collections or create your own collection.

✔ Tip

- You can rename collections, including the three default ones Adobe provides. To do so, click the collection name once to select it, then click it again to put the name into editing mode and type the new name.

To create a new collection:

1. Click the New Collection icon, located beneath the Categories column (**Figure 13.10**).

   Acrobat inserts a new collection named something like "Untitled 1."

2. Type a name for your collection.

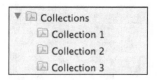

Figure 13.9 The Collections pane lists virtual folders that contain PDF files pertaining to a particular task.

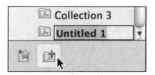

Figure 13.10 You create a new collection by clicking the New Collection icon below the Places column.

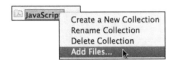

Figure 13.11 You add files to a collection by right-clicking the collection name and choosing Add Files from the contextual menu.

Figure 13.12 When you click a collection, the files it contains are displayed in the Files column.

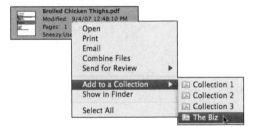

Figure 13.13 An alternative way of adding a file to a collection is to right-click the file in the Files pane, choose Add to a Collection, and choose the collection to which you want to add the file.

To add files to a collection:

1. Right-click the collection name in the Categories column to obtain a contextual menu (**Figure 13.11**).

2. In the contextual menu, choose Add Files. Acrobat presents you with the standard pick-a-file dialog box.

3. Choose the file you want to add to the collection.

    When you click the collection's name in the Category column, the Files column lists all the files you've placed in that collection (**Figure 13.12**).

✔ Tips

■ Note from Figure 13.11 that you can also rename or delete a collection by right-clicking it in the Categories column and choosing the appropriate option from the contextual menu.

■ An alternative way to add a file to a collection is right-clicking that file in the Files column and choosing Add to a Collection (**Figure 13.13**). The resulting contextual menu has a submenu that lists all existing collections; choose the collection to which you want to add the file.

■ You can also add files to a collection by dragging them from the Finder or Windows Explorer onto the collection icon in the Collection pane.

CREATING FORMS WITH ACROBAT PRO

Acrobat Pro has long provided tools that let you define interactive form fields that can collect data from a reader and send that data back to you.

We could write an entire book (or two) about creating Acrobat forms. This chapter introduces you to the basics of creating a functioning form with Acrobat. Happily, you can get very far with just the basics.

And with Acrobat 9, it is now absolutely, mindlessly simple to distribute your forms to a group of people and then retrieve their responses. The secret? That newly introduced wonder of wonders: Acrobat.com. Acrobat 9 automatically handles all the details of posting your form online, sending out notices to your list of responders, and then collecting the information they provide.

Creating and distributing Acrobat forms has never been easier.

About LiveCycle Designer

Acrobat 9 Pro has a large number of auto-mated processes that create useful forms without your necessarily having to become an expert.

Much of this ease of use is a result of integra-tion between Acrobat and Adobe LiveCycle Designer, a visual form editor that lets you create a form with the ease of laying out a page in a desktop publishing application. LiveCycle Designer is a separate program that ships with the Windows version (only) of Acrobat 9 Pro.

Note that LiveCycle Designer isn't avail-able in the Macintosh version of Acrobat. Bummer, but true. The biggest impact of this is that the Macintosh lacks access to Acrobat's form templates (more about these later). Still, the Mac version of Acrobat lets you create forms from electronic files and images, and it provides full support of the important form-distribution features.

Acrobat, together with LiveCycle Designer, lets you create forms from three sources:

Templates. Acrobat provides a large collec-tion of form templates that can be custom-ized to your needs. This functionality is Windows only, because it requires LiveCycle Designer.

Electronic documents. You can con-vert regular PDF files, Excel spreadsheets, scanned paper forms, and other files into interactive forms.

Paper forms. Acrobat uses your scanner to convert a paper form into an image and from there to a PDF form.

We won't be discussing in detail scanning to a form. Once you understand the tem-plates and, especially, converting electronic documents, the procedures for scanners are relatively easy.

✔ **Tip**

■ Forms created with LiveCycle Designer can't be dependably filled out with Acrobat 6 or earlier; the recipients of your form must have Acrobat 7 or later. If you need to make a form that is compatible with earlier versions of Acrobat, you must create your form fields using Edit Form mode; we shall see how to do this.

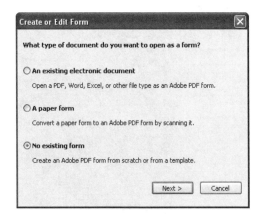

Figure 14.1 When you choose Forms > Create New Form, you are presented with a dialog box that lets you specify your starting point in the process.

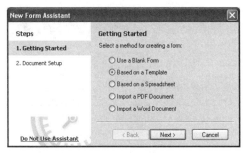

Figure 14.2 The New Form Assistant starts by asking you how you want to create your form; we'll start with a template.

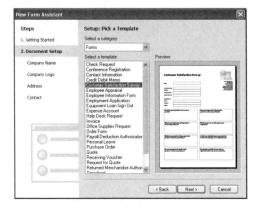

Figure 14.3 The next step in the wizard is to pick a template.

Creating a Form from a Template

Most of the actions you'll take regarding forms—creating, distributing, collecting— are accessible through the aptly named Forms menu.

Let's start by creating a form from one of the large number of templates Acrobat supplies. This will give us an opportunity to examine LiveCycle Designer.

Again, the templates aren't available on the Macintosh.

To create a form from a template:

1. Choose Forms > Start Form Wizard.

   Acrobat displays the Create or Edit Form dialog box, which asks what the starting point for your form will be (**Figure 14.1**).

2. Click the "No existing form" radio button, and click Next.

   Acrobat launches LiveCycle Designer and displays the first step in that program's New Form Assistant wizard (**Figure 14.2**). This step asks you how you want to create your form.

3. Click the "Based on a Template" radio button, and click Next.

   The next panel of the Create New Form wizard opens (**Figure 14.3**) and asks you to pick a template.

   Acrobat ships with an awe-inspiring collection of templates for everything from invoices to requests for unpaid leave.

   There is also a Blank category, which drops you directly into LiveCycle Designer with a blank form.

   Continues on next page

CREATING A FORM FROM A TEMPLATE

4. Choose a category and then a template within that category.

The preview in the dialog box displays the template you've chosen.

5. Click Next.

The next step in the New Form Assistant wizard opens (**Figure 14.4**), which asks for your company name.

6. Type your company's name in the text field and click Next.

The next panel asks for an image file containing your company's logo (**Figure 14.5**).

7. Click the Browse button, and choose the TIFF, JPEG, or other image file that contains your logo.

8. Click Next.

The next two panels ask for your company's contact information: address, telephone number, e-mail address, and Web address.

9. Supply your company's address, and click Next.

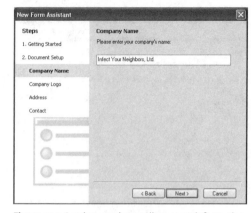

Figure 14.4 Acrobat needs to collect some information about your company to incorporate into the template. This includes your company's name and contact information.

Figure 14.5 You can supply an image file that contains your company logo.

10. Supply your telephone number and e-mail and Web addresses, and click Finish.

Acrobat thinks for a short while and then shows you your new form in LiveCycle Designer (**Figure 14.6**). We shall discuss the features of this window in the next section.

11. Reposition and resize the template's form fields by dragging the fields and their handles (**Figure 14.7**).

You can edit the field labels as you would any other text. You can also add new form fields to the template-based form; we'll see how to do that in the next section.

12. Choose File > Save to save the form.

Toolbar

Edit pane

How To pane

Library pane

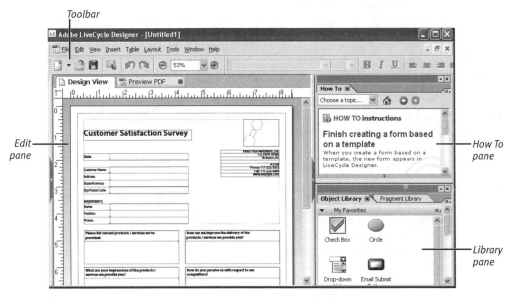

Figure 14.6 The LiveCycle Designer window has three panes. Clockwise from left, these are the Design pane, the How To pane, and the Library pane.

Figure 14.7 When you create a form field, you can move and resize it by dragging its border and its handles. You can also edit the label.

Editing Forms with LiveCycle Designer

When you have a form open in LiveCycle Designer, as at the end of the previous task, you're looking at a graphic representation of your form (Figure 14.6). The window has three panes:

Design. This largest pane presents a view of your form's page. Two views are available here; select one by clicking the appropriate tab at the top of the pane:

◆ The **Design View** pane presents the page in editable format. This is the view you use to place your form fields (**Figure 14.8**).

◆ The **Preview PDF** pane shows what the final form will look like when displayed in Acrobat.

How To. This pane presents a complete and useable help system for LiveCycle Designer. Refer to this early and often.

Library (**Figure 14.9**). The Library pane supplies premade components you may add to your form. The pane has tabs giving you access to two libraries:

◆ The **Object Library** supplies form fields and controls (check boxes, text fields, and so on) you can place on your Acrobat page. Choose a control type, and then click the form page to place a form field. (We'll discuss this more later.)

◆ The **Fragment Library** contains collections of form fields that you have saved as a *form fragment*. When you drag a fragment from the Fragment Library onto your form's page, all the form fields that make up the fragment are placed on the page.

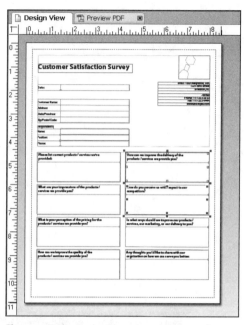

Figure 14.8 The Design View pane shows your form in an editable state. You can move, resize, and otherwise edit the form fields.

Figure 14.9 The Library pane allows you to add predefined objects to the page.

Figure 14.10 To add a form field to the page, you click on the field type in the Object Library pane and then click on the page.

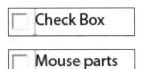

Figure 14.11 When you first place a form field, it has a generic label (top). Edit this label text so it's the way you want it on the form.

Figure 14.12 You can reposition and resize the form field by dragging the border and its handles.

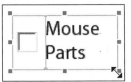

Figure 14.13 If you make the label's box too short, the label may wrap to multiple lines.

Most of the time, you'll use LiveCycle Designer to adjust the position and size of form fields created by one of the templates, as you did in the previous section. You can also add your own form fields to pages you created from a template.

To place a form field on the page:

1. In the Library pane, click the form field type that you want to add to the page (**Figure 14.10**).

2. In the Design View pane click the page to indicate where you want the control to go.
   Acrobat places the new control on the page with a generic label (**Figure 14.11**).

3. Select the label's text as you would in a text editor, and change the label to whatever you want (Figure 14.11).

4. Click the border of the control to get a border rectangle and handles (**Figure 14.12**).

5. Reposition and resize the form field by dragging the border and its handles.

✔ Tip

- If you reduce the width of your control too much, LiveCycle Designer wraps the label to a second line (**Figure 14.13**).

Having placed your form field, you can modify quite a few of its visual characteristics by right-clicking the field. For example, you can specify the font of the form field and its label.

To change a field's text properties:

1. Right-click the form field to display its contextual menu.

2. Choose Palettes > Font (**Figure 14.14**). The Font palette opens (**Figure 14.15**).

3. From the pop-up menus, choose the font and size you want for the label's text.

   You can also choose from a variety of styles, such as bold and italic.

4. Click the Windows close box to dismiss the palette when you're finished.

✔ Tips

- If you click the Paragraph tab in the Font palette, you can change a number of properties affecting the placement of the label text (**Figure 14.16**), such as alignment (left, right, centered). Many of these paragraph properties have an effect only if the label text has wrapped to multiple lines.

- There are a number of other palettes available from the contextual menu (Figure 14.14). The most routinely useful one is the Border palette, which lets you change the appearance of the form field's border.

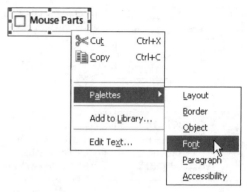

Figure 14.14 You can change a variety of a control's properties with contextual-menu options. Here we're changing the font.

Figure 14.15 The Font palette lets you change the font, size, and style of the form field's label.

Figure 14.16 If you click the Paragraph tab, you can specify the label's alignment, as well as other, less-frequently-used properties.

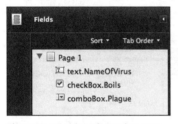

Figure 14.17 When you convert an electronic document to a form, your starting document looks like a form but isn't one. The lines and squares are just lines and squares, not form fields.

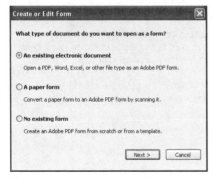

Figure 14.18 Although Acrobat automatically creates many of the form fields, you will need to add the rest of them using the Fields navigation pane.

Figure 14.19 To convert a PDF file or scanned paper form to an Acrobat form, choose "An existing electronic document."

Converting Electronic Documents to Forms

Many corporations today find themselves with a collection of paper forms they want to convert to PDF forms that can be filled out electronically.

Acrobat 9 has made this a relatively easy task; the only prerequisite is that the form must be in electronic format. It must be scanned or, if it was designed with software, it must be exported to PDF. The resulting PDF or image file looks like a form (**Figure 14.17**), but there are no active form fields on the page; the fill-in-the-blank lines are just graphic lines.

Converting the electronic file to a PDF interactive form is easy. Acrobat 9's Form Field Recognition feature analyzes the file and automatically places appropriate form fields on the new PDF page. Although Form Field Recognition gives you an excellent start, you'll probably need to add some additional form fields manually, using the Fields pane (**Figure 14.18**); Acrobat often fails to recognize some of the fill-in spaces in the original document. We'll see how to do this later.

Still, Acrobat does an amazingly good job for a first pass; you're left, relatively speaking, with just clean-up.

I'm pleased to report that this feature is available on the Macintosh as well as in Windows.

To convert an electronic file into a form:

1. Choose Forms > Start Form Wizard.

   The Create or Edit Form dialog box opens (**Figure 14.19**).

   Continues on next page

CONVERTING ELECTRONIC DOCUMENTS TO FORMS

2. Choose the radio button "An existing electronic document" and click Next.

Acrobat presents you with the first pane in the Create or Edit Form wizard, which asks you to locate the document you want to convert (**Figure 14.20**).

3. Click the Browse button, and choose the PDF or image file you want to convert; then click the Next button.

Acrobat displays a progress bar and spends some time importing the document. Although this process is usually fast, it can sometimes take a remarkably long time, so don't cancel the process until several minutes have elapsed.

When Acrobat is finished processing the file, it presents you with the document window in Edit Form mode (**Figure 14.21**). The PDF pages will have many form fields already in place, put there by the Form Field Recognition feature.

4. Resize and reposition the existing form fields so that they fit the page's artwork appropriately.

Acrobat will have probably missed some of the form fields we need on the page; for example, in Figure 14.21, Acrobat did not place any check boxes, so we shall need to add those fields by hand.

You will need to add the missing form fields, using the following steps.

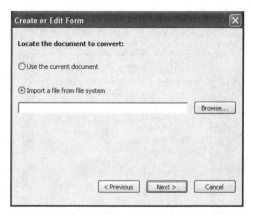

Figure 14.20 The Create or Edit Form wizard asks you to pick the document you want to convert. Or you may use the currently open PDF file, if you wish.

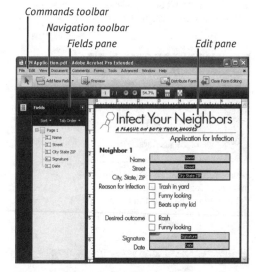

Figure 14.21 Once Acrobat has converted your file, you will see in Edit Form mode that many form fields have already been placed on your page.

Figure 14.22 To place a new form field on the page, select the appropriate form field type from the Add New Field button.

Figure 14.23 When you place your form field, it appears as a rectangle with handles and has a palette next to it, in which you can type a name for the field.

Figure 14.24 When you return to the Acrobat Hand tool, your form fields are in place and functioning on the page.

5. Click the Add New Field button (in the Edit Form mode toolbar) to get a drop-down list of available form fields (**Figure 14.22**); select the type of field you want to add to the page.

The pointer turns into a peculiar-looking ghost-rectangle with a dotted-line crosshair.

6. You may either click once on the PDF page, which places a form field on the page the same size as the "ghost," or drag out a rectangle, which gives you a new form field the size of the rectangle you dragged.

Either way, you get a form field on the page with a floating palette immediately adjacent to it (**Figure 14.23**).

7. Type a name in the palette's Field Name field.

8. If this field represents required data— that is, data that the user must supply before closing the form, such as name or zip code—click the "Required field" check box.

9. Reposition and resize the new field so it matches the page's artwork.

You can nudge the position of the field with your arrow keys and nudge the size with Control-arrow keys.

10. Repeat Steps 4 through 9 for each of the form fields you need to add to the page.

11. When all is to your liking, click the Close Form Editing toolbar button.

Acrobat displays your document page with all its form fields in place (**Figure 14.24**).

Continues on next page

✔ Tips

- If you are partway through creating a form and have to put it aside (there are only so many hours in a day), you can resume adding fields to it by opening the file in Acrobat and selecting Forms > Add or Edit Fields. Acrobat drops you into Edit Form mode (Figure 14.21).

- If you click the Show All Properties link visible in Figure 14.23, Acrobat displays a Field Properties dialog box specific to the type of field you just created (**Figure 14.25**). Most of the controls here have reasonable defaults, but I suggest you take a look at them in your idle moments. You can get to the same dialog box by right-clicking on a field in Edit Form mode and selecting Properties in the resulting contextual menu (**Figure 14.26**).

- You can add a set of Create Form Field tools (one for each form field type) to the Edit Form toolbar by choosing Add New Field > Show Tools on Toolbar. The Add New Field button is replaced by a series of buttons, one for each type of form field (**Figure 14.27**). I find these useful when I am making a large number of new form fields; it's a bit more convenient just to click on the Text Field button, rather than to select Text Field from the Add New Field button's menu.

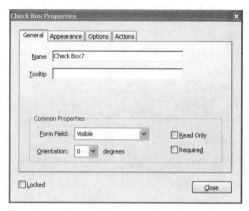

Figure 14.25 The Field Properties dialog box (here shown for a check box) lets you specify the appearance and other properties of a form field.

Figure 14.26 You can get to the Field Properties dialog box by right-clicking on a form field and choosing Properties.

Figure 14.27 You can replace the Add New Field toolbar button with a series of Add Field buttons, one for each form field type.

Distributing Forms

In times past, one of the most troublesome parts of using Acrobat for your forms was distributing them and then somehow getting information back from your respondents.

With Acrobat 9, distributing your form to a group of respondents has never been simpler. Acrobat does all the bookkeeping necessary to send the form to your readers and collect the responses from them.

Acrobat lets you distribute your form in three ways:

E-mail. Acrobat sends the form to your list of recipients attached to an e-mail message. The recipients open the attachment, fill out the form, and click a Submit Form button in the document window; then the completed form is automatically e-mailed back to you. You can open the returned form and examine the responses.

Acrobat.com. Acrobat uploads your form to Acrobat.com and then e-mails a link to the file to your list of recipients. They click on the e-mailed link, fill out the form, and then click the Submit Form button in the document window. Their responses are uploaded to Acrobat.com. You can examine the responses anytime in Acrobat.

Your own server. This is the same as distributing a form by Acrobat.com, except that you use your own server to store the form and its responses. We shall not be discussing this option in this book; Acrobat.com is free and easy and is a much better way to distribute forms.

Note in all cases that Acrobat tracks your form's progress: To whom has the form been sent? Who has responded? What information did they type in the form fields? All of this is handled by Acrobat and accessible through the Tracker window, which we last saw when discussing document reviews in Chapter 8.

As one who has worked with people for years setting up form distribution and response workflows, let me assure you this is way cool.

Distributing forms by e-mail

As outlined earlier, Acrobat can distribute your form as an attachment to an e-mail message you send to your recipients.

To distribute a form by e-mail:

1. With the form open in Acrobat, choose Forms > Distribute Form.

   The Distribute Form wizard opens (**Figure 14.28**). This dialog box lets you choose how to distribute the form.

2. In the drop-down menu, choose "Manually collect responses in my email inbox" and then click the Next button.

   Acrobat displays the second panel in the Distribute Form wizard, which asks if you want Acrobat to e-mail the form to your recipients or if you want to do it yourself (**Figure 14.29**). Here, we shall have Acrobat do the mailing.

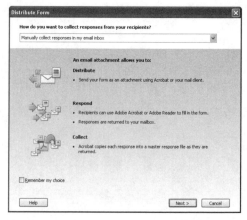

Figure 14.28 When you choose Forms > Distribute Form, Acrobat presents you with a dialog box that lets you specify how to distribute your form. We'll send our form by e-mail.

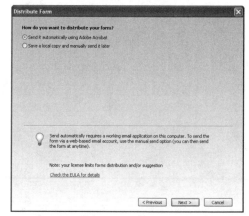

Figure 14.29 First, the Distribute Form wizard asks whether Acrobat should e-mail your form to your recipients or whether you want to do it.

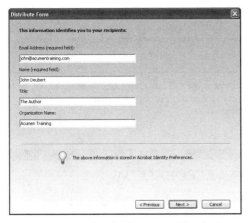

Figure 14.30 Next, the Distribute Form Wizard asks you for the name and e-mail address to which form replies should be sent.

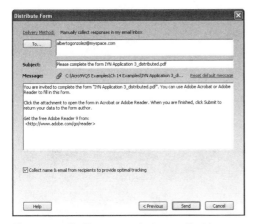

Figure 14.31 Finally, you supply the e-mail addresses of the people to whom the form should be sent. You can also edit the subject and message body.

Figure 14.32 Whoever receives your form sees a brief set of instructions and two buttons at the top of the form's page.

3. Choose "Send it automatically using Adobe Acrobat" and click Next.

Acrobat displays the next step of the Distribute Form wizard (**Figure 14.30**).

4. Type in the pane the return e-mail address to which responses should be sent, and click Next. Acrobat may skip this step if it already knows your return address from earlier forms you have distributed.

The last step of the wizard appears, asking you for the e-mail addresses of the form's recipients (**Figure 14.31**). This step will be missing if you earlier opted to e-mail the form yourself, rather than let Acrobat do it.

5. Type in the To field the e-mail addresses of all the people to whom the form should be sent.

The addresses may be on separate lines within the field or separated by semicolons. Note that you can also click the To button and take addresses from your system's address book.

6. Type a subject and message in the appropriate fields, and click Send.

Acrobat sends your form as an attachment to the e-mail addresses you provided. Depending on your system and e-mail client, Acrobat may send the e-mail directly or it may open your mail client with an appropriate message already open, ready for you to click Send.

When recipients receive the form and open it in Acrobat, they see an instruction panel at the top of the document window (**Figure 14.32**). This panel contains instructions on what to do with the form.

Having filled out the form, the recipient clicks the Submit Form button. Acrobat uses the recipient's mail client to send the completed form back to you.

Distributing a form with Acrobat.com

Arguably, the most efficient way to distribute a form is using Acrobat.com as a server. In this case, your form and all the bookkeeping information associated with it (including the responses from your recipients) are stored on Acrobat.com. The advantage is that you don't need to receive each and every responder's information one at a time; you can simply use the Tracker periodically to get the currently submitted responses.

Furthermore, all the recipients' responses are compiled into a single file, rather than being scattered among a series of individual PDF files.

See the "Acrobat.com" sidebar in Chapter 8 for more information.

To distribute a form with Acrobat.com:

1. With the form open in Acrobat, choose Forms > Distribute Form.

   The Distribute Form dialog box opens (Figure 14.28).

2. In the drop-down menu, choose "Automatically download & organize responses with Acrobat.com" (**Figure 14.33**), then click the Next button.

   Acrobat displays the next panel in the Distribute Form wizard, which asks you to sign in to Acrobat.com (**Figure 14.34**). You can also create a new Acrobat.com account, if necessary.

3. Provide your Adobe ID (which is just your e-mail address) and password, then click the Sign In button.

   Acrobat spends a few seconds talking to the Acrobat.com server and then displays the next panel in the Distribute Form wizard (**Figure 14.35**).

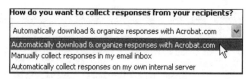

Figure 14.33 You can use Acrobat.com to distribute your forms by choosing this option in the Distribute Form wizard.

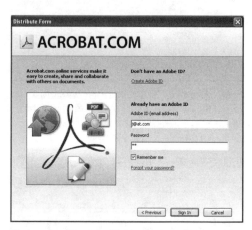

Figure 14.34 You are asked to sign in to Acrobat.com. Remember that your Adobe ID is just your e-mail address.

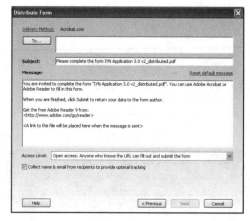

Figure 14.35 You supply the e-mail addresses of the people you want notified of your form's availability.

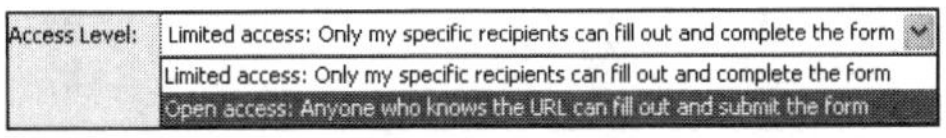

Figure 14.36 You can specify that your form may be viewed by anyone who knows your form's URL or only by people to whom you sent notices.

4. In the To field, enter the e-mail addresses of all the people you want notified of the form's availability. You may modify the subject and message text, as well.

   An e-mail containing a link to the copy of your form stored on Acrobat.com is sent to all the people whose e-mail addresses you supply.

   Note that this panel of the wizard has a drop-down menu that lets you specify who should have access to this form: anyone who knows the URL or only the people whom you notified by e-mail (**Figure 14.36**).

5. Click Send.

   Acrobat uploads your file to Acrobat.com, sends your e-mail notifications, and then opens the Tracker window so you can see the status of your newly posted form (**Figure 14.37**).

   Your form is now available to your audience of responders.

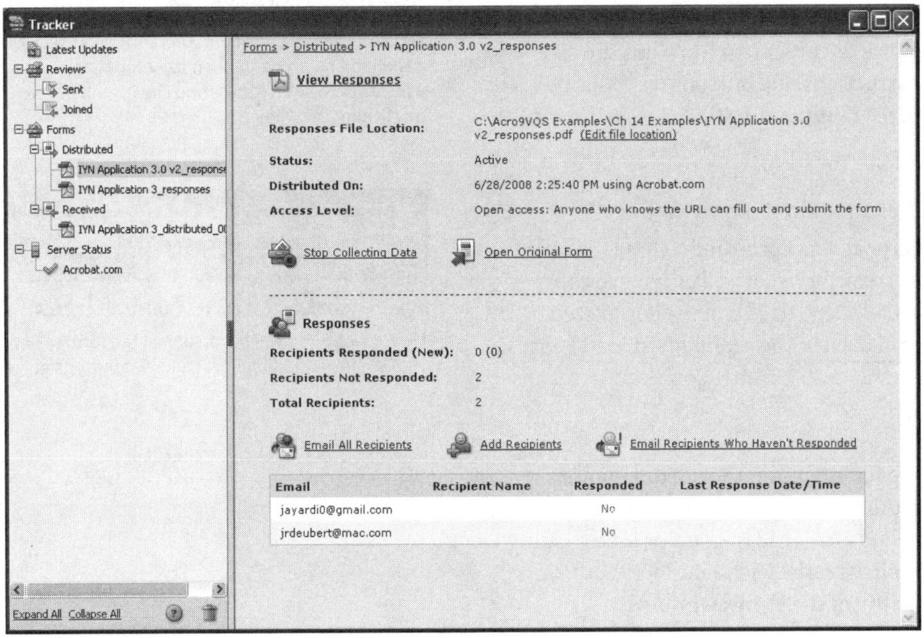

Figure 14.37 You can later see your recipients' replies through the Forms Tracker.

Responding to a Distributed Form

If you are one of the recipients of a form distributed by Acrobat 9, you will receive an e-mailed
notice, similar to that in **Figure 14.38**.

Depending on how the form was distributed,
the e-mail message will either have the form
file as an attachment or contain a link to the
form file's location on Acrobat.com.

To respond to a distributed form:

1. Open the form in Acrobat 9; you will do
   this one of two ways:
   - ▲ If the form file is attached to the e-mail
     message, then simply open the attach-
     ment in Acrobat 9.
   - ▲ If the e-mail contains a link, click on that
     link; your Web browser opens and takes
     you to Acrobat.com, which presents you
     with a button that automatically down-
     loads and opens the file (**Figure 14.39**).
     Click this Download button.

   You are now looking at the PDF form,
   whose document window has the
   instructions and buttons we described
   earlier (**Figure 14.40**).

2. Fill out the form.

3. Click the Submit Form button.

   Acrobat acts according to how the form
   was distributed: it will either use your
   e-mail client to e-mail the completed
   form back to the sender or upload your
   form data to Acrobat.com.

✔ Tip

- The form fields in the document are
  initially shaded a blue tint to make them
  obvious. You can toggle this blue shading
  by clicking the Highlight Fields button at
  the top of the form's window.

Figure 14.38 Your recipients receive an e-mail that
contains a link to the form on Acrobat.com.

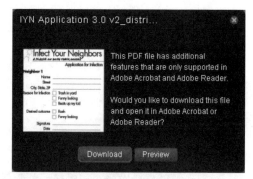

Figure 14.39 As a recipient of a form, you click on the
e-mailed link and are taken to Acrobat.com, which
asks if you want to download the form file. Tell it Yes
by clicking Download.

Figure 14.40 You will be looking at the form's window
with some instructional text and two buttons at the top.

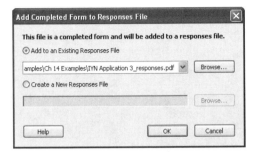

Figure 14.41 When you receive an e-mailed response to your form, Acrobat asks if you want it added to the other responses for that form. To do so, click the top radio button and click OK.

Receiving and Viewing Results

Acrobat 9 also makes it remarkably easy to receive and view responses to your form. The secret is to use the Forms Tracker, which takes care of all the grunt work entailed in managing the form data returned by your recipients. Furthermore, the Tracker handles all your forms, whether you sent them by e-mail or you distributed them through Acrobat.com.

Receiving form responses

Responses to forms distributed through Acrobat.com are retrieved from the server automatically when you ask to see those responses in the Tracker.

For forms that were distributed by e-mail, you must open the returned form (which was e-mailed back to you as an attachment) and tell Acrobat to add that file's form data to the collection of responses.

To receive form results returned by e-mail:

1. In your e-mail software, open the e-mail with the attached, completed form.

2. Open the attached PDF file.

   In most systems, you can do this directly from the e-mail client. In other systems, you may need to download the attachment to a file and then open that.

   A dialog box opens, notifying you that the form belongs to an ongoing form distribution and asking permission to add the data to that form's collection of responses (**Figure 14.41**). Note that you will see references to a "responses file" in this and other forms-related dialog boxes; this is a file in which Acrobat keeps bookkeeping information about a distributed form.

Continues on next page

3. Click OK.

Acrobat adds the form's responses to the collection. You're now looking at the completed form, which you can examine, if you wish.

Viewing form responses

The Forms Tracker is Grand Central Station for viewing the responses to all of your distributed forms. You access the Forms Tracker by choosing Forms > Track Forms. The resulting Tracker window (**Figure 14.42**) gives you access to all the forms you have distributed, whether by e-mail or by Acrobat.com.

Currently active forms

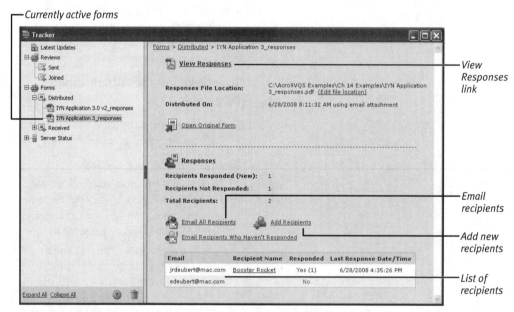

View Responses link

Email recipients

Add new recipients

List of recipients

Figure 14.42 The Forms Tracker is the tool you use to manage the replies to your form.

Figure 14.43 The Tracker window has a list of all your currently distributed forms. Select one of these to examine its responses.

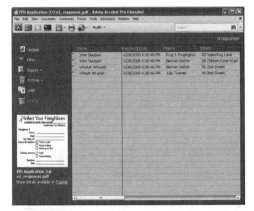

Figure 14.44 Clicking on the Tracker's View Responses link yields an Acrobat portfolio that lists all the replies received so far.

Figure 14.45 Double-clicking on a reply in the Responses portfolio displays the form page with the recipient's responses in place.

The left side of this window displays a hierarchical list of all the forms you have in distribution (**Figure 14.43**). When you click on one of the forms in the list, the right side of the window fills with information and a collection of links leading to more information about that form, including a list of who has and who has not responded to the form.

This is the same Tracker we used earlier in the book to examine responses to document reviews.

To view the responses for all returned forms:

1. Choose Forms > Track Forms.

   The Tracker window opens (Figure 14.42).

2. In the left side of the window, select the distributed form whose responses you want to examine.

   The right side displays that form's respondents.

3. Click the View Responses link in the right side of the window, at the top.

   Acrobat creates a portfolio that lists all the responses received for this form and provides tools for examining, archiving, and otherwise working with those responses (**Figure 14.44**).

4. Double-click one of the responses in the list.

   Acrobat displays that filled-in form, along with a toolbar containing navigation tools that let you zoom in on the current response and move from one returned form to the next (**Figure 14.45**).

5. Click the Next Form button to step through each returned form or repeat Step 4 for each response you wish to examine.

✔ Tips

- The Responses portfolio (Figure 14.44) has a toolbar (**Figure 14.46**) and a set of command buttons (**Figure 14.47**) that provide several functions, such as saving individual responses to a file on your hard disk and printing the responses.

- The Responses portfolio's Update button (Figure 14.47) is particularly useful for forms distributed by Acrobat.com. It checks to see if there have been any more responses posted.

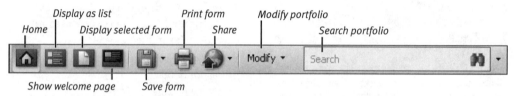

Home *Display as list* *Display selected form* *Print form* *Share* *Modify portfolio* *Search portfolio*

Show welcome page *Save form*

Figure 14.46 The Responses portfolio has a toolbar that lets you navigate around the list of replies.

Figure 14.47 The Responses portfolio also has a collection of controls that carry out a variety of tasks.

PASSWORD PROTECTION

15

An increasing proportion of the world's documents are distributed as PDF files, many of which are to a greater or lesser extent confidential. Banks don't want their customers' financial statements read by just anyone; software companies need to keep new product specifications from the eyes of their competitors; and most of us don't want our love letters broadcast for the world to read.

Acrobat offers three types of security to control the opening and viewing of a PDF file:

Password security. You assign a password that is required to open the file. This is simple and effective and is the method we'll discuss in this chapter.

Certificate security. This approach restricts the reading of the file to a specific list of people. Each person on the list must have a *digital ID*, which we'll discuss in Chapter 16.

LiveCycle Policy Server security. Adobe's LiveCycle Policy Server software manages digital IDs and permissions on a server. This allows an administrator to restrict or loosen permissions on the fly.

You can also restrict the actions a viewer can perform with the document and require a password to overcome those restrictions. For example, certain readers may be able to open a file but not print it unless they know the "secret word."

Restricting File Access

The most effective protection you can apply to a file is to password-protect access to it; viewers are not allowed to see the file's contents unless they know the password. The file is encrypted, so that even if you open it with a text editor and try to look at the PDF code (always a treat), all you see is gibberish.

The encryption applied to the file's contents has gotten more sophisticated as Acrobat has matured. The more secure your document is, the later the version of Acrobat a reader must have to open it.

To password-restrict access to a document:

1. With the document open, choose File > Properties.

   The Document Properties dialog box opens (**Figure 15.1**). Choose the Security tab.

2. In the Security Method pop-up menu, choose Password Security.

   The Password Security Settings dialog box opens (**Figure 15.2**).

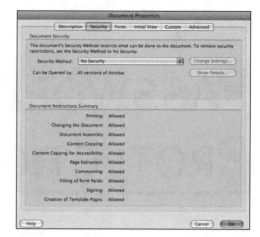

Figure 15.1 The Document Properties dialog box's Security pane lets you specify what method to use to secure your document.

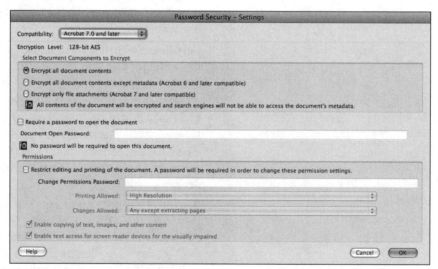

Figure 15.2 The Password Security Settings dialog box has all the controls to restrict access to your document.

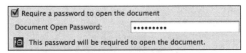

Figure 15.3 To prevent your document from being opened by unauthorized personnel, type a password in the Document Open Password text box.

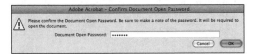

Figure 15.4 When you close the Password Security Settings dialog box, Acrobat asks you to confirm your password.

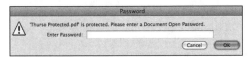

Figure 15.5 When someone opens your password-protected document, Acrobat demands the password of them.

✔ Tips

■ The document isn't actually password protected until you save it to your disk. Until you do so, you can freely change your security settings by clicking the Change Settings button in the Document Properties dialog box (Figure 15.1).

■ When readers attempt to open your protected file, they're asked for a password (**Figure 15.5**). If they type an incorrect password, they aren't allowed to open the file.

3. In the Compatibility pop-up menu, choose the earliest version of Acrobat a reader can have and still be able to open the document.

Here you decide how strong the encryption applied to your document must be; later versions of Acrobat use stronger encryption than earlier versions.

You may choose compatibility with Acrobat 3, 5, 6, 7, or 9. The later the version of Acrobat you require, the harder it will be to read your encrypted content, but also the more often you'll have readers who can't read your document without updating their Acrobat or Reader software.

4. Decide what parts within your document should be encrypted: everything, everything except metadata, or nothing except attached files.

See the sidebar "What to Encrypt?" below for a discussion of what to encrypt. Personally, I tend to encrypt everything.

5. Click the "Require a password to open the document" check box.

6. Type a password in the Document Open Password text box (**Figure 15.3**).

The password you type appears as a row of bullets on the screen.

7. Click OK.

A dialog box opens, asking you to confirm your password (**Figure 15.4**).

8. Type your password into the text box, and click OK.

Acrobat returns you to the Document Properties dialog box, which now displays your security settings.

9. Click OK to return to your PDF document.

Restricting Reader Activities

Acrobat lets you restrict what readers can do with your file once they have opened it. The Permissions controls in the Password Security Settings dialog box (**Figure 15.6**) allow you to restrict the editing and printing of your file and to assign a password that must be typed in before the permissions can be changed.

These permissions and their password are completely independent of the password needed to open the document. You can have an Open password, a Permissions password, both, or neither.

You can allow three levels of printing permission:

High Resolution. This option allows unrestricted printing of the document.

Low Resolution. The document is always printed as a 150-dpi bitmap. Thus, a reader can print a proof of this document but not a high-quality copy.

None. The document may not be printed.

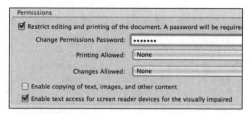

Figure 15.6 The Permissions controls let you specify the degree to which readers may edit your document.

What to Encrypt?

When you assign an Open password to a document, Acrobat encrypts the contents of the document, making it impossible to read the document without knowing the password. Acrobat gives you three choices in deciding how much of your PDF file to encrypt (**Figure 15.7**):

Encrypt all document contents. Acrobat encrypts everything in your file. This is the option I generally choose because it has the lowest requirements for reading the document: a reader must have only Acrobat 5 or later.

Encrypt all document contents except metadata. Acrobat leaves keywords and other metadata unencrypted so that they're searchable. This requires the reader to have Acrobat 6 or later.

Encrypt only file attachments. The Comments toolbar lets you attach a spreadsheet or other file to your document. These attached files are encrypted, but nothing else is. This requires at least Acrobat 7 to be read.

> ◉ Encrypt all document contents
> ○ Encrypt all document contents except metadata (Acrobat 6 and later compatible)
> ○ Encrypt only file attachments (Acrobat 7 and later compatible)

Figure 15.7 You have control over what parts of your password-protected document are encrypted.

Editing permissions

You can also allow one of five degrees of permission for editing the file:

None. The reader isn't allowed to modify the file.

Inserting, deleting, and rotating pages. The reader may change the orientation or presence of pages, but may not modify the contents of those pages.

Filling in form fields and signing existing signature fields. This option is appropriate for a distributed form. It allows recipients to input information in a questionnaire but prevents them from playfully changing the wording of the questions using the TouchUp tools.

Commenting, filling in form fields, and signing existing signature fields. This option lets readers fill in a form and attach comments. Thus, an expense report form would allow the attachment of scanned receipts (as an "attachment" comment).

Any except extracting pages. Readers can modify the document in any way they wish except pulling the pages out into another document. Note that readers can use the TouchUp tools to change the content of the PDF file.

In addition to these editing and printing permissions, you may allow readers to copy text and other content from your file and, presumably, paste it into another document.

Finally, if you restrict copying of the content of your document, you may nonetheless allow screen readers and other devices for the visually impaired to extract the text.

Permissions Caveat

One important thing to remember about setting permissions is that obeying the restrictions is the responsibility of the PDF-viewing software, which includes not only the Adobe Acrobat products but also such programs as Apple's Preview and the free Ghostscript program. The permissions exist as a series of "flags" in the PDF file that tell the PDF viewer which actions are restricted and which are allowed. Absolutely nothing enforces these restrictions; if a PDF viewer chooses to ignore them, then it may allow its user to print, edit, and otherwise modify the PDF file regardless of the permissions settings.

RESTRICTING READER ACTIVITIES

To assign permissions to a document:

1. Choose File > Properties.

   Acrobat displays the Document Properties dialog box (Figure 15.1).

2. In the Security Method pop-up menu, choose Password Security.

   The Password Security Settings dialog box opens (Figure 15.2).

3. Click the "Restrict editing and printing" check box (**Figure 15.8**).

4. Type a password in the Change Permissions Password field.

5. Choose the degree of printing permission you want from the Printing Allowed pop-up menu (**Figure 15.9**).

6. From the Changes Allowed pop-up menu, choose the permission you wish to allow for editing your file (**Figure 15.10**).

7. If you want to allow readers to copy text and images from your PDF file, click the "Enable copying" check box (Figure 15.6).

8. If you choose to *not* allow readers to copy text from your file, but you still want screen readers for the visually impaired to work, then click the "Enable text access" check box.

9. Click OK.

   Acrobat asks you to confirm your password (**Figure 15.11**).

10. Enter a password and click OK.

    Acrobat returns you to the Document Properties dialog box.

11. Click OK to return to the document page.

    Once you've saved your file, the Document Properties dialog box reflects your security settings (**Figure 15.12**).

Figure 15.8 You must supply a password to restrict the editing of your file.

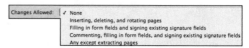

Figure 15.9 You may forbid a reader to print your document, allow a low-resolution proof, or allow high-quality printing.

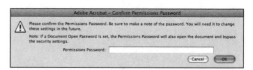

Figure 15.10 You may choose from a variety of degrees to which a user may modify your PDF file.

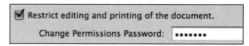

Figure 15.11 When you close the Password Security Settings dialog box, Acrobat asks you to confirm your password.

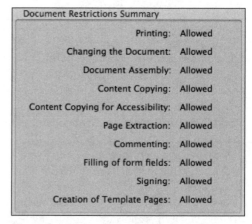

Figure 15.12 Once you've saved your document, the Permissions settings are put in place and the Document Properties dialog box reflects this.

DIGITAL SIGNATURES

From the early days, Adobe has wanted contracts and other agreements in PDF format to be legally binding documents. To do this, there needed to be some way of electronically signing a PDF document so that it was unimpeachably certain that a particular person had agreed to its contents.

This problem has been thoroughly solved; electronically signed PDF files are accepted as legally binding documents by many federal agencies and state governments, including the Internal Revenue Service and the State of California. In this chapter, we shall see how to sign a PDF document and how to confirm that the signature on a signed document is valid.

About Adobe Self-Sign Security

Acrobat's electronic signature mechanism is open-ended. Third-party companies, such as Cyber-SIGN and Entrust, can implement their own ways of identifying the signer of a document using Adobe Acrobat's plug-in technology.

In this chapter, we'll discuss the use of the electronic signature mechanism that ships with Acrobat: Adobe Self-Sign Security.

You need to understand the following concepts and terms before you can use Adobe Self-Sign Security:

Digital ID. A collection of data that electronically identifies a person. This is the data that is embedded in the signed document to identify the signer.

Certificate. A file that contains digital ID information. This file can be sent to another person for installation into their copy of Acrobat as a *trusted identity*.

Trusted identity. A certificate that has been installed in your copy of Acrobat and can be used to validate a signature. It's "trusted" in the sense that you know the certificate actually came from the person whom it's supposed to represent.

Signature validation. The process of confirming that a signature was created with a particular digital ID. When you receive a signed document, validation confirms that the signature was created by one of your trusted identities.

Setting up to use signatures

Some preparation must be carried out before you can digitally sign PDF documents. We'll examine each of these steps in greater detail as we go through the chapter:

- ◆ You create on your computer a digital ID that you'll use to sign documents. You must also create a password that you'll use every time you use this ID.

- ◆ You create a digital certificate from this ID.

- ◆ You send the certificate to people who will be recipients of your signed documents.

- ◆ The people to whom you send your certificate must import it into their copies of Acrobat as a trusted identity that represents you as a signer.

  They should also confirm that it was you who sent the certificate, perhaps by calling you on the telephone and asking if you just e-mailed a certificate to them.

With this preparation in place, signing a document is relatively easy:

- ◆ You supply your digital ID and password; the ID's identifying information is embedded in the signature.

- ◆ You send your signed document to a recipient.

- ◆ The recipient opens the document; Acrobat automatically validates the signature, confirming that it corresponds to your certificate and, therefore, really was placed on the document by you.

Let's see how to accomplish all this.

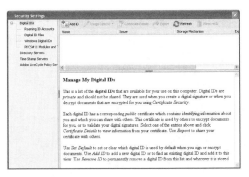

Figure 16.1 You create a digital ID by going to the Security Settings dialog box.

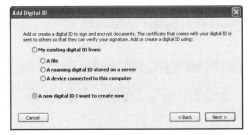

Figure 16.2 In the Add Digital ID dialog box, you tell Acrobat that you want to make a new self-signed ID.

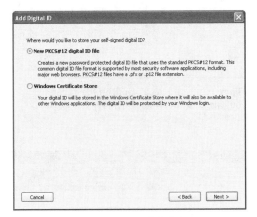

Figure 16.3 You can store your digital ID as a standard-format file or in the Windows Certificate Store. The latter works only in Windows, of course.

Creating a Digital ID

The first bit of preparation you must do when you intend to sign one or more PDF documents is to create a digital ID. You can do this on the fly when you sign a document, but if signing a document will be a common activity for you, you should create your ID ahead of time.

To create a digital ID:

1. Choose Advanced > Security Settings.

   The Security Settings dialog box opens (**Figure 16.1**).

2. Click the Digital IDs heading in the column on the left side of the dialog box.

   Acrobat displays all the digital IDs currently defined on this computer. This list is initially blank, of course.

3. Click the Add ID icon.

   The first panel of the Add Digital ID wizard opens, which asks what you want to use to create your ID (**Figure 16.2**).

4. Click the radio button "A new digital ID I want to create now," and click Next.

   The next panel asks whether you want the ID you create to be stored as a file or in the Windows Certificate Store (**Figure 16.3**). For the purpose of this book, the digital file is preferable, because it's a cross-platform industry standard.

   Continues on next page

CREATING A DIGITAL ID

5. Click the radio button "New PKCS#12 digital ID file," and click Next.

   The next panel asks for some professional information, such as your name and title (**Figure 16.4**). This information can be displayed as part of your signature.

6. Type in as much of the information as you like (I suggest at least your name), and click Next.

   Acrobat displays the next panel, which asks where the data file for the ID should be placed (there's no good reason not to accept the default); it also asks for a password (**Figure 16.5**).

7. Type a password in the Password and Confirm Password fields, and click Finish.

   You'll need to supply this password every time you sign a document.

   When you click the Finish button, Acrobat returns you to the Security Settings dialog box, which now displays your new digital ID (**Figure 16.6**).

8. Click the window's Close button to finish the process.

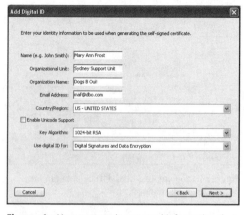

Figure 16.4 You can type in personal information that may be displayed as part of your digital signature. You should supply at least your name.

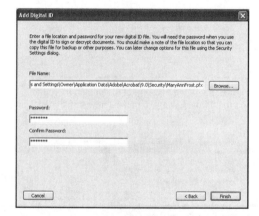

Figure 16.5 Type in a password for the signature; you'll need to supply this whenever you sign a document.

Figure 16.6 When you return to the Security Settings dialog box, it lists your new digital ID.

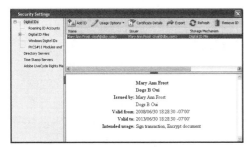

Figure 16.7 You create a certificate for your digital ID from the Security Settings dialog box.

Figure 16.8 Choose your digital ID in the Security Settings dialog box, and click the Export icon.

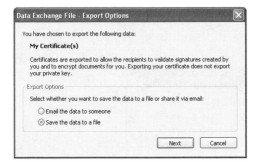

Figure 16.9 Acrobat gives you the choice of saving your certificate to a file or immediately e-mailing it to someone.

Creating a Certificate from an ID

A certificate is a digital file you can send to the people to whom you'll be sending signed documents. They can import this certificate into their copies of Acrobat to create a trusted identity, which represents you to their systems.

Everyone to whom you send a signed document must have a certificate from you before they can validate your signature.

To create a certificate:

1. Choose Advanced > Security Settings.
   The Security Settings dialog box opens (Figure 16.1).

2. Click the Digital IDs heading in the column on the left side of the dialog box.
   Acrobat displays all the digital IDs currently defined on this computer.

3. Select the digital ID for which you want to create a certificate.
   Acrobat displays information about the person whose ID this is (**Figure 16.7**).

4. Click the Export icon at the top of the dialog box (**Figure 16.8**).
   Acrobat displays the Export Options dialog box (**Figure 16.9**). This presents you with the choice of exporting your certificate as a file or immediately e-mailing the certificate to someone.

Continues on next page

CREATING A CERTIFICATE FROM AN ID

5. Click the "Save the data to a file" radio button, and click Next.

A standard Save dialog box opens.

6. Specify a name and location on your hard disk for the certificate file, and click OK.

Acrobat creates the certificate file in the location you specify. You now have a file that you can send to recipients of your signed documents.

✔ Tip

■ If you click the "Email the data to someone" radio button in Step 5, Acrobat creates a certificate and immediately e-mails it to a recipient. When you click the Next button, the Compose Email dialog box opens, which lets you supply an address, a subject, and a message body for the e-mail (**Figure 16.10**).

Figure 16.10 If you have Acrobat e-mail your certificate, the software asks for an address and subject for the e-mail. You can also modify the e-mail's message body.

Figure 16.11 To import a certificate as a trusted identity, you go to the Manage Trusted Identities dialog box and click Add Contacts.

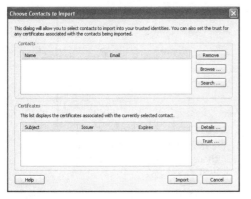

Figure 16.12 The Choose Contacts to Import dialog box lets you choose a certificate to import. Just click the Browse button and choose the certificate file.

Importing a Certificate as a Trusted Identity

In the previous section, you created a certificate that encapsulates your digital ID. When you send this file to another person— presumably someone to whom you'll be sending electronically signed documents— they must import the certificate into Acrobat as a trusted identity.

The presence of a trusted identity allows Acrobat to identify the signer of a PDF document. Acrobat can confirm that a digital signature was placed on the page by the same person who is identified by the trusted identity.

The trusted identity is "trusted" in the sense that you know it really came from the person it claims to represent. This can be confirmed relatively simply: Telephone the person you believe sent you the certificate, and ask that person if they actually did so.

The following task assumes the certificate file is somewhere on your hard disk, having been e-mailed to you, perhaps.

To import a certificate as a trusted identity:

1. Choose Advanced > Manage Trusted Identities.

   Acrobat presents you with the Manage Trusted Identities dialog box (**Figure 16.11**). This dialog box lists all the trusted identities your copy of Acrobat knows about.

2. Click the Add Contacts button.

   The Choose Contacts to Import dialog box opens (**Figure 16.12**). This dialog box allows you to choose as many certificates as you wish to import into your copy of Acrobat.

3. Click the Browse button.

   A standard Open dialog box opens.

Continues on next page

IMPORTING A CERTIFICATE AS A TRUSTED IDENTITY

4. Choose the certificate file you want to import, and click OK.

Acrobat returns you to the Choose Contacts to Import dialog box, which now lists the certificate you want to import (**Figure 16.13**).

5. Click the Import button.

Acrobat returns you to the Manage Trusted Identities dialog box, which lists your new trusted signer (**Figure 16.14**).

You've installed a new trusted identity, but you need to explicitly tell Acrobat that it can be used for signatures.

6. Choose the newly installed trusted identity and then click the Details button.

The Edit Contact dialog box opens, which presents a one-element list with the name of the certificate (**Figure 16.15**).

7. Choose the name in the list and then click the Edit Trust button.

The Import Contact Settings dialog box opens (**Figure 16.16**). This dialog box has check boxes that indicate the items for which this identity can be trusted.

8. Click the "Use this certificate as a trusted root" and the "Certified documents" check boxes.

You shouldn't click the check boxes for dynamic content, embedded JavaScript, or privileged system operations, since these would allow a signature to "validate" documents that may change dynamically after signing.

9. Click OK to return to the Edit Contact dialog box (Figure 16.15) and OK again to return to the Manage Trusted Identities dialog box (Figure 16.11).

10. Click Close to close the dialog box.

Your copy of Acrobat will now recognize signatures placed on a PDF page by the person whose certificate you imported.

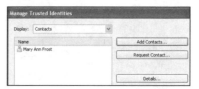

Figure 16.13 Once you've selected a certificate, the name of the contact appears in the Choose Contacts to Import dialog box.

Figure 16.14 To specify the actions for which the identity should be trusted, choose the contact, and click the Details button.

Figure 16.15 In the Edit Contact dialog box, choose the trusted identity, and click Edit Trust.

Figure 16.16 In the Import Contact Settings dialog box, you can specify that the identity should be used to verify signatures.

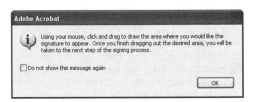

Figure 16.17 When you first sign a document, Acrobat presents a dialog box that reminds you of the procedure.

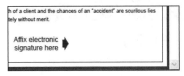

Figure 16.18 The document page usually has a place reserved for your electronic signature.

Figure 16.19 When you sign the document, Acrobat presents you with a dialog box that lets you specify the digital ID you want to use and to type the corresponding password.

Signing a PDF Document

Having created your digital ID and sent certificates to the appropriate people, the actual signing of a document is pretty easy.

Once you've signed a PDF document, Acrobat immediately saves the file in what is called an *increment-only* form. The contents of this type of PDF document cannot be removed from the file. New items can be added to the signed file, but Acrobat can always revert to the original, signed version of the document. This is what makes it possible to use a signed PDF file as a legal document: you can always see the document as it was when people affixed their signatures.

To sign a PDF document:

1. With the document open, choose Advanced > Sign & Certify > Place Signature.

   Acrobat reminds you how to place a signature on the page (**Figure 16.17**). This gets annoying after you've signed a few documents, so you should make use of the "Do not show this message again" check box.

2. Click OK in the reminder dialog box to return to your document, with the pointer changed to a crosshair.

3. Drag a rectangle on the page where you want the signature to go.

   The location of the signature is often a reserved place on a page within the document (**Figure 16.18**).

   When you release the mouse button, the Sign Document dialog box opens (**Figure 16.19**).

Continues on next page

4. Choose a digital ID from the Sign As drop-down menu.

5. Type the ID's password in the Password field.

6. Choose an appearance from the Appearance pop-up menu.

   There is initially only one appearance in this menu: Standard Text. You'll see how to create new appearances in the next section.

7. Click the Sign button.

   Acrobat presents you with a standard Save As dialog box, forcing you to immediately save the signed document.

8. Save the document in the usual fashion.

   Acrobat returns you to the document page, which now has the electronic signature placed on it (**Figure 16.20**).

✔ Tips

- If the person who created the PDF document intended it to be signed (which is true for contracts and similar documents), then they will almost certainly place a signature form field on the page, which eliminates a step or two in this process. We'll discuss signature fields later in this chapter.

- When you open a signed document, Acrobat places text and a button at the top of the page (**Figure 16.21**). The text tells you whether the document's signatures are valid; the button opens the Signatures navigation pane. We shall discuss validating signatures and the Signatures pane later in the chapter.

Figure 16.20 When you return to the document page, the signature appears as a bit of text with either your name in large print or a graphic.

Figure 16.21 Whenever the signed document is opened, Acrobat will put some text at the top of the window that indicates the document has been signed; there is also a button that opens the Signatures navigation pane.

Figure 16.22 The Sign Document dialog box lets you choose an appearance to use with your signature.

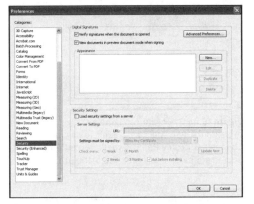

Figure 16.23 You create appearances in the Security Preferences.

Creating a Signature Appearance

By default, the visible representation of a signature on a PDF page is a generic icon accompanied by a collection of text information, as in Figure 16.20. You can change the appearance of the signature, if you wish: you can specify what information should be presented as text, and you can choose an image or other graphic that becomes part of the signature.

You do this by creating one or more named *appearances* in your Acrobat preferences. The appearance consists of a list of the text information and the image that should visually identify your signature on the page.

When you sign a document, one of the controls that appears in the Sign Document dialog box (Figure 16.19) is a pop-up menu of all the appearances available to your copy of Acrobat (**Figure 16.22**). Simply choose the appearance you want to use for the signature.

✔ Tip

- The visual marks don't make up the electronic signature itself. The actual signature is a wad of binary information that is embedded in the PDF file and isn't directly visible on the page. A signature appearance is just the visible indication that a signature is placed on the page.

To create an appearance for your signature:

1. On the Macintosh, choose Acrobat > Preferences; in Windows, choose Edit > Preferences.

   The Preferences dialog box opens (**Figure 16.23**).

Continues on next page

CREATING A SIGNATURE APPEARANCE

2. Choose Security in the Categories list on the left side of the dialog box.

3. Click the New button.

The Configure Signature Appearance dialog box opens (**Figure 16.24**).

4. Type a name for your appearance in the Title field at the top of the dialog box.

This name will appear in the pop-up menu when you sign a document.

5. If you want to have a picture appear as part of your signature, click the "Imported graphic" radio button, and click the File button.

A standard Open dialog box opens, letting you choose the image, PDF, or other graphic file you want to use for your signature. Acrobat lets you use a wide variety of file types for your signature graphic, including PDF, TIFF, and JPEG files.

6. In the Configure Text section, choose the check boxes corresponding to the information you want to appear in the text part of your signature. I recommend selecting at least your name and the date.

The Preview in the dialog box reflects your choices (**Figure 16.25**).

7. Click OK to return to the Security Preferences, which now lists your new appearance (**Figure 16.26**). Click OK again to dismiss the Preferences dialog box.

Now, when you sign a PDF document, you can choose your appearance in the Sign Document dialog box, and the new signature is displayed on the page using your appearance details (**Figure 16.27**).

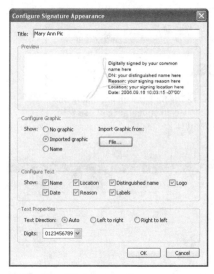

Figure 16.24 When you configure an appearance, you specify a graphic to use in your signature and itemize what information should appear in the signature's text block.

Figure 16.25 The Configure Signature Appearance dialog box presents a preview of what your signature looks like, based on the control settings.

Figure 16.26 Your new appearance is in the list in the Security Preferences pane.

Figure 16.27 When you sign a document, Acrobat applies the appearance you chose to the signature.

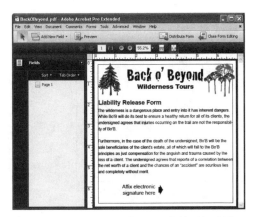

Figure 16.28 You create a signature field with within Edit Forms mode.

Figure 16.29 Choose Digital Signature from the options presented when you click the Add New Field button.

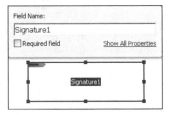

Figure 16.30 The signature field initially appears as a rectangle with handles, accompanied by a palette in which you should type a field name.

Creating a Signature Field

If you're creating a PDF file that contains a contract or other document that must be signed by the reader, you'll make things easier if you provide a *signature field* as part of the document. This is the electronic equivalent of a "sign here" line on a paper document; when the reader clicks this form field, it presents the Sign Document dialog box (Figure 16.19) so the reader can sign the document.

Having created your PDF document, you place a signature field on the page in Edit Form mode (**Figure 16.28**). (See Chapter 14 for a reminder of the ins and outs of Edit Form mode.)

To create a signature field on a document page:

1. With your document open, choose Forms > Add or Edit Forms.

   Acrobat displays the document in Edit Form mode (Figure 16.28).

2. Click on the Add New Field button and choose Digital Signature (**Figure 16.29**). The cursor turns into a crosshair.

3. Drag a rectangle on the page, indicating where the signature field should go.

   The field is displayed as an outline with handles and an adjacent palette with a Field Name text field (**Figure 16.30**).

4. Type a field name in the Field Name text field.

   The field name can be anything you want, although I suggest you use something appropriate to the field's purpose. The default "Signature1" isn't actually too bad.

Continues on next page

5. Click the Show All Properties link.

Acrobat displays the Digital Signature Properties dialog box (**Figure 16.31**).

6. Select the Appearance tab.

7. Use these controls to specify the color you want for the border and fill.

8. Select the Signed tab.

Acrobat displays the controls that dictate what should happen when the user signs the document (**Figure 16.32**).

9. Click the "Mark as read-only" radio button, and choose "All fields" in the pop-up menu, which ensures that no further changes can be made after the reader has signed the document.

10. Click the Close button.

Acrobat returns you to the document page. The new signature field is visible as a rectangle with handles, though the floating palette is now gone.

11. Reposition and resize the field by dragging the rectangle and its handles.

12. Click the Close Form Editing button in the Edit Form mode toolbar to leave Edit Form mode.

The new, functional signature field is visible as a rectangle with a small icon in the upper-left corner (**Figure 16.33**). When the pointer moves over the field, it turns into a pointing finger; if you leave it over the field for a half-second, a tooltip appears, letting the reader know that this is a signature field.

When users clicks inside the field, the Sign Document dialog box opens so they can sign the document.

Figure 16.31 In the Appearance tab of the Digital Signature Properties dialog box, you can specify the color and width of the field's border and fill.

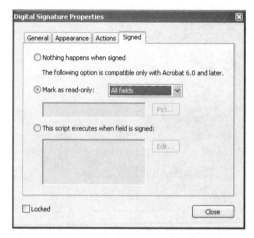

Figure 16.32 In the Signed tab, specify what should happen when a signature is fixed to the field.

Figure 16.33 When you leave Edit Form mode, the pointer becomes a pointing finger whenever it passes over the field. Tooltip text appears after a half-second.

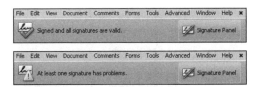

Figure 16.34 When you open a signed document, Acrobat supplies one of two messages at the top of the window, indicating that all signatures are valid (top) or that at least one signature may not be valid (bottom).

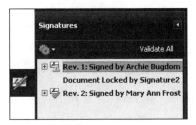

Figure 16.35 The Signatures navigation pane lists all the signatures in the current file, each labeled as valid or not.

Figure 16.36 To validate all the signatures in the current file, click the Validate All link in the Signatures navigation pane.

Validating a Signed Document

When you receive a signed document, you need to verify that the signature was placed on the page by the correct person. In Acrobat, this means verifying that the signature was placed on the page by someone who is one of your trusted identities. This process is referred to as *validating* the signature.

When you open a signed document, Acrobat automatically compares the digital ID of all the document's signers with your list of trusted identities. If they all match, then Acrobat puts an appropriate message at the top of the document window (**Figure 16.34**, top).

The validation process happens automatically when you open the signed document. The only time you need to do anything special is if one or more signatures fail to validate, indicated by the message "At least one signature has problems," at the top of the document window (Figure 16.34, bottom). In this case, you must validate the signature manually using the Signatures navigation pane (**Figure 16.35**). This pane lists all the signatures in the current document, together with an icon indicating whether each signature is valid.

To validate all signatures in a document:

1. Click the Signatures navigation pane icon to make the pane visible.

2. Click the Validate All link at the top of the pane (**Figure 16.36**).

   Acrobat attempts to validate all of the document's signatures, placing a Valid or Invalid icon next to each one in the Signatures pane.

A signed document can still be changed using the touch-up and commenting tools. However, even if extensive changes have been made to the document since its signing, it's always possible to revert to the document as it was at signing.

To revert to the original signed version of a document:

◆ In the Signatures pane, right-click the signature you're interested in, and choose View Signed Version (**Figure 16.37**).

The document reverts to the signed version; you're looking at the document exactly as it was when it was signed. Acrobat places a notice at the top of the window, telling you that you are looking at an earlier, signed version of the document (**Figure 16.38**); next to this text is a button that presents a report on any dynamic components (such as JavaScripts) or external dependencies (such as unembedded fonts) in the document that would invalidate the signature.

✔ Tip

■ You should also try out Compare Signed Version to Current Version in the contextual menu (Figure 16.37). It shows you the signed and current versions of the document side by side, with the differences highlighted. Quite cool.

Figure 16.37 Using the Options menu in the Signatures navigation pane, you can always see the document exactly as it was when it was signed.

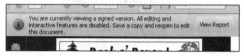

Figure 16.38 Acrobat reminds you that you are viewing the earlier, signed version of a document.

CONVERTING PAPER TO PDF

We have spent this book discussing the wonderful things you can do with PDF documents; however, most of the important official documents we all receive are printed on paper. Professionals are particularly wedded to paper: contracts, estimates, invoices, and the like are most frequently distributed as paper documents. Until relatively recently, even Adobe insisted that some of its developer applications be printed, signed, and faxed back; PDF files weren't accepted. For that matter, most companies have many years' worth of paper stored in warehouses, documenting all of their past transactions and business.

What if you want to store these documents on your disk or fill them out electronically? You'll scan the paper and then store or otherwise deal with the scanned image. Because Acrobat can open image files, automatically converting them to PDF, scanned paper documents can be treated entirely as PDF files.

In this chapter, you'll see what you can do with a scanned paper document. Acrobat provides tools for conveniently filling out scanned paper forms and for converting scanned text into searchable, real text.

This chapter assumes you've already scanned the paper document with which you're working.

CONVERTING PAPER TO PDF

Typing on a Paper Form

If you scan a paper form that you need to fill out, (or, for that matter, if you receive a PDF-format form that doesn't have form fields), you have a document that looks like a form but, in an Acrobat sense, isn't one. The lines and boxes where you're supposed to write your information are just graphic objects, not interactive form fields that collect information (**Figure 17.1**).

You can lay form fields on top of the scanned pages (see "Converting Electronic Documents to Forms" in Chapter 14), but if the form is something you need to fill out only once and then forget about, placing form fields on the page seems like unnecessary work. What you'd really like to do is type your responses on top of the page contents, exactly as though you were printing or typing on a paper page.

The Typewriter tool allows you to do exactly that. This is a truly useful little gadget for those of us who prefer to do everything electronically if at all possible. Every time you click the page with the Typewriter tool, you get a blinking cursor, which lets you type text on the page (**Figure 17.2**).

This makes it easy to fill in one-off forms that you'll never see or bother with again. The form you fill in can be e-mailed to another person or, of course, printed and faxed. The typed-on form can be opened with Acrobat 5 or later.

The Typewriter tool is most easily used through the Typewriter toolbar (**Figure 17.3**).

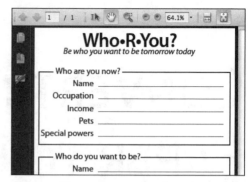

Figure 17.1 When you scan a paper form, the result may look like a form, but it isn't, in an Acrobat sense. The lines where you type your data are merely lines, not Acrobat form fields.

Figure 17.2 The Typewriter tool lets you type text on top of the PDF page, exactly like typing on a paper form.

✔ Tip

- Although here we're discussing the Typewriter tool with regard to scanned paper documents, you can use it to type on any PDF document.

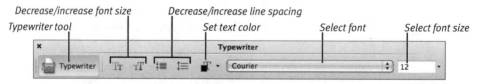

Decrease/increase font size *Decrease/increase line spacing*
Typewriter tool *Set text color* *Select font* *Select font size*

Figure 17.3 The Typewriter toolbar contains the Typewriter tool and icons that let you select the font, point size, and other text characteristics.

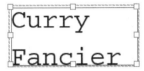

Figure 17.4 Having typed your text, you can click it with the Hand, Select, or Typewriter tool to get a border with handles. These let you resize and reposition the text.

Curry

Fancier

Figure 17.5 If you shorten the text's border too much, the text wraps into multiple lines.

To type form responses onto a PDF page:

1. With the document open, select the Typewriter tool from the Typewriter toolbox.

   The pointer turns into an I-beam cursor.

2. Click the page where you want to type your text.

   Presumably, this will be above or in some graphic element on the page, such as a line or a box.

3. Type your text.

   If you click the typewritten text with the Typewriter, Selection, or Hand tool, Acrobat places a rectangle with handles around the text (**Figure 17.4**). You can now reposition the text by dragging the rectangle around the page. You can resize the bounding box of the text by dragging the handles; if you make the box too narrow to accommodate the text, Acrobat wraps it into multiple lines (**Figure 17.5**).

✔ Tips

- You can edit your typewritten text by double-clicking it with either the Hand or the Typewriter tool.

- The Typewriter toolbar (Figure 17.3) also has icons to change the font, point size, and the spacing between typewritten lines. Click the typewritten text to select it, and then click the icon.

TYPING ON A PAPER FORM

Creating a Searchable Image

When you scan a paper document—a contract, say—the result is a bitmapped picture of the original text and graphics (**Figure 17.6**). Although it looks like text, there is, in fact, no text there.

If you're simply reading the document, this technicality doesn't matter; the eye doesn't care if it's looking at text or a picture of text. However, if you're hoping to use common text functions with the document—in particular, if you want to be able to search the document for words or phrases—then a picture of the text won't do. You must have pages of actual text.

Acrobat has a built-in optical character recognition (OCR) function that can analyze an image and convert the picture of the text into real text that can be searched.

The appearance of the page remains the same as the scanned text; the real, searchable text occupies an invisible layer that lies under the scanned text. This preserves the original appearance and relieves Acrobat of having to guess at the font, point size, and other characteristics of the original text. This combination of an image and an invisible text layer is called a *searchable image*.

In a searchable image, all of Acrobat's text-related tools and features (in particular, the Find feature and the Select tool) work as usual, applying themselves to the invisible text layer. Thus, in addition to searching for text, you can copy and paste text from the PDF page into another application (**Figure 17.7**).

To create a searchable image PDF file:

1. With the image file open in Acrobat, choose Document > OCR Text Recognition > Recognize Text Using OCR.

   The Recognize Text dialog box opens (**Figure 17.8**).

Figure 17.6 When you scan a paper page, the result may look like text, but it's really a bitmapped picture of the text.

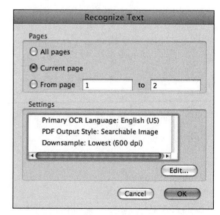

Figure 17.7 In a searchable image, the original bitmap image is unchanged, but there is an invisible layer whose text can be selected, searched for, copied, and pasted. Here, we've apparently selected some bitmapped text with the Selection tool; in fact, we've selected the underlying real text.

Figure 17.8 You specify the pages you want to convert in the Recognize Text dialog box lets you specify the pages to be converted. Clicking the Edit button lets you specify the details of the conversion.

Figure 17.9 The Recognize Text – Settings dialog box lets you specify the language and style you want for the OCR process.

Figure 17.10 The PDF Output Style menu lets you specify what kind of file should result from the text recognition.

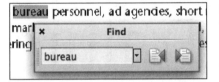

Figure 17.11 Having converted your document to a searchable image, you can search for words and phrases within the document.

2. Choose which pages you want Acrobat to convert: all pages, the current page, or a specific range of pages.

You'll nearly always click the "All pages" radio button.

3. In the Settings section of the dialog box, click the Edit button.

The Recognize Text – Settings dialog box opens (**Figure 17.9**).

4. In the PDF Output Style pop-up menu, choose Searchable Image (**Figure 17.10**).

5. If necessary, choose the language of the text in the Primary OCR Language pop-up menu.

6. Click OK to return to the Recognize Text dialog box, and click OK once more to have Acrobat convert your document.

Acrobat analyzes your pages' bitmaps and creates the invisible text layer. When Acrobat is done converting your document, the pages look unchanged; but if you search for a phrase, Acrobat can find it and highlight it (**Figure 17.11**).

✔ Tips

■ The PDF Output Style pop-up menu (Figure 17.10) presents two additional choices: Searchable Image (Exact), which is the same as Searchable Image but uses a more sophisticated (and slower) OCR method; and ClearScan, which is a new Acrobat feature we'll discuss in the next section. In the context of this discussion, choosing Searchable Image is a good compromise between OCR speed and accuracy.

■ OCR works best with a 300-dpi monochrome (1-bit, black-and-white) scan. I find it works acceptably with 150-dpi scans, as well. Adobe claims that 72 dpi is adequate, but you'll find some mistakes in the character recognition with such a coarse bitmap.

Converting a Scan with ClearScan

In the previous section, we showed how Acrobat creates a special, invisible text layer beneath a scanned bitmap. This leaves the scanned image visually unchanged but lets you search for phrases in the scanned text.

Keeping the page as a bitmap maintains the look and feel of the page; however, you cannot edit the text, and zooming in on the text makes it look jagged and unpleasant.

If you'd like to convert your scanned pages into something that can be edited using Acrobat's TouchUp tools, you need to convert your scan to a combination of actual text and line art, discarding the bitmap altogether. This is the purpose of Adobe's ClearScan feature.

ClearScan is new to Acrobat 9. When you convert a bitmap page with ClearScan, the result is a PDF file with real line art and real text. The method of text conversion is what's new to Acrobat 9: Acrobat creates a new font on the fly whose metric and artistic characteristics closely match the scanned text. The results are interesting and not appropriate for all circumstances or scanned pages, as **Figure 17.12** shows; the new text can look misshapen. However, it *is* actual text: scalable, selectable, searchable, and editable (ran out of *s* words).

✔ Tip

- Scan resolution has an enormous effect on the usability of ClearScan results. The paper page in Figure 17.12 was scanned at 150 dpi; compare that with the text in **Figure 17.13**, converted from a 300-dpi scan. The higher the resolution, the better your converted text will look.

Figure 17.12 Converting your image with ClearScan makes the text smooth and searchable and tries to match the original character shapes, but can yield misshapen characters. Compare this with Figures 17.6 and 17.13.

Figure 17.13 The higher the resolution of the original scan, the better ClearScan does. Compare this result, from a 300-dpi scan, to Figure 17.12, which used a 150-dpi scan.

Figure 17.14 Choose ClearScan in the PDF Output Style menu.

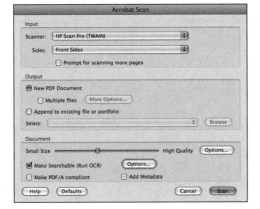

Figure 17.15 Click the "Make Searchable (Run OCR)" check box to scan a paper document directly to searchable text.

To convert a scanned document to text and graphics:

1. With the image file open in Acrobat, choose Document > OCR Text Recognition > Recognize Text Using OCR.

   Acrobat displays the Recognize Text dialog box (Figure 17.8).

2. Choose which pages you want Acrobat to convert: all pages, the current page, or a specific range of pages.

   You'll nearly always choose "All pages."

3. In the Settings section of the dialog box, click the Edit button.

   The Recognize Text – Settings dialog box opens (**Figure 17.14**).

4. In the PDF Output Style pop-up menu, choose ClearScan.

5. If necessary, choose the language of the text in the Primary OCR Language pop-up menu.

6. Click OK to return to the Recognize Text dialog box and click OK again to have Acrobat convert your document.

✔ Tip

■ Acrobat can scan a document directly to searchable text. The Scan dialog box has a "Make Searchable " check box that tells Acrobat to apply OCR to the scan results (**Figure 17.15**). This is extremely convenient if you are converting a large number of paper documents to PDF. See Chapter 4 for a reminder on how to scan paper documents directly to PDF.

CONVERTING A SCAN WITH CLEARSCAN

INDEX

A

access. *see also* password protection
  file restrictions, 234–235
  shared portfolios, 88
  shared reviews, 130
Acrobat 5 compatibility, legacy animations, 193
Acrobat menu, 6
Acrobat Pro, creating forms with. *see* forms
Acrobat Scan dialog, 65
Acrobat.com
  creating account with, 130, 138
  distributing forms with, 223, 225–226
  features of, 136–138
  reviewing shared document on, 132
  sharing portfolio on, 87–88
  starting shared review on, 128–131
Action menu, Pages pane, 139
actions. *see* link actions
Add Digital ID wizard, 241
Add Folder button, 74
Add Header and Footer dialog, 156–158
Add ID icon, 241
Add Movie dialog, 192–193
Add New Field button, 222
Add Note to Selected Text tool, 103
Adobe Buzzword, 136
Adobe Illustrator, 154–155
Adobe PDF 9.0 virtual printer
  options, 61
  PDFMaker using, 63
  printing to PDF file, 60
Adobe PDF Files (vector), 47
Adobe PDF Files, Optimized (vector), 47
Adobe Reader, enabling comments, 110
Adobe Self-Sign Security, 239
Advanced Editing toolbar
  Article tool, 179
  defined, 9, 150
  Link tool, 173, 176, 186
  Sound tool, 200
  TouchUp Object tool in, 152–154
  TouchUp Text tool in, 150–151
Advanced menu, 7
Analysis toolbar, 9, 38
appearances
  creating signature, 249–250
  signing PDF document, 248
Append button, adding scanned page to PDF, 65
Area tool, 38, 41
Arrow tool, 98
Articles pane
  creating articles, 178–190
  defined, 13
artifacts, 48
artwork
  creating Next Page button for presentation, 186–187
  creating Play Movie button, 196–198
  editing in Adobe Illustrator, 154
Assemble PDF Portfolio, 74
attachments, encrypting, 236
Autodesk AutoCAD, 109
Autorotate and Center, printing, 56

B

background, adding to pages, 159–160
Basic Grid layout, portfolios, 77
Binding menu, 58
bitmap vs. vector files, 47
booklets, printing documents as, 58
bookmarks
  adding, 170–172
  adding advanced actions, 175

creating when merging PDF files, 70
searching for text in, 31
using, 37
Bookmarks pane, 13, 170–172
Border palette, 218
borders
  Callout comments and, 97
  cropping, 146
  digital signature appearance, 252
  form field, 215, 217–218
  hiding in Acrobat presentation, 183
  link, 173
  measuring, 38, 40, 42
  modifying line art, 152
  Next Page button, 187
  placing movie as Flash animation, 192
  redaction selection, 164
  selecting, 153–154
  Text Box color, 95
  typing on paper form, 257

C

Callout comments, 97
cascade, open document windows, 33
case-sensitivity, searching for text, 31
certificate security, 233
certificates
  creating from digital ID, 243–244
  defined, 240
  importing as trusted identity, 245–246
  setting up to use signatures, 240
Change Scale Ratio, 42
chat collaboration, 131, 135
Check Spelling dialog, comments, 108
check-marks, comment, 115
Choose Contacts to Import dialog, 245–246
ClearScan, 259, 260–261
Clipboard, pasting onto page as Stamp, 107
Close button, drag bar, 5
Cloud tool, comments, 100–101
codes, redaction, 164
Collaborative Live navigation pane, 135
Collapse/Collapse All buttons, Comments List, 113
Collate check box, 53
Collections pane, Organizer, 212–213
color
  changing bookmark, 171–172
  changing Text Box, 95
  choosing background, 160
  choosing portfolio, 83
  setting redaction properties, 163
Combine Files button, Organizer, 205

Combine Files dialog, 69–70, 74
Command/Ctrl-Q, 3
Comment & Markup toolbar
  adding underline and cross out text tools to, 103
  commenting tools in, 90
  defined, 9
commented documents, reading, 111–122
  examining Comments List, 112–113
  managing Comments List, 116
  marking, 115
  migrating, 122
  printing, 119–121
  replying to comment in Comments List, 114
  searching for text, 31, 117–118
comments
  adding Callout, 97
  adding lines and arrows, 98
  adding ovals and rectangles, 99
  adding polygons and clouds, 100–101
  adding Stamp, 104–107
  adding Sticky Note, 93
  adding Text Box, 94–96
  e-mail-based reviews, 124–127
  enabling in Adobe Reader, 110
  exporting and importing, 109
  indicating text edits, 102–103
  shared reviews, 128–132
  spell checker, 108
  tools for, 90–91
Comments and Forms menu, 54, 120
Comments List
  choosing visible comments, 116
  examining, 112–113
  marking comments, 115–116
  printing summary of comments, 121
  replying to comment, 114
  searching for text, 117–118
  sorting items, 116
Comments menu, 7, 90, 121
Comments pane, 14
compatibility
  placing movie as legacy animation, 193
  restricting file access, 235
Configure Signature Appearance dialog, 250
ConnectNow, 137
controls, printer, 54–56
Create Form Field tools, 222
Create Go To View dialog, 174
Create Link dialog
  creating links, 173–174
  creating Next Page button, 186
  radio buttons in, 175

Create New Form wizard, 213
Create or Edit Form dialog, 213, 219–220
Create PDF, PDFMaker, 62
Create Web Links command, 177
cropping pages, 146–148
Crossout Text for Deletion tool, 102
cross-platform compatibility, legacy animation, 193
Custom link button, 175
Custom Stamp dialog, 106–107
Cyber-SIGN, 240

D

date, on page, 158
deadlines, shared review, 131
descriptive text, portfolios, 74
Design pane, LiveCycle Designer, 215–218
Design view pane, LiveCycle Designer, 216–217
desktop, converting screen shots to PDFs, 68
digital IDs
    creating, 241–242
    creating certificate from, 243–244
    defined, 240
    setting up to use signatures, 240
    signing PDF document, 248
Digital Signature Properties dialog, 252
digital signatures, 239–254
    Adobe Self-Sign Security and, 239
    creating certificate from ID, 243–244
    creating digital ID, 241–242
    creating signature appearance, 249–250
    creating signature field, 251–252
    importing certificate as trusted identity, 245–246
    overview of, 239
    setting up to use, 240
    signing PDF document, 247–248
    validating signed document, 253–254
Disable Measurement Markup, 42
disk, saving document to, 44
Distance tool, 38, 39
Distribute Form wizard, 224–226
distributed forms
    creating, 223–227
    receiving and viewing results, 229–232
    response to, 228
    restricting reader activities, 237
distributed presentation files, 181
Document menu, 6, 139
Document pane, 4
Document Properties dialog
    assigning permissions, 238
    file access restrictions, 234–235

Open in Full Screen mode, 189
open options, 182
drag bar, 4–5
drivers, and scanning, 65
duplex, 56
Dynamic Stamps, 104
Dynamic Zoom tool, 25

E

Edit Contact dialog, 246
Edit Form toolbar, 222
Edit menu, 6
Edit PDF Portfolio window
    adding header, 81–82
    adding welcome page, 79–80
    choosing color scheme, 83
    choosing layout, 77–78
    creating PDF portfolio, 73
    publishing portfolio, 85–86
    setting file information, 84
    sharing with Acrobat.com, 87–88
Edit toolbar, 9
editing
    in Adobe Illustrator, 154–155
    forms with Live Cycle Designer, 216–218
    permissions for readers, 237
electronic documents, converting to forms, 212, 219–222
e-mail
    attaching portfolio to, 86
    certificates to recipients, 244
    distributed forms, 223–225, 228–230
    Office documents as PDF files, 63
    review of PDF documents, 124–127
    shared portfolios on Acrobat.com, 88
    shared reviews on Acrobat.com, 129–132
Email button, Organizer, 205
Email PDF, PDFMaker, 62
Email-Based Review Wizard, 124
embedded movies in PDFs, 193, 195
Encapsulated PostScript (vector), 48
encryption, 234–236
End key, 19
Entrust, 240
EPS format, 45–46, 49
Examine Document pane, 165
Expand/Expand All buttons, Comments List, 113
Export icon, 243
exporting
    comments, 109
    to other formats, 45–49
extracting pages, 140

F

Favorite Places folder, Organizer, 207
FDF (Form Data Format) file, 109
Field Properties dialog, 222
File menu, 6, 18
File radio button, 159, 162
File toolbar
  defined, 9
  opening file from, 18
  saving and printing tools on, 44
filename, saving documents, 44
files
  adding to collection, 209
  converting to PDFs, 64
  creating portfolio, 73–76
  password protection, 234–235
  setting information for portfolio, 84
  sharing on Acrobat.com, 137
Files column, Organizer, 204, 206
fill, selecting, 153
Find toolbar, 30
Finder, opening file from, 18
First Page command, 19
Fit Page command, 22
Fit to Printable Area, 53, 56
Flash animations, 190–192, 199
Flash tool, 190, 199
folders
  creating portfolio with, 73–76
  Favorite Places, 207
font
  adding header or footer to document, 157
  bolding bookmark, 172
  changing text, 151
  changing Text Box, 96
  editing form, 218
  text watermark, 161–162
footers, 156–158
Form Data Format (FDF) file, 109
Form Field Recognition, 219
form fields
  converting electronic documents, 219–222
  laying on top of scanned pages, 256
  placing on page, 217–218
  signature, 248, 251–252
  text properties for, 218
form fragments, 216
formats
  conversion file types, 64
  exporting to other, 45–49
forms, 211–232
  about LiveCycle Designer, 212
  converting electronic documents to, 219–222
  creating from template, 213–215
  distributing, 223–227
  editing permissions for readers, 237
  editing with LiveCycle Designer, 216–218
  receiving and viewing results, 229–232
  responding to distributed, 228
Forms menu, 7, 213
Forms Tracker, 230–232
Fragment Library tab, LiveCycle Designer, 216
Full Screen mode
  Reading mode vs., 33
  self-running presentation in, 188–189
  slide show in, 184–185
  turning on and off, 185
  when to use for presentations, 183

G

Go to a page view, link action, 175
graphics. *see also* artwork
  adding watermark, 161–162
  background, 159–160
  converting scanned document to, 261
  editing in Adobe Illustrator, 154–155
  modifying line art, 152–154
  signature appearance, 250
group presentations, 181

H

H.264 video standard, 190–192
Hand tool, 94, 196–197
headers
  PDF, 156–158
  portfolio, 81–82
Help menu, 7
Highlight Selected Text tool, 102
highlight style, links, 173
History pane, Organizer, 206
Home button, Portfolio toolbar, 75
Home key, 19
How To pane, LiveCycle Designer, 215–218

I

I-beam cursor, 257
icons
  Add ID, 241
  for comments, 91
  Export, 243
  New Bookmark, 170
  New Collection, 208
  Next Page, 19
  Oval and Rectangle tool, 99
  Sticky Note, 92–93

Identity setup dialog, 91
images
    adding company logo to form, 214
    converting to PDF files, 64
    creating searchable, 258–259
    editing in PDF document, 154–155
    portfolio welcome page, 80
    signature appearance, 250
Import Contact Settings dialog, 246
importing
    certificate as trusted identity, 245–246
    comments, 109
    electronic documents to forms, 220
    vs. migrating comments, 122
imposition, 56
increment-only forms, 247
Initial View tab, Document Properties dialog,
        182–183
Insert Flash dialog, 199
Insert Sound dialog, 200–201
Insert Text at Cursor tool, 102
Insert Video dialog, 191–193
inserting pages, 142, 237

J

JPEGs (bitmap), 48, 80

K

kiosk presentations, 181, 183, 188–189

L

landscape pages, rotating, 145
Last Page command, 19
layouts
    header, 82
    page, 28–29
    portfolio, 73, 77–78, 84
    printing reference pages of, 57
    rotating pages in, 144
    single page for presentations, 183
    TIFF and EPS options, 46, 49
legacy animations
    defined, 190
    placing on PDF, 192–193
    playing with visible controls, 196–198
Library pane, LiveCycle Designer, 215–218
lines
    adding, 98
    modifying, 152–155
link actions
    creating links, 174

creating Next Page button, 186–187
creating Play Movie button, 196–198
overview of, 175
Link tool, 173–174, 176, 186–187
links
    creating, 173–175
    creating Play Movie button, 196–197
    making automatic Web, 177
    modifying existing, 176
    viewing documents, 36
List view, Portfolio toolbar, 75, 83
LiveCycle Designer
    creating forms from templates, 213–215
    editing forms with, 216–218
    overview of, 212
LiveCycle Policy Server security, 233
Logo and Structured Text header, portfolios,
        82
Loop after last page check box, presentations,
        188–189
Loupe tool, 21, 26

M

Macintosh
    creating portfolio with packages, 74
    PDFMaker and, 62
Manage Custom Stamps dialog, 107
Manage Trusted Identities dialog, 245–246
margins, 147–148, 157
Mark for Redaction tool, 164–165
Mark with Checkmark, comments, 115
marking, commented documents, 115–116
markups, printing, 54, 120
Marquee Zoom tool, 23–24, 25
measurement markup, 39, 40, 42
Measuring Info window, 41
measuring sizes and areas
    Area tool, 41
    Measurement palette, 38–39
    Perimeter tool, 40–41
    settings, 41–42
menu bar, 5
Menu Item dialog, 187
menus, types of, 6–7
merging
    comments, 126, 127
    PDF files, 69–70
Microsoft Office, creating PDF files in, 62–63
Microsoft Word, exporting comments to, 109
migrating, comments, 122
minimizing file size, 50–51
Modify, Portfolio toolbar, 76
movies, placing on page, 190–193

INDEX

moving
    bookmarks, 171–172
    existing links, 176
    links, 174
    pages from one location to another, 140
MP3 files, 201
Multimedia Operations dialog, 196–197, 198
Multimedia toolbar, 9, 190–192
multimedia, placing movie on page, 190–193

N

navigation, 169–180
    articles, 178–180
    automatic Web links, 177
    bookmarks, 170–172
    Full Screen mode, 185
    links, 173–175
    modifying existing links, 176
navigation panes
    closing, 12–13
    converting into palettes, 14
    converting palettes into, 14
    customizing list of, 13
    hiding for presentations, 182–183
    most useful, 13–14
    opening, 5, 12–13
New Bookmark icon, 170
New Collection icon, 208
New Form Assistant wizard, 213–214
New Search button, 32
Next Page button, 186–187
Next Page icon, 19

O

Object Library tab, LiveCycle Designer, 216
OCR (Optical Character Recognition), 64,
    258–259
On an Image layout, portfolios, 77
online conferencing, Acrobat.com, 137
opacity
    background, 160
    watermark, 162
opening
    Acrobat, 3
    files, 175
    Organizer, 205
    PDF files, 18
    presentations, 182–183
    Web pages, 175
Optical Character Recognition (OCR), 64,
    258–259
Organizer, 203–209

changing width of columns, 206
Collections pane, 212–213
examining, 204–205
History pane, 206
overview of, 203
Places pane, 211
Oval comment tool, 99

P

packages, creating portfolio in Macintosh, 74
Page Display toolbar, 10, 28–29
Page Down key, 19
page layout, 28–29
Page Navigation toolbar, 10, 19
page numbers
    specifying appearance on page, 158
    specifying background, 160
Page Properties dialog, 198
Page Scaling menu, 53, 55, 57–58
Page Up key, 19
page-handling controls, 55–56
page-manipulation, 139–148
    cropping, 146–148
    extracting, 141
    inserting one file into another, 142
    overview of, 139
    rearranging, 140
    replacing, 143
    rotating, 144–145
pages
    moving around among, 19
    printing multiple per sheet, 57
    restricting reader activities, 237
    setting layout for presentations, 183
    sharing, 131, 135
Pages column, Organizer, 204–205
Pages pane, 14. *see also* page-manipulation
Pages per Sheet menu, 57
Pan & Zoom tool, 27
paper
    changing size for document, 148
    converting to PDF. *see* scanned paper,
        converting to PDF
    forms, 212
password protection
    assigning permissions, 238
    creating digital ID, 242
    editing permissions, 237–238
    overview of, 233
    restricting file access, 234–235
    restricting reader activities, 236
Patterns Radio button, Search and Redact,
    168

PDF files
  migrating comments into modified, 122
  opening, 18
  portfolios. *see* portfolios
  printing. *see* printing
  printing with comments, 119–120
  saving, 44–49
PDF files, creating, 59–70
  on Acrobat.com, 137
  converting images and other files, 64
  converting screen shots, 67–68
  converting Web pages, 66
  merging, 69–70
  printing to PDFs, 60–61
  scanning directly, 65
  using PDFMaker in Microsoft Office, 62–63
PDF Output Style menu, 259, 261
PDF Portfolio button, 74
PDF/A (vector), 48
PDF/E (vector), 48
PDF/X(vector), 48
PDFMaker, 62–63
Perimeter tool, 38, 40–41
permissions, 236–238
Places column, Organizer, 204
Places pane, Organizer, 211
Play button, adding sound, 201
Play Media dialog, 196–198
Play Movie button, 196–197
Polygon comment tool, 100–101
Polygon Line comment tool, 100–101
Portfolio toolbar, 75–76
portfolios, 71–88
  color scheme, 83
  creating, 73–76
  file information, 84
  header, 81–82
  layout, 77–78
  opening, 72
  overview of, 71
  publishing, 85–86
  sharing with Acrobat.com, 87–88
  welcome page, 79–80
portrait pages, rotating, 145
poster frames
  Flash animation, 191–192, 199
  legacy animation, 192–193
  for non-MP3 sounds as markers, 201
preferences
  comments, 91
  converting files to PDFs, 64
  editing software for graphics and images, 155
  self-running presentations, 188–189

  setting, 15–16
  signature appearances, 249–250
presentations, creating Acrobat, 181–201
  to embed or not embed, 195
  full-screen slide show, 184–185
  Next Page button, 186–187
  overview of, 181
  placing Flash animation on page, 199
  placing movie on page, 190–193
  placing sound on PDF page, 200–201
  playing movie, 196–198
  self-running presentations, 188–189
  setting open options, 182–183
Preview Document, Portfolio toolbar, 75
Preview PDF pane, LiveCycle Designer, 216–217
preview picture, Print dialog, 53
Previous Page icon, 19
Print Color As Black setting, 52
Print Production toolbar, 10
Print to File setting, 52
printer controls, 54
printing
  assigning permissions for, 238
  booklets, 58
  miscellaneous settings, 52–53
  multiple pages per sheet, 57
  options, 54–56
  overview of, 52
  to PDF files, 60–61
  to PDF files with comments, 119–120
  restricting reader from, 236
  selected portfolio file, 75
  summary of all comments, 120–121
  terminology, 56
print-range controls, 55
properties
  adding advanced actions to links, 175
  article, 180
  automatic playing of movie, 198
  editing forms, 218
  form field, 222
  modifying existing links, 176
  Next Page button, 186–187
  open options for presentations, 182–183
  Play Movie button, 196–197
  redaction, 163–164
  Sticky Note, 93
  text, 151
  Text Box, 95–96
Properties bar, 10
publishing
  comments on shared document, 132
  portfolios, 85–86

Q

quitting Acrobat, 3

R

readers, restricting activities of, 236
Reading mode, viewing documents in, 34–35
real-time collaborative review, 134–135
Recognize Text - Settings dialog, 259, 261
Recognize Text dialog, 258–259, 261
Rectangle comment tool, 99
rectangles
    creating link, 173–174
    creating Play Movie button, 197
    resizing/repositioning movie on page, 192
redaction
    of items in document, 164–165
    overview of, 163
    search and, 166–167
    setting properties, 163–164
redaction overlay, 163
Redaction toolbar, 10, 163–167
Reduce File Size dialog, 50–51
Remove Checkmark, comments, 115
Replace Selected Text tool, 103
replacing pages, 143
Reply to Comment icon, Comments List, 114
repositioning objects, 152
resolution, and scanning, 261
response, to distributed forms, 228
Responses portfolio, 232
review status, comments, 115
reviewing PDF documents
    e-mail-based, 124–127
    features of Acrobat.com, 136–138
    real-time collaboration, 134–135
    shared. see shared review, on Acrobat.com
Revolve layout, portfolio, 78
Rich Text Format (vector), 48
rotating objects, 154
rotating pages, 144–145, 237

S

Save As dialog
    export file types in, 47–49
    saving document, 44
    saving file to other formats, 45–46
Save, Portfolio toolbar, 75
saving files
    background settings, 160
    header and footer combination, 158
    minimizing size, 50–51
    to other formats, 45–49

overview of, 44
scanned paper, converting to PDF, 255–261
    converting scan with ClearScan, 260–261
    creating searchable image, 258–259
    overview of, 255
    typing on paper form, 256–257
scanning, paper documents to PDF, 65, 261
screen
    arranging documents on, 33
    converting shots to PDFs, 67–68
    examining initial, 4–5
Search and Redact tool, 166–167
Search tool, 117–118
Search, Portfolio toolbar, 76
searchable image, creating, 258–259
searching for text, 30–32
security
    digital signatures. see digital signatures
    password protection. see password
        protection
    types of, 233
Security Settings dialog. see digital signatures
Select & Zoom toolbar
    defined, 10
    moving Text Box comment, 94
    using zoom tools in, 22–27
    zooming by fixed amount with, 22
Selection tool, 94
self-running presentation, creating, 188–189
Send Comments dialog, 126
Send for Review button, Organizer, 205
Send Invitation button, e-mail-based review,
        125
Send PDF for Shared Review Wizard, 129
Sends Comments button, e-mail-based review,
        126
server-based distribution, of forms, 223
server-based review. see shared review, on
        Acrobat.com
Set Link button, 174
Set Status tool, Comments List, 115
Share Wizard, 87–88
Share, Portfolio toolbar, 76
shared review, on Acrobat.com
    overview of, 128
    receiving, 133
    reviewing shared document, 132
    starting, 129–131
sharing portfolio, with Acrobat.com, 87–88
Show Cover Page During Two-Up layout, 29
Show tool, Comments List, 116
Show Welcome Page, Portfolio toolbar, 75
Shrink to Printable Area, 53, 56
Sign Document dialog, 247–248, 250, 252

Sign In button, 225–226
signature fields, 248, 251–252
signature validation, 240
Signatures pane, 14, 248, 253–254
simplex, 56
Single Page Continuous layout, 28
Single Page layout, 28
size
    links, 174
    modifying existing links, 176
    object, 152
    open options for presentations, 183
    pages for printing, 53, 55–56
    PDF file, 38–42, 50–51
    Stamp, 105, 107
    Text Box comments, 94
    Text Box text, 96
slide shows, 184–185
Sliding Row layout, portfolio, 78
Snap Types, 38
software, movie playing, 190
sorting, Comments List, 116
Sound tool, 190, 200–201
Specify File Details button, portfolios, 83
spelling checker, comments, 108
Stamp comments
    applying to page, 105
    creating own, 106–107
    deleting custom, 107
    overview of, 104–107
    printing document and, 120
Stamp menu, 104–107
Start Form Wizard, 213, 219
Start Page Sharing button, 135
Sticky Notes, 93
Submit Form button, 228
Summarize Options dialog, 121

T

target rectangles, 26, 27
Tasks toolbar
    converting file to PDF, 64
    converting Web pages to PDF, 66
    creating portfolio, 74
    defined, 10
    merging several files into single PDF file, 69
    scanning directly to PDF, 65
    starting e-mail-based review, 124
    starting shared review, 129
templates, 212, 213–215
terminology, printing, 56

text
    changing in document, 150–151
    converting scanned document to, 261
    creating bookmark from selected, 171
    creating portfolio with descriptive, 74
    creating searchable image PDF, 258–259
    creating signature appearance, 250
    editing forms, 218
    header or footer, 157–158
    indicating edits to, 102–103
    searching and redacting, 166–168
    searching for, 30–32
    setting redaction properties, 163–164
    typing on paper form, 256–257
    watermark, 161–162
Text (Accessible) format, 49
Text (Plain) format, 49
Text Box comments, 94–96, 97
Text Edits tool, 102–103
Text radio button, 161–162
text styles, 96, 171–172
thumbnails, 140–141, 204–205
TIFF format, 45–46, 49
tile, open document windows, 33
Tips, troubleshooting, 52
toolbars
    adding or removing, 11
    converting into palette, 9
    hiding for presentations, 183
    location of, 5
    as stand-alone palette, 8
    types of, 9–10
Tools menu, 7, 90
TouchUp Object tool, 152–154
TouchUp Text tool, 150–151
touch-up tools
    backgrounds, 159–160
    headers and footers, 156–158
    line art, 152–155
    redacting documents, 163–167
    text, 150–151
    watermarks, 161–162
Tracker window, displaying, 133
transitions
    in Full Screen Mode, 185
    self-running presentations, 188–189
troubleshooting Tips, 52
trusted identity, 240, 245–246
TWAIN drivers, 65
Two-Up Continuous layout, 29
Two-Up layout, 29
Typewriter tool, 256–257
Typewriter toolbar, 10, 256–257

U

Underline Selected Text tool, 103
Units menu, 148
Update button, Responses portfolio, 232

V

Valid All link, 253
validation, 248, 253–254
vector files, 47–48
Video tool, Multimedia toolbar, 190–193
View Comments link, shared reviews, 133
View menu, 6, 34
View Responses, 231
View Signed Version, 254
viewing documents, 17–42
    arranging on screen, 33
    choosing page layout, 28–29
    measuring sizes and areas, 38–42
    moving from page to page, 19
    moving from view to view, 20
    opening PDF files, 18
    results from distributed forms, 229–232
    searching for text, 30–32
    using bookmarks, 37
    using links, 36
    using Reading mode, 34–35
    zooming in and out. *see* zooming
views
    defined, 170
    moving between, 20

W

watermarks, 161–162
Web links, automatic, 177
Web pages, converting to PDFs, 66–67
welcome pages, portfolios, 79–80
WIA (Windows Image Acquisition) drivers, 65
Window menu, 7
windows
    converting screen shots to PDFs, 68
    setting for presentations, 183
Windows Certificate Store, 241
Windows Explorer, 18
Windows Image Acquisition (WIA) drivers, 65
Word processing, Acrobat.com, 136

X

X control, 84

Y

Y control, 84

Z

zooming
    with Dynamic Zoom tool, 25
    to fit document window, 22
    by fixed amount, 22
    with Loupe tool, 26
    with Marquee Zoom tool, 23–24
    overview of, 21
    with Pan & Zoom tool, 27

INDEX